Front cover concept and design La Staunton. Dust jacket graphics Sean De Sparengo. Original cover photographs provided by Lou Smith

ISBN 978-1-8381567-1-8
Secure Publishing Limited Reg. No. 12790078
Contact: well.secure@securepublishing.co.uk

i

Grateful acknowledgement is made to the following for permission to reproduce previously published material:

Lyrics for "Brixton Hill Revisited" by Milk Kan reproduced with kind permission of Scrappy Hood/Milk Kan.

Lyrics for "Brother", "Mannaggia la Miseria", "The Wicker- man" and "The Other Side of a Wonderful World" reproduced with kind permission of Zsa Zsa Sapien/Warren Mansfield and Meatraffle.

Lyrics for "Rock Fishes", "Is It Raining in Your Mouth?", "Whitest Boy On The Beach", "I Am Mark E. Smith", "Tin- foil Deathstar", "Feet" and "Vagina Dentata" reproduced with kind permission of Lias Saoudi and Fat White Family - published by Domino Publishing Ltd.

Lyrics for "Drink and Glide" reproduced with kind permission of Paddy Austin, Graham Bendel and Snapped Ankles.

Lyrics for "Mama Power", "Human Baby", "Free the Naked Rambler" and "Bite the Apple" reproduced with kind per- mission of Jamie Taylor and Phobophobes.

Lyrics for "Elocution", "Tweet Tweet Tweet", "Just Like We Do", "B.H.S.", "Firewall" and "OBCT" reproduced with kind permission of Jason Williamson and Sleaford Mods.

Lyrics for "It's All Free" reproduced with kind permission of William Hung, John S. Procter and I, Ludicrous.

Lyrics for "The Truth" reproduced with kind permission of David Martin and I Like Trains - published by Schubert Music Publishing Ltd.

Lyrics for "Lose It" reproduced with kind permission of Dom Keen, Blang Records and Jack Medley's Secure Men.

Lyrics for "Miami" reproduced with kind permission of Baxter Dury - published by Downtown Music Publishing.

Praise for WOO!

"Only a vibrant cultural scene like the one covered by Thomson can produce such a memorable scene. The book succeeds because Thomson has found a way to tell stories from his recent past with a keen eye on the immediate future. He may not offer answers to our vexing philosophical questions, but he certainly knows how to present the questions in the context of his stories. He wisely leaves the deliberations, and any conclusions reached, to each reader. As we head into a winter of flu and COVID machinations, Woo! is an excellent curl-up with at night book. You'll travel shoulder to shoulder with Thomson as he goes to places we'd all enjoy visiting, and as we refigure our new normal."

Frank Pizzoli (Independent Book Review)

"London is a hillbilly backwater, Seamus is God and I love this book"

Saul Adamczewski (Fat White Family)

"Dave has taken me back to my own album launch night, and in this quantum boomerang of a book he takes us on a journey into and out of his mind. He was there and now so are you."

"Beth Soan (Madonnatron)

"A written kiss on the pinkest parts of South London."
Clams Baker (Warmduscher)

"This book sums up what it's like to be involved in the Windmill scene and the crazy situations that you end up in. Dave Thomson has done this without being cultish about it and for that reason I fully endorse this book."
Haydn Davies (Pink Eye Club)

"A love letter to music, friendship and questionable life choices."
La Staunton (Reprezent FM)

"I suggested to Dave he call the book 'The Chronicles of The Windmill', but he just kneed me in the balls and said, "That sounds like the title of a f***ing Rush album!"
Zsa Zsa Sapien (Meatraffle)

"Get this vital piece of propaganda."
Jamie Taylor (Phobophobes)

"It's great to finally read the book Dave's been using as a social crutch these past three years."
Seamus McCausland (Landlord, Windmill Brixton)

Hey Carorine
   + Kasper!

May the
   WOO!
   be with you!

Love + Peace,

Darcey

WOO!

Strange Happenings at the Windmill and Other Tangential Rants

DAVE THOMSON

Secure Publishing

Contents

PART TWO

LATER...

Introduction

15TH APRIL 2020, HOME

Do you know that feeling? When everything is happening too fast, information's raining in, shouting at us, demanding attention, deserving more than we could ever give? Do you not find it impossible to keep up? News of epic proportions washed away by more news of epic proportions: 9/11, banking crisis, planet in meltdown, half of it flooding, half on fire, war after war after war, corporate monopolies exploiting the world, refugees everywhere made homeless by never-ending wars, oppressive regimes, climate calamities, or all three.

On top of this, our data is harvested, credit profiles monitored, social platforms analysed, predilections targeted, all demanding input because we need the likes, the comments, the validation.

Amongst all this, we must wrestle with time, like hamsters in a wheel keeping it all moving, our lives functioning, chasing dreams never satisfied, futures never actualised, for as fast as we run it is never fast enough. And when the pressure is at us from all sides, when it's all too much, too overwhelming and we can no longer cope, we just want it all to STOP. For someone, *anyone* to hit pause on the entire fucking world.

Well, someone has. Okay, not someone. Something. A living organism a mere 0.0005 of a millimetre in size has managed to bring the entire human world to a shrieking halt. Charmingly named Severe Acute Respiratory Syndrome Coronavirus 2, rebadged to the slightly less alarming Covid-19, an infinitesimal lifeform, but technically not alive at all, more like a zombie in its bionomy, replicating at an alarming rate once inside the warm bosom of our respiratory systems. A zoonotic virus, believed to have travelled through a bat then an anteater, on its journey to us, has successfully called a halt on pretty much all human activity, smashing apart free market dogma and blindsiding world government into a state of ideological confusion.

World leaders have deliberated over legislation designed to reduce carbon emissions. A woefully slow response to what is spectacularly obvious to all: we are destroying this little blue planet's ability to keep our species alive. Then, quite unexpectedly, this teeny viral eco-warrior springs forth from a lab or wet market in Wuhan or wherever and within a matter of months carbon emissions plummet; planes are grounded, drivers fined for unessential journeys and an economic system dependant on all of this in confused chaos, shining a light on the sheer simplicity of the problem.

Where we go from here, no one knows. Covid-19 has force us all to stop in our tracks and take a long hard look at our lives, our motivations, as we all recalibrate our hierarchy of values. The psychological impact far greater than the banking crisis, for alongside the economic devastation, a shadow looms large over our health and of those we hold dear. We have no clue what lies ahead, yet deep in our bones we all know one thing: humankind's future trajectory has been forever changed.

It feels more like a real war, but this time with a mystery enemy, for no one knows who is next in this pathogen lottery, if we will soon be grieving the loss of a friend or family member. Tragedy dealt out in huge swathes all over the globe, America brought to its knees by their intellectually challenged President, powerfully exemplifying why private health is a societal failure of profound proportions. Governments are nervous, even with their *Police State emergency powers*, as there's more of us than there are of them. They know too well every culture has its breaking point; every dog has its day.

We've been flung through a wormhole into a parallel universe, where every holiday, every concert, every new job, every house move, every visit to our mum can no longer happen. The future's been cancelled. Any plan that involves leaving our homes to do anything other than what the State considers essential, is now illegal. Still, there's no fear of missing out as there's fuck all to miss. Instead, we occupy a new reality, where the simple act of nipping out for groceries has become an alien concept fraught with unseen peril. Institutionalised within our own homes, we inhabit a digital universe where apps like Zoom and Houseparty are everyday tools for a continued social life – meetups, gigs, even raves. Friends, colleagues, relatives reduced to visual avatars with delayed audio as the fibre optics buckle under the strain of it all.

Meanwhile, in the analogue world, like Big Brother contestants in a house they cannot escape, relationships are tested and much like Amazon, divorce lawyers have found themselves on the winning side of this pandemic.

I cannot say this lockdown has *no* upside. Everything is just so chilled and time feels weirdly fluid. Even the weather's decent enough to create the illusion of an extended holiday; a staycation at least.

I do miss going out though. Took it all for granted, assumed nothing would ever change, well, at least not in such a fundamental way, our entire existence reduced into this half-life within an utterly lame yet insane new universe, this *new normal*. Grappling with our health and our sanity, bouncing off the walls as we try to create some meaning in all this. I so miss my family. And my mates. All of it. The larks, the giggles, the arguments, the hugs, the wind-ups, the dramas, the drinks, the smokes, the gigs, the craic, the smell of beer and piss and perfume and sweat. . .

PART ONE

Earlier...

Chapter One

The Roof Dog, The Train Driver, Burnt Human Hair, Meat Raffle Tickets

Oh the chainless sea is a-clanging
From the Lefty's windowsill
Ole Billie's brewin' brimstone
Up there on Brixton Hill
"Brixton Hill Revisited" – Milk Kan

29TH JULY 2017, BRIXTON UNDERGROUND STATION
Woo! I fly up the escalator, the two flights of gold-encrusted stairs, weave my way through the commuters towards the exit and out into the hot damp muggy NOx-infused summer air of Brixton Road, already crackling

with tension and Saturday night anticipation. So am I and with good reason, two musical happenings: one big, one small, both in Brixton, eight different bands. To see everything will be a physical impossibility, can't be in two places at once, but better to be spoilt for choice than bugger all happening.

First stop, the Windmill in Blenheim Gardens just off Brixton Hill. A shitty looking flat-roofed seventies breezeblock construction surrounded by gentrification which would have also faced the bulldozers had it not managed to achieve iconic status on the musical map of London, often listed in top ten London venue lists – just duckduckgo it. Now, no one dare touch it, for to do so might cause a riot. A bit of a walk from Brixton station, just long enough to clear my psyche of travel stress and get in a crafty smoke. Unlike most London venues, you don't have to grab a decent beer on the way, as they offer up a fine selection, including their rather exceptional Guinness. Okay, not as cheap as Spoons, but that's the price you pay for Independence and not supporting an exploitative, Farage supporting Gammon.

Now, for the uninitiated, the Windmill is not just a pub and is not just a music venue, it is both of course but so much more. It's a veritable microculture, a disparate melting pot of musicians, artists, poets, chancers, DJs, bloggers, blaggers, filmmakers, producers, youtubers, self-abusers and oholics of all colours, all persuasions. It takes in the young, the old and every imaginable slice of humankind in between. No one is judged, all and everyone's accepted, except, perhaps, anyone who turns out to be a cunt.

The Windmill has found itself at the epicentre of this whole south London happening, along with a string of other pub venues, all connected by the bands they support and their couldn't give a toss leftfield attitude. It is, without doubt, my favourite London musical hangout and in my view takes the London small venue crown.

It's a meeting place, a community, brimming with creativity, experimentation, utter lunacy and flashes of sheer genius. The role the Windmill plays in a band's development is significant, for they are channelling something fantastically unique, an interstellar nursery for all manner of burgeoning talent or any nutter with a mad idea. It makes other London venues feel unsatisfying, especially north of the river where it no longer feels authentic, not since money crept in and fucked it all up with contrived authenticity, like distressed furniture whose journey through time is a work of deceit.

I turn off Brixton Hill into Blenheim Gardens and can already make out the silhouette of Tim the train driver, standing by the benches near the entrance, sucking hard on a rollie. Tim Perry's his name and he's not really a train driver. My bro dubbed him that because he has played (and continues to play) such a key role in creating this whole wonderful thing, whatever this thing is (and yes, I am strenuously resisting the word "scene"). Tim is the Windmill's events manager and he does *look* like a train driver. Not a modern one, more like an old-fashioned steam train, except Tim isn't stoking an engine with coal, but a music venue with a weird and wonderful ragbaggle of musicians, performers, artists and DJs.

"Tim, how's it going?"

He turns to me.

"All right, Dave, you're nice and early tonight," he observes, in his soft Northern Irish lilt, because I'm usually reliably late.

"So, I haven't missed Zsa Zsa?"

Zsa Zsa Sapien is a mate of mine and the first act on the Windmill menu this evening. More on him later, much more.

"No, not yet we're running a bit late tonight." He looks at me, chuckles and sighs. "Because Zsa Zsa's running a bit late."

Tim is wearing his special T-shirt with the words ". . .*And You Will Know Us by The Bark of Roof Dog*" emblazoned across the front. This is one of many T-shirts specially made when, in 2015, the Windmill's iconic Roof Dog – a Rottweiler named Ben – sadly barked his last bark and is now immortalised as the venue's website logo, as well as the pub's own brew "Roofdog" (of course).

Tim's knowledge of music is wide and weird, his opinions strong and unforgiving (just ask him what he thinks of Bob Marley or Nick Cave), but he truly is a lovely gent and seems to know every unsigned band on the circuit at any given time. He fills this place up pretty much every night of every week, year in, year out and has tirelessly done so since 2002. All this, yet still he finds time for a Sunday afternoon live punk barbeque.

There is none of this "pay to play" bullshit, the venue takes just 10% of the door, barely covering the cost of the doorman, the remaining 90% divvied up amongst the bands.

On the downside, Tim's a fervent supporter of the band HMLTD, previously known as Happy Meal Ltd, until the fast-food chain's corporate lawyers caused them to rebrand, making them sound more like a Swedish clothing retail out-fit. Maybe I've been around too long but I find their art school-infused gender-warping image pretty unoriginal, yet still they act as if they're spearheading a cultural revolution, "dressing" their environment, burning human hair during their set to create "atmosphere", describing their shows as a "4D experience" - if, that is, you still have a sense of smell.

All I can smell is bullshit.

My relationship with Tim can be a little complex, our encounters often descending into ruthless banter and like a couple of old anoraks we often argue over music, even if we largely agree. Yet, what I love about Tim the most, is his total indifference to his own importance within all this, for none of what he has created here, or the significant role he plays in nurturing and encouraging so many of south London's finest, has ever gone to his head and he's visibly embarrassed when complimented, far more comfortable trading insults.

I pay the £5 entrance to Nasos, the friendliest doorman in London by a long yard. Yet, it must be said, a stickler for the rules. You can offer him a crafty smoke and he will gladly accept, but it'll buy you no favours. He's protecting the band's income and the venue's licence, so you can only respect him for that. He smiles and hands me a raffle ticket, though I forget to ask why (no cloakroom here – only trust), before branding my wrist with the Roof Dog paw print stamp.

I head for the bar, order a stout and look around, see who's about. I greet Seamus, the gruff, troll-like proprietor perched in his usual spot at the end of the bar by the entrance to the beer garden, undoubtedly the best vantage point in the whole place and with good reason, for together with his wife Kathleen, he runs the Windmill.

Seamus lifts himself off his stool using the bar for support. "Better check the barbie," he barks in his thick Cork accent.

"Is there a barbie?" I quiz.

Seamus stares at me like I'm stupid.

"Did ya not get yer ticket?"

"What ticket?" I ask, confused.

He pulls out a handful of raffle tickets.

"One of these."

"Ha-ha," I laugh, "meat raffle tickets!"

Seamus shakes his head, chuckling, before disappearing through the door and into the beer garden.

Chapter Two

Fleapit Feng Shui, Musical Pulp and the Brother from Another Mother

Paintings by Pre-Raphaelites
You like that sort of thing
We got lots of things in common
Like staying off heroin
"Brother" – Meatraffle

29TH JULY 2017, WINDMILL, BRIXTON

According to the rules, this is the point where I should describe the Windmill's interior using all the literary descriptive prose at my self-educated disposal. But there really is nothing aesthetically extraordinary about this place.

In many respects, it's just your average fleapit rock/punk pub venue: walls littered with graffiti, peeling posters, the odd bit of artistic flourish (no doubt daubed on the walls by various Windmill attendees). They either go to great lengths to make it look unremarkable, or more likely don't give a toss about aesthetics and even less about feng shui. The layout of the place is pretty haphazard, the bar dominating most of the available space, plonked awkwardly along one side of this long, rectangular room and stretching all the way to the stage at the far end. There's no glamourous backdrop, only what appears to be large linen dust sheets (the kind you use to protect furniture when decorating) draped along the rear wall, upon which a small Windmill logo has been hastily pinned. There's faded art on the ceiling signifying a once more glamourous time, now scattered with remnants of shredded gaffer tape, a living history of past events. The toilets, behind two adjacent doors, are smothered in promo stickers, with nothing to indicate which door belongs to which gender. Outside, you'll find a covered smoking area known to all as simply "The Shed" and beyond that a lovely walled beer garden, generally full of music-obsessed revellers.

All in all, the Windmill could not be described as special, but the magic conjured up here makes it very special. Plus, they have a thumping sound system, so I guess it's all about priorities.

I wonder if Tigger's in yet. Perhaps he's in the beer garden sampling the barbeque or maybe he's gone straight to the Academy. Nothing has been arranged, it's rare we do nowadays. Not like a few years back when we first stumbled into all this. Intrepid explorers at the musical coalface in search of all things alternative, avant-garde, anything in touch with the zeitgeist. You couldn't separate us back then as we dug around for music that holds a mirror to this cultural malaise, this political clusterfuck: Trump, Brexit, wars without end, rampant terrorism, neoliberal economics and a planet being physically and psychologically torn apart by all of the above.

The skies appeared to be darkening on our world, but with Tigger none of these topics were up for discussion, only music.

Was this our version of escapism? Perhaps. Of course. But more than anything else we wanted something real, outsider outsiders with authentic voices, something to challenge the mediocrity of the musical pulp dominating the mainstream and rammed down our throats at every opportunity. We explored the weirdest and grimiest musical corners, unearthing new and forgotten gems, something, anything that hadn't been hijacked, dumbed down and packaged into saccharine shite with barely a morsel of cultural relevance beyond a couple's first shag or a blockbuster film soundtrack.

Our friendship took some time, a forced relationship pushed together as our wives had become close. We socially orbited one another, resistant and reluctant support actors in our respective partner's friendship movie. You know what it's like when they really want you to get on with their best mate's other. It feels like an arranged marriage and something inside repudiates. Neither Tigger nor I wanted or expected any kind of meaningful friendship to develop. I thought he was an arrogant prick. And he is, but then I guess so am I. He has a wild dishevelled look about him, like a sort of late Cobain had Kurt survived another 10 years whilst continuing his particular brand of rock star lifestyle.

Initially, our relationship remained safely superficial, but over time we discovered in each other a shared musical heritage stretching back more than two decades before we met. In fact, whilst utterly oblivious to each other's existence, we both saw Spiritualized's legendary Royal Albert Hall gig in '97, both off our tits on acid. And if there is one album that truly connects us, it has to be *Ladies and Gentlemen, We Are Floating In Space*. It was our album, our ground zero.

Having a mate get this close was a big thing for me. I've always found friendships tough, for as much as I try and resist, I'm drawn to the crazy ones and them to me. It always starts out okay as we winch to the top of our new friendship roller-coaster, but inevitably one of us ends up being too loopy for the other. Sanity is so fucking relative. I find it tough relating to straight people, having normal conversations about normal things, small talk and the concentrated effort it requires. My mind gets super-bored, super-quick and wanders off before they've even finished a sentence. I really try to hang on to what's being said, sometimes all the way to the end, even though it feels dull and predictable. I have a tendency to butt in, which people see as me being rude or not listening, but I just know how the sentence is going to end and don't want to go through the pointless ritual of waiting. Though try I must, for these are the rules of social engagement. Over the years, I've learnt to be better at feigning interest and responding appropriately. But, sometimes they notice the light in my eyes flicker out as my unruly mind coaxes me away with a more interesting tangential thought. I have a condition, you see. On the spectrum, somewhere, but then I guess we all are to some degree, aren't we?

Aren't you?

I'm a kick junkie, a pleasure seeker, some would say a he-donist, but that's an all-too-convenient label. I'm just like everyone else with a constant need for dopamine to help life feel more tolerable. Enjoyable even. The only trouble is the tap in my brain that regulates the flow is faulty and it takes a little more stimulus to kickstart it. I find people on the edge of this or some other condition more interest-ing, more fun and more likely to help release my own happy hormones. What is sanity anyway? Conforming to society's norms? Accepting mundanity? Being debt slaves? Clocking in, clocking off? Devouring mind-numbing entertainment? Filling the hole, the emptiness, the lost sense of purpose, just passing time and waiting to die?

Fuck that. At least those touched by madness make life a bit more interesting, more thought-provoking, more stim-ulating. At least they inject some colour into this otherwise grey, tedious world. As Jeffrey Lewis says in his Leonard Co-hen homage: "It's the ones who've cracked that the light shines through".

Whenever Tigger and I got together, it turned into a part, even if the crowd had whittled down to just the two of us. We'd end up pogoing around the kitchen to The Gun Club, The Cramps, The Fall, The Velvets, Wasted Youth, all sorts of old shite. But the band that truly nailed our friendship and dragged us from what was good back then, to what is good right now, was Fat White Family. We would feast upon their live YouTube footage and their twisted fucked-up videos, giggling our tits off at keyboardist Nathan Saoudi's gliding in and of shot on a skateboard, naked from the waist down as Lias sneers out the vocals to "Touch the Leather". Or the video to "Cream of the Young" with its stomach-churning table manners and blood-curdling lyrics. Or the truly insane footage accompanying "Special Ape".

It was all so wrong. Which is why, to us, it was all so right.

Before we knew it, we were hanging out at each other's pretty much all the time, smoking, drinking, fighting over the next track to play, both intent on blowing the other's mind with something new or unheard or just plain nuts. We were going to gigs all over town and whenever there was a party we'd be there or one of us would be throwing one. Wherever, whatever, it was always a celebration, always a blast. It was also a rare and some would say perfect scenario, our wives and kids all mates and Tigger was my surrogate brother – my brother from another mother.

Chapter Three

Anti-Fashion, Fighting Cocks, Shit Live Music, Warm Flat Beer

With a bottle of orange Lucozade
Showing all the kids how the other kids live
Give 'em all the pop, but take away the fizz
Is this Rome, Babylon, or ancient Belfast?
"Rock Fishes" – Fat White Family

"Would you like to pay for this, Dave?"

I snap out of my thoughts, sucked back into the moment, blinking, readjusting, bringing forth the outward version of me, the one that interacts with the world. It's Piotr, welcoming, friendly, always smiling, with long wavy locks like a surf dude or a 70s rocker. Piotr is sharp as they come, nothing gets past him, he's seen it all having run the Windmill bar for the past fourteen years, before most of the Fat Whites were old enough to even drink. He's smiling, my stout resting before me, already settled.

"Ah sorry, Piotr, for a minute there I lost myself." He laughs as I hand over a tenner.

"Have one on me?" I offer.

He is not really used to that, it's not really a tipping place. Mainly just down to economics but also, at the risk of sounding like a fucking hippie, money's not the primary currency around here.

"I'm fine thanks, bit early for me anyway."

I don't want to make it awkward, so I take my change, grab my drink and nod.

"Okay, before the night's out. . ."

"Sure," he smiles.

He really is the polar opposite of that other barman, the surly death metal fan, whom I eventually discovered is called Toby, a name that does not befit this man's demeanour in any way, shape or form – *way* too friendly. For reasons unclear, Toby just hates everyone. I used to think it was just me, but no, it's everyone, the entire human race. It's as if the nihilism of his music has seeped into his general world view. I've seen him get into many futile spats along the way. I do get it, I've worked a bar and the drinking public can be arseholes to deal with, it goes with the territory. We all have to find a coping mechanism, a way of dealing with all the alcohol-pickled knobheads. This is Toby's chosen method.

I take a large glug of stout and survey the interior of the Windmill again. Still not many in, but a healthy amount considering it's only around 7:45 p.m. I do so love this venue. Watching a band here is not just intimate – it's immersive. This is why I am always conflicted, initially rooting for a band, wishing them all the success, but when it comes, I end up mourning for the good old days. As their audience grows, they move beyond these intimate venues to the next level up; the moment it all begins to change.

You know the places: the show ends, we want a drink, need a drink, deserve a drink – but no, the music stops, lights go bright, bar's closed and unfriendly bouncers shepherd us out like naughty children, "*You can piss off now, party's over*". So, we pour onto the streets, the cold, brittle air killing the buzz, snapping our party heads into sobriety and bringing the evening to an abrupt and disappointing end.

Then you move up the venue trajectory to the 1,500 plus capacity, a journey any aspiring young band naturally yearns for. Yet also the point where the audience experience begins to seriously diminish. You know the gigs: bands perform, audiences observes, mostly passive, apart from some clapping between songs and the obligatory "I was there" shot on their phones, for upload to the more exciting, more fulfilled online versions of themselves. The mosh pits are invariably lifeless, occasionally a small crowd by the stage are dancing, sometimes moshing, but only in that rugger-bugger, let's make a circle, we're so edgy, bullshit way, totally missing the point and so involved in their stupid and frankly irritating game, they forget about the band they've spent their hard-earned cash to go and see.

The bigger the band, the larger the venue, the wider the physical gulf, until you can drive a Sherman tank in front of the stage without hitting a single flailing limb. Any human connection between band and audience distanced to the point of there being . . . no fucking point.

Worse still, when a band is fully embraced by the mainstream, helped along by the promotional machinates afforded to such rock/pop luminaries, they play these massive stadium concerts. Most of the audience only get to see these gangly stick dudes strutting about in the distance. They don't even bother watching the stage. No, their "live" experience is via a ginormous pixelated screen.

Seriously people, why do you bother? So much for the economy of scale, paying stupid amounts for your tickets just to stand in some damp field or stadium; mouth dry cos the queue for warm shitty flat beer is no longer viable, bladder bulging, as the beers you had on the way have arrived at their internal destination and seek immediate release. The toilets a tortuous mission where you find yourself in another queue in which you practically piss yourself. And all of this to watch your favourite fucking band, on a big fucking telly, surrounded by morons who won't shut the fuck up.

And that's supposed to be fun?

Fuck that. At the Windmill, there is no gulf, no distance at all and at times the entire venue is a mosh pit. Also, no green room, so when the bands are not performing, they mix with the audience, in fact, half the audience *are* performers. Most people here know how tough it is to put yourself on the line and this invites higher levels of creative tolerance, a rare thing in today's competitive, commoditised, neoliberal world. Bands here have the freedom to explore, experiment, swap members, try shit out. Sometimes it *is* shit, sometimes they hit upon some thing truly special and unique, other times they go ape-shit-crazy to the point of falling apart – and that just has to be the most exhilarating music, when it can all fall apart at any moment yet somehow doesn't.

Who wants perfection? Who wants their live music polished and safe? Check out the Windmill, let it readjust your set. I promise you will never be fully satisfied when you return to those carefully choreographed, perfectly produced, soul-deadening gigs.

I look around again and right behind me, bent over his lap-top, intensely hammering on the keyboard, I spot the crazy, anti-fashion, overall nut-job that is Angus Knight. Eyes encircled with badly applied black eye shadow and accompanying black lips. He looks like he's about to play Dr Frank-N-Furter in in a local production and I reckon he could just about pull it off.

He's so engrossed in his laptop he hasn't seen me, so I walk towards him, lean over the table to speak and note his large naked hairy legs poking out the bottom of his jacket. Is he wearing no trousers? This place is a backlash to this brand-obsessed culture, so anti-fashion with a touch of am-glam is the order of the day round here, the dodgier the better, even if that means being partially naked.

"Hey, Angus!"

He briefly looks up.

"Hey, man." He quickly returns to his screen. "So, you're not wearing trousers tonight, then?"

Angus looks up again and then smiles theatrically like a bad transvestite, before standing up to reveal his skimpy denim shorts – unreasonably short shorts.

"I'm wearing shorts! I always wear shorts at No Friendz gigs!"

They are in fact women's hot pants and it's also a total lie, which is Angus's default setting, yet delivered with such camp am-dram boldness it's just not worth arguing. He's worn all manner of garb: glam rock, pinstripe suits, dresses, even good old jeans and T-shirt. Tonight, though, denim hot pants will surely finish off the weird look Angus is after and it is without doubt an unbridled success – he does look properly insane.

"Aw shit, I forgot you guys were on tonight."

"For fuck's sake, of course we fucking are!"

"What time?"

"I dunno? Nine fortyish?"

"Oh bollocks. I'm gonna catch The Moonlandingz at the Academy after Zsa Zsa's set – they're on at nine thirty."

"Well, it's up to you," he shrugs, hammily. "Moonlandingz are yesterday. No Friendz are now."

I do love Angus's self-belief, his arrogant pomp. I find it infectious and oddly charming. When I first met him, I thought he was a bit of a dick, in fact, we clashed swords, which looking back was ironic, since it was in a pub called The Fighting Cocks. They were hosting a Meatraffle gig and Angus was standing in for Cloudy Truffles, their bass player and "The Bird Song" vocalist, their biggest hit to date. After the gig, he and I were chatting, during which he quite forcibly attempted to convince me that he'd seen Nirvana's legendary *Reading* performance back in 1992.

"What, on DVD?"

"I was fucking *there*, man."

"No, you weren't."

"I was! Kurt was amazing – came on in a wheelchair wearing a white frock!"

It's true, he did, but you'd only have to watch the DVD to know that.

"What were you then, a foetus?"

He looked at me, a twinkle in his eye. At the time, he looked to be in his early 20s, but found out later he was just 18, so when Kurt wheeled onto Reading's stage twenty five years ago, he wasn't a twinkle in *any-one's* eye. This is the moment I realised Angus is full of shit, yet it is one of his traits I've grown to love and simply come to expect. It can be quite endearing, except perhaps when he inhabits his DJ alter ego "Angus Steakhouse", during which between, say, Joy Division and The Fall, he'll play some of the cheesiest pop possible, including Bucks Fizz, then with a poker face insists his ridiculous musical choices are completely devoid of irony.

Here's a less annoying thing about Angus, he's an incredibly talented musician and can turn his hand to pretty much any instrument. He'll get up to all sorts of Hendrix theatrics when on lead guitar – okay, not nearly as good, but he's got the attitude. His band, No Friendz, are a ridiculously attired glam-infused garage punk band, knocking out crowd-pleasing anthems about being useless, having no friends and wanting to be hedgehogs, which is better in real life than it sounds on paper. The whole band are great musicians: their drummer, Dan GB, turns the cliché on its head by being the sanest and most level- headed member. Then there's Adam Brennan, their sensitive, slightly precious lead guitarist, a true virtuoso, a Vini Reilly for our times and undoubtedly one of the finest guitarists in this whole south London collective. Fronting it all is the at- tention- seeking, fully formed prima donna that is An- gus Knight and as a frontman he's a shit-kicking rock star. Whether No Friendz break through, break up, ex- plode or implode is hard to judge at this stage, but they're great fun live and Angus is definitely one to watch. . .

I grab my stout and then, speak of the devil, Zsa Zsa appears with Madame HiFi.

"Zsa Zsa! Madame HiFi!"

I greet them both with a hug.

"You're late, apparently."

"Aw fackin' hell, Dave. I've had a nightmare day."

"Need any help bruv?"

"Nah fanks, mate. I'll be alwright."

I nod and Zsa Zsa heads to the stage with his equip- ment, then turns back and says something incoherent. Madame HiFi is nearer, so I ask her.

"What's he say?"

"He said wait for him after. He'll walk to the Academy with you."

"Cool. I'm gonna go spend my golden ticket," I reply, presenting my cloakroom ticket as if a precious thing – which it is considering it represents a plate.

"Good idea. Line your stomach for once." Madame HiFi chuckles and continues towards the stage area.

I head the opposite way towards the beer garden.

As I approach, the door flies open and Tigger crashes into me, his new girlfriend, Sadie, is close behind, both in a frenzied hurry.

"Tigger!"

"Heyyy!"

He throws himself at me. I look at his eyes, he's clearly well on the way if not already there.

"You okay?"

"Yeah, but we're off now, dude."

"Where?"

"We gotta go. Uber."

"Where you going?"

"Moonlandingz!"

"You're not gonna catch Zsa Zsa? He's on any minute?"

"No, we don't wanna miss The Moonlandingz."

"You won't, they'll not be on for a good hour."

"We gotta go, dude. Uber's 'ere."

"Why d'you need a fuckin' Uber?" Sadie pipes up.

"Cos it's fookin' raining."

Is she cross? Who with? Tigger? Me?

"Ah, it's only spitting."

I probably shouldn't have said that.

Sadie gives me an icy stare. Time momentarily freezes, then jerks back into action as she tugs Tigger's arm.

"Come on, we gotta go."

And off she trots, Tigger bouncing behind.

As he disappears through the door, a fleeting sense of loss washes over me, a sulky resentment.

Now, where did that come from?

Chapter Four

Trumpet-Wielding Marxists, Lifestyle Fascists and Alien Couture

Pour that guilt into those big wine glasses
Drop your mirrors for scales and bus passes
Well! They've done some mind-expanding
But let's just discuss the benefits of famine
"Drink and Glide" – Snapped Ankles (Austin/Bendel)

29TH JULY 2017, WINDMILL BEER GARDEN

"Well, fancy meeting you here!" comes a voice.

I turn to find Ollie Cookson, keyboardist from the band Honkies standing before me, managing to simultaneously look like a neo-Nazi and an Auschwitz survivor. This man's responsible for introducing me to the dark gothic-country-punk sounds of Country Teasers, whose influence and DNA runs through many of the bands peddling their wares on this south London circuit, particularly here at the Windmill.

"All right, Ollie? We must stop meeting like this."

After constantly bumping into each other at various south London gigs, we soon realised that we might have something in common.

Ollie is quiet but fiercely intelligent, most of it all going on beneath the surface. He is an occasional scribe for The Quietus and plans to interview Ben Wallers of Country Teasers pretty soon. A big fan with a tattoo to prove it, designed by Ben Wallers who twisted one quarter of the swastika and somewhat bizarrely discovered it took on the look of a man running in terror, arms aloft. The eccentric nutter's rather proud of it, calling his creation the "Spak-enkreuz", not after the original Hindu symbol, but the Third Reich's subverted rebrand, the "Hakenkreuz". Ben's solo vehicle is called The Rebel and his "Spakenkreuz" decorates the cover of his 2008 album *Prawns*. It is also the tattoo adorning Ollie's forearm, the mad fucker. It does make me wonder how long Ben Wallers had been experimenting with this Third Reich symbol before discovering this – and more to the point, why? But then you only have to go through his back catalogue to find it is part of an overall theme, for Ben likes to explore the darker side of humanity, whilst ridiculing the fake morality of the mainstream.

I follow Ollie into the beer garden towards the barbie, where I exchange my raffle ticket for an empty plate and join the small, but growing queue for barbecued food, served up by our gruffly jovial host, Seamus. Apparently, the barbie's his thing, but to be frank, apart from sitting on his stool, I don't know what else he does around here. Still, the mere fact that he and Kathleen enable this musical community to thrive is more than enough, to be sure, to be sure.

I'm not particularly hungry, but my stomach needs something more than stout to work with and if I don't eat there'll be payback later, normally in the form of acid reflux. Fresh salad, sweet potato chips and various forms of barbecued dead animal are on offer. So no, this ain't no hippie hang-out. But what a result, five bands (good bands), a slap-up meal, wonderful company, which is quite often the bands you're about to see – and all for a fiver. From the music to the free food, this is something authentic, honest and uncommodified, beyond the reaches of supply–demand capitalism.

I've arrived at the front of the barbie queue. "Burger?" enquires Seamus.

"No thanks."

"Sausage?"

I shake my head. I have this rule you see, to not eat minced or reconstituted meat on account of the fact you've no clue what other shit's been thrown into the mix. Not a critique of Seamus's food, more the whole meat production industry, which is evil in so many ways I'm fighting hard to resist a prolonged rant.

"Just a piece of chicken, please, Seamus."

Seamus usually takes a hard line on the meat front – a piece of chicken, a burger and a sausage is what you get – but he gives me a wink and serves up two pieces of nicely browned chicken. I smile and thank him before moving over to the salad table.

Okay, I'm a hypocrite for eating any meat, but having tried full-on vegetarianism for over 15 years, ending up white, pasty and a barely functioning immune system, I've reverted to the occasional plate of flesh. Not an admission we need to eat meat, because we don't, I'm simply fessing up to being a crap vegetarian, not giving enough attention or proper dietary thought to the project. Plus, I hate all the labels, being confined, boxed in, then constantly judged by your own values. I lean in a vegan direction, but I ain't no vegan. So, all you nutritionists, food fundamentalists and lifestyle fascists, keep your wagging fingers away. I neither crave nor require your condescending, righteous advice.

Mark E. Smith once described vegetarianism as *"just another way of leaving your trolley of normality behind,"* which at the time was on point – of course it was, it was Mark E. Smith. But over the decades the axis of ordinariness has significantly shifted and being vegan has become a mainstream endeavour. And despite how annoyingly self-righteous they can be, it is, of course, a good thing. Just look at the stats: 15,000 litres of water, 25 kilogrammes of grain, just to spit out only a paltry kilogramme of cow steak. It's easy to see that eating meat is borderline insanity and although there is much debate as to the numbers, the people who could be fed with vegetable protein, currently used to rear livestock, runs into billions.

Whilst tucking into a chicken drumstick, I look up to find John Clay standing before me, like he's just beamed in from a 70's space movie.

"Hey, John!"

He looks up, a fine-looking man with so much attention-grabbing style and such a warm friendly smile. Tonight, he is wearing a red leather coat, designed by what can only have been fashion-conscious aliens. His afro curls sculpted into three points, emboldening his otherworldliness, like he's just stepped out the pages of a Marvel comic.

"Yo, Dave!"

"You filming tonight?" I ask, noting the bag of equipment hanging off his shoulder.

"Yeah, some of it. I think Lou will be along later."

John is one of the two key videographers who both play a crucial role in recording and uploading all that is happening here. Lou Smith was first on board and John's been playing catch-up, darting all over south London, recording, editing and uploading various acts of note onto his YouTube channel "Clark Kent's Rock and Roll Revue" (of course). Check it out, especially his series set in producer Margo Broom's living room. More importantly (sorry, John), check out Lou Smith's channel for some very excellent vintage (and recent) Fat White Family footage.

John peers into his phone, which could just as easily be a teleporting device, then slickly inserts it into his pocket and looks up. Something's on his mind.

"I gotta go, catch you later."

Before I can say anything, he skips away. Not rudely, more purposefully – something important needs doing. Saving the planet, a girl from a burning building, something.

I sit down at Ollie's table, who together with Tara and James make up 75% of Honkies; a deranged, synth-infused, honky-tonk, psycho-country outfit. The remaining 25% is their rabid drummer, Lincoln Barrett. He'll be along later, he's been out rehearsing with his other band, Sorry. I'm not apologising, it's actually their name. Like Girl Band, Sweat, Shame and Insecure Men, totally unGoogleable and having potentially undesired effects on your algorithmic profile.

Sorry have developed a unique sound, like Throwing Muses or Breeders put through a London filter. They are often heard on 6 Music, especially by the bright and sunny Lauren Laverne, seemingly a keen fan of their work.

We're sitting around a picnic table enjoying our al fresco fine dining, discussing, comparing, unravelling and guffawing over Country Teasers' lyrics, after which we head inside to catch Zsa Zsa Sapien's set.

Sporting his "Spiritual Gangster" T-shirt, Zsa Zsa has already begun his one-man show, involving trumpet, poetry, samples and singing. A brilliantly brave thing to do, executed without a jot of fear, well, at least none visible on his rugged exterior.

We became friends from pretty much the moment we met. Tigger introduced us and we just clicked into this easy relaxed rhythm, as if we'd always been mates. Zsa Zsa's also another key player in all this, so I should tell you a bit more about him. Perhaps a good place to start would be a very brief bio used on SoundCloud to introduce his composition "Foreign Muck":

"Trumpet-wielding Marxist Zsa Zsa Sapien is the frontman of Meatraffle. He spends his time trolling the EDL, making music and creating communist propaganda with oil paints and stained glass. This particular piece, Zsa Zsa claims, was commissioned (and paid for) by Nigel Farage to play at the UKIP party conference."

All of which is true, apart from the UKIP part, which, I'm sure you appreciate, is ironic, as is the song.

Zsa Zsa is an incredibly prolific creative force, with a Buddha-like quality. I don't mean he's fat, well, he's a tad cuddly and could no doubt pack a punch. In fact, he's an ex-boxer, so most definitely could. I just mean he has a more

Zen-like way of looking at the world, seeing things others don't and then writing a song about it – or painting it. He sees beauty in ugliness, but then again, he probably has to, for as good as Zsa Zsa is at oil painting, he ain't one. In fact, he has the look of someone who's done time for murder. This makes him all the more beguiling, for underneath his menacing demeanour, you discover a loveable, charming and disarming gent. In fact, everyone who knows him loves him and Zsa Zsa seems to know everyone.

He puts on an inventive performance, new compositions alongside interesting interpretations of Meatraffle songs, all well received by the growing audience. One new song, "The Day the Earth Stood Still", is sublime – undoubtedly a future Meatraffle classic.

John Clay is out front, camera on shoulder, taking a well-earned break from bringing a halt to planet Earth's imminent destruction so he can record some of Zsa Zsa's set for later upload onto his Superman-themed channel. He moves around like a Ninja in his quest to capture every conceivable angle, whizzing the lens around the room, adding to the thrill factor of the resulting video. Just don't watch them when you're pissed, you'll be sick – seriously, you will.

As I watch Zsa Zsa, I feel a presence to my left and look around to find a striking young lady very attentively taking in Zsa Zsa's performance. She's wearing thick gothic make-up, with blonde hair poking out from under her black beret. I get a strong sense she could be a Madonnatron fan.

She becomes aware of me gawping, so I quickly speak to break any awkward tension.

"You lookin' forward to Madonnatron?"

Just to be clear, I'm not trying to pull. I'm happily married and even if I wasn't, I'm just not into all that shit.

The truth is, I talk to any*one*, can't help it, it's part of my condition. In fact, my wife's relieved when someone else is on the receiving end.

She smiles, laughing modestly.

"Er. . . I guess."

I look at her puzzled.

"You guess?"

"I'm *in* Madonnatron."

This confuses me. She looks different and much younger than I recall. In fact, I don't recall her at all.

"Really? Have we met?"

"I'm not sure. I joined at the beginning of the year."

"Ah, then we haven't. The last gig I saw was late last year."

She smiles coyly.

"So, what do you play?" I probe.

"I sing."

"What? Lead?"

"No there's three vocalists."

"What happened to the other singer?"

"Er. . . she left."

"Really? I didn't know that."

"Yes, before I joined"

I turn to her conspiratorially.

"Well, she couldn't sing for shit anyway," I say, realising too late how dangerous such talk is, having no clue of their relationship dynamic, or who might be in earshot.

Thankfully, she giggles, then holds out her hand semi-formally, princess-like.

"Joanie."

I take her hand and introduce myself.

"Dave."

We turn to the stage to find Zsa Zsa glaring at us both, he hates people chatting through his set. Joanie and I grimace at each other like naughty children and settle back into Zsa Zsa's performance. He introduces a new Meatraffle composition called "London Life". He'd sent me a rough demo of it a while back, demanding feedback – positive feedback only, that is.

I look around to see if John Clay's recording, but he's disappeared, so I take out my phone, my black mirror, my technological talisman and hit record for later upload to the entire world, should the world care to look. Redemption for chatting through some of his set. I've become an occasional, albeit amateur, videographer too. Although, out of respect, I try not to film if Lou or John are already on the case. They're way better than me and have all the tackle, whereas I just have a phone with a cracked screen. Also, if I plan to record anyone else tonight, I have to record some of Zsa Zsa's set or he'll just sulk. I don't mind though, I love this song, a catchy little ode comparing urban living to country life, describing the regulars of a stereotypical village pub as "dirty kippers drinking in their Little England lounge", instantly bringing to mind the worst characteristics of living in the countryside. Not just the bugs and the pollen, but the wax-jacketed, four-wheel-driving, white reactionary UKIP-voting wankers who inhabit these places. I'm generalising, of course and fully accept this all changes when you get beyond the commutable reach of the capital, like the wilder parts of Cornwall where my mum and bro have pitched their tents. And, of course, there's the North, where healthy layers of creative insanity still thrive.

After Zsa Zsa's set comes to a close, Joanie turns to me.

"Nice to meet you, Dave. Hope to see you later."

"And you, Joanie. I'm off to see Moonlandingz shortly but coming back to catch your set."

"You'd better!" Joanie laughs.

I shrug my shoulders and smile, she kisses my cheek and heads to the bar, but I hold back for Zsa Zsa. If the truth be told, I only have a vague plan and I'm trying not to get too fixated on detail, it only gets me in trouble. I wait as Zsa Zsa gathers his equipment; a trumpet and a Roland SP555, before joining me so we can hoof down Brixton Hill to catch The Moonlandingz set at Brixton Academy; their biggest gig to date.

I do realise it's not *called* Brixton Academy anymore, but who decided these places could be rebranded and corporatised in this way? The Carling Academy? The O2 Academy? It'll be the Goldman Sachs Academy next. In my view, we have a collective duty to only refer to this venue as Brixton Academy. Okay, for any of you rock venue historians out there, it was originally called The Astoria, but at least Simon Parkes' rebranding in 1981 (the chap who paid all of £1 to purchase the venue) was untainted by corporate branding and product placement.

I'm not sure Angus notices us quietly leave. Perhaps it's just my imagination, but I can feel his disappointment boring into our backs as we slip away, slightly ashamed to be going to the bigger widescreen gig at the Academy than remain here, within the warm bosom of the Windmill, for an incendiary slice of No Friendz.

Chapter Five

Kitchen Earthquakes, Mythical Suburbs and King of the Humble Brag

The future isn't what it used to be
I was a bird that preferred to walk
I was a monkey that learnt to talk
"Mama Power" – Phobophobes

29TH JULY 2017, BRIXTON HILL

As I said earlier, it's a difficult night for us. Apart from Zsa Zsa, the Windmill has four other great acts. As we stroll down Brixton Hill towards the Academy, Sex Cells will be hitting the infinitesimally smaller stage. A beautiful, sexy, yet oddly surreal duo, banging out infectious, trashy electro-punk with hyperactive commitment. I have seen them a few times already, so feel less conflicted over their omission from this evening's roster.

Following on from Sex Cells is No Friendz, recently picked up by Liam and Luke May's Trashmouth Records, the first to release albums by Fat White Family, Warmduscher, Meatraffle and now of course Madonnatron.

The Windmill's penultimate act is Ghost Car, a punky outfit reminiscent of "Dead Pop Stars" era Altered Images, yet with more bite. So long as they don't follow the same awful musical trajectory and refrain from "Happy Birthday" songs, they could mature into something interesting. Listening to their lyrics, they do seem to have an issue with men, but I'm pretty sure that doesn't include me, though I willingly accept it might simply by being one.

Finally, we have Windmill headliners Madonnatron, to whom this night belongs, for it marks the day their eponymously titled debut album is released into the world. The cover artwork based around an idea that bubbled to the surface of Zsa Zsa's fertile brain, a striking cover of a Godzilla-sized holy Madonna, lasers projecting from her eyes onto the urban landscape below.

True to the original punk ethos, Madonnatron cut their teeth, learnt their chords and developed their sound totally on the fly. They couldn't play a note when they began, well, none except Beth Soan who played guitar, so she became their drummer – obviously.

"Like listening to a kitchen falling apart in an earthquake," was Fat White Family's, Lias Saoudi's brutal assessment of their early days and having witnessed a few of their early

gigs it's hard not to agree, their departed singer in a wavering key of her own, like Nico when bombed.

Judging by their recent output, it sounds like they've mastered their instruments, found their sound, along with a new-found swagger and suddenly everyone is taking note of these four sexy, sassy, sequined ladies, harmonising dark gothic poetry over post-punk guitar-driven psychedelia, like a witch's choir in a Tim Burton movie.

Brothers Liam and Luke May of Trashmouth Records felt they were on to something (though it was hard to see what, at first), producing and releasing their singles "Headless Children" and "Tron". It seems they were right, 6 Music's Marc Riley and Gideon Coe both latched onto them and now a sessions in the offing.

It will mean a major sacrifice, but I shall endeavour to stay on plan and give the Academy's headline act a swerve so I can return to the Windmill to catch Madonnatron 2.0.

What Brixton Academy's roster lacks in quantity it certainly makes up for in quality. First up, Jane Weaver, having just released her fourth album *Modern Kosmology*, a slow burner but a real corker that has the critics in a tizz of excitement. If you haven't already, you should check it out, though a more mellow perhaps even trippy mood is required. Unfortunately, we've already missed her, sacrificed for Zsa Zsa's performance.

See what a good mate I am to the moany old fucker? Oh, have I not mentioned that? Zsa Zsa can be a right proper moaner.

Then there's The Moonlandingz, who are due on any minute, so we'd better get a wiggle on. Formed purely as a concept for an album by anarcho-electronic outfit Eccentronic Research Council (ERC), who invited Lias Saoudi and

Saul Adamczewski of Fat White Family to create a fictional band with them, based in mythical Sheffield suburb, Valhalla Dale. Their combined efforts produced four songs featured in ERC's snappily titled *Johnny Rocket, Narcissist and Music Machine. . . I'm Your Biggest Fan.* Driving the narrative is Maxine Peake (actor, Labour activist and all-round National Treasure), who takes on the role of a fanatical stalker obsessed with the band's singer Johnny Rocket – a character deftly inhabited and clearly embellished by Lias, who saw his Ziggy moment and hurled himself at it with glam-sleaze fucked-up relish. The Moonlandingz tracks were scooped together for an EP which caught the attention of 6 Music's Marc Riley, particularly "Sweet Saturn Mine" which he played on rotation, clearly oblivious to its dodgy lyrics. An ode to the milk of life and yes, I do mean semen. Now, Marc Riley is broadcast weekdays from 7 p.m., so teatime, family time, practically daytime radio and not an easy lyric to explain to the kids. Arguably, Riley kicked the whole buzz off, bringing them into the slightly more mainstream culture and in April this year, he invited this fictional band to step out into the real world (well, a BBC studio) and perform these songs live for the first time. They also caught the attention of Sean Lennon and so fascinated was he by their whole schtick, he invited them all to stay over at his gaff where they messed around in the Beatles' son's studio. Spurred on by all this excitable attention, The Moonlandingz came kicking and screaming into the world, like one of Dr Frankenstein's monsters, fully-formed, fictitious backstory already in place, all in character – especially Johnny Rocket – and took the whole shebang on the road.

So, for this and for the interest he has shown in so many emerging south London bands, including Phobophobes,

Goat Girl, Meatraffle and Madonnatron, I doff my cap to Marc Riley.

The Moonlandingz are playing support to Goat, a mask wearing psychedelic afrobeat outfit from Sweden, tonight's headliners and a spectacle like no other; two women out front, wildly dressed from head to toe, not one bit of flesh on display yet somehow incredibly sexy. I saw them at Field Day last year, visually and aurally stunning, banging out psychedelic world music like nothing I've seen or heard before. The sort of thing that would send 6 Music "Freak Zone" DJ Stuart Maconie into spasms of ecstasy and probably does. Though, it's hard to tell with him, for even his resting face has the look of a man wanking.

In the interest of balance, it needs to be said that not everything about 6 Music is good. It still has playlists (though their DJs appear to have way more influence than any commercial station would allow) and some of their DJs can be particularly irritating. Like, for example, Elbow's Guy Garvey. It was my bro who pinned down why and once you see it, you can never un see it – or, in Garvey's case, unhear it. If you think he's a top bloke and want to hang on to that, I suggest you move to the next chapter now, otherwise this new awareness will make listening to his show as hard for you as it is for me now.

Accompanying almost every song, Garvey offers up a personal anecdote connecting him to the performer. Always someone he knows, has met, went to school with, played footie with, recorded with, played support to, was supported by, met on a train, met in a pub. His show is a never-ending stream of *"Lovely chap"*, *"Really good pal o' mine"*, *"I met PJ Harvey on a plane once and I asked her. . ."*, *"I used to frequent the same pub as him and he told me. . ."*, *"We went to school together"*, *"He taught me how to play guitar"* and so on. And it's not just an occasional thing , he does it ALL THE FUCKING TIME.

For all his "bloke down the pub" delivery, I can no longer ignore his anecdotal blatherings as he recounts the turgid details of each and every unremarkable encounter.

So, who put Garvey on the radio?

The beeb, that's fucking who.

Chapter Six

Lord Snooty, False Prophets and George Osborne's Arse

I wish I had the time
To be a wanker just like you
And maybe then
I'd be somewhere lovely and warm
Just like you
"Elocution" – Sleaford Mods

ERC are political, more so than the Fat Whites, but then they're from in and around Sheffield, where it's a criminal offence to vote Tory. Almost.

I recall when Tigger sent me the SoundCloud link to ERC's track "Loathsome Dave" around the time of the 2015 election. You know, the one Miliband lost, all because someone had managed to make him look like a rubber-mouthed Nick Park animation whilst eating a bacon sandwich. No doubt a publicity-driven staged event cooked up by Miliband's campaign manager to show the voting public he wasn't actually *that* Jewish, trying to woo those leaning in a UKIP direction, politically expedient to fan the embers of racism, shamefully aglow after all these years.

Miliband's bacon sandwich stunt totally backfired, of course, as an already unsympathetic, predominantly right-wing press decided to make him look like a twat. It's too easy nowadays, especially when someone's eating, just film them and then go through each frame until you find the money shot.

Have you ever noticed how the visual narrative in the media is *the* most compelling and persuasive? Just look at the way it changed during Theresa May's ill-fated snap election. Once the media got up-close and personal they discovered May to be not just frustratingly evasive but devoid of intellect, sincerity and humanity. Conversely, Corbyn came over as honest, genuine, engaging and, rather ironically, strong and stable. So, when, to everyone's utter astonishment, the tide of opinion changed and the popularity stakes altered, so did the visual media. The sands were shifting in disorientating ways and they'd lost control of the narrative. "Oh, so you hate May now? Don't trust her? You'll like these shots, then." Gone were the pictures projecting Corbyn as a tinfoil-hat-wearing buffoon (remember the one they kept trotting out of him in his allotment shorts?), instead, we had shot after shot of Maybot grimacing like she'd just eaten a freshly squeezed turd from the bony arse of her nemesis, George Osborne. The nation's shifting sentiments reflected by the choice of news imagery. They only want to be on one side, the one that sells papers, regardless of their own political bias. Of course, they're only teasing us, for they will *never* let Corbyn into Number 10.

ERC's "Loathsome Dave" was a timely piece of biting poetry spat out with appropriate venom by Maxine Peake, alongside a fucked-up electronic, industrial soundscape. Not what you'd call a song, more a slice of anger at Cameron projecting himself as a normal guy, when we all knew he was just the *Beano*'s Lord Snooty all grown up.

It is no small wonder people are apathetic over the effort of voting when nothing ever really changes and you end up hating the government, whatever colour their flag.

Do you remember Russell Brand telling us not to vote, then changing his mind, then writing a book called *Revolution*? It even proclaimed on the cover "*This book is the beginning of a conversation that will change the world.*" which, by anyone's standards is one fuck of an oversell, particularly when you discover it's really about how good he is at meditating, with a cover shot of him looking deep and thoughtful, illustrating in capital letters the brazen vanity driving this project, pissing on any hope it might be something more noble, more profound, more life-changing. Revolution, my arse. *My Booky Wook 3* more like. Just another narcissistic wank-fest. And yes, I have read it. I'm an optimist. I'd clung onto the hope that he *did* have something to say, we were just building up to it. Surely Brand was heading *somewhere* with all this. Somewhere a little more, I dunno, *revolutionary*?

For a while, there was a real sense he might be on to something. Do you remember how it felt? Brand getting up all the right noses, tapping into decades of frustrated, thwarted anger. Momentum was building, bubbling under the surface, like magma beneath Yellowstone Park. You could feel the Establishment's sphincter clenching, the smell the panic and a whiff of revolution. Could this be it? Could this be our moment?

Sadly not. The foreplay was way better than the shag. Way fucking better. Even poor ill-fated Miliband found himself swept up in the hysteria, believing viewers of *The Trews* could turn his election fortunes around and like a desperate salesman trying to close a deal before his company deadline, he turns up at Brand's door. This transitory transfer of power gave Brand a hard-on and you didn't need to see the bulge in his pants, it was written all over his smug, manicured face. Maybe, just maybe, this episode of *The Trews* would be seismic, the tipping point, the day Britain woke up and finally gave the Tory's the kicking they deserved, all because of Russell Brand's YouTube channel.

We all know how it turned out. Drunk on power, Brand went from deriding the system, encouraging non-participation in the upcoming election, to endorsing a politician and contradicting his entire fucking premise. Miliband spectacularly lost to the pig-fucking Lord Snooty and Brand, visibly deflated, was left holding his soggy flaccid cock, messiah complex reversed; embarrassed, naked, pathetic. Disappointing does not describe how it felt.

Much like after the 2010 election when Tigger let slip he'd voted Tory. . .

* * *

Yes, that is what I said. And I was stunned, too.

8TH MAY 2010, TIGGER'S KITCHEN

"Are you fucking winding me up?"

"What did *you* vote, then?" snaps Tigger defiantly.

"Is that seriously a fucking question?"

His faced suggests it is a fucking question.

"Labour for fuck's sake!"

"Wasted vote round here, dude."

This is technically true, but if we all took that view, nothing would ever change.

"You'd have had more chance voting Lib Dem, dude," he continues.

This is also technically true, but now they've slept with the devil, they're forever off my list.

"You think I'm gonna trust those power-hungry wet tossers with a tactical vote?" I snap.

He's winding me up. Surely?

"You're fucking yanking my chain you twat!" I say, staring into his eyes.

He holds firm and says nothing, just stares smugly, cocking his head back with an air of insolence.

"Seriously?"

"Yeah," he retorts, like an obstreperous teenager.

I shake my head, confused, look up at him, still hoping his face will crack and end this torment.

It doesn't. He *is* serious. I want to hit him.

"What the fuck, man! Why?"

"Got to think of me business, innit."

Clearly being with the majority has emboldened his confidence sufficiently enough to go public over his brainless ballot box choice.

"What have the Tories ever done for your business?"

Tigger ran a plumbing business, which to be frank was struggling.

"Sometimes you have to put yourself first, dude."

I was gobsmacked, betrayed – politically betrayed. Is there such a thing? I had never actually asked, just assumed he was a socialist. I'd often go off on one of my rants and he'd rarely disagree or proffer an alternative view, so this new information was hard to assimilate.

"You stupid cunt! Look at the shit-show they're making of this, we're all worse off, we're all miserable and yet, somehow, like proverbial Christmas turkeys, idiots like you vote these black-hearted fuckwits back in!"

"Yeah. . . but they've been good for the economy."

"Says who? The government? So, GDP's improving? What does that even mean? Growth is no gauge of success, it's not a quality measure, it has zero meaning in our lives. Look around, see how people are really living, for fuck's sake!"

"They're more efficient," asserts Tigger.

"They are tearing the heart out of everything we've fought for. Everything that made us civilised." I shake my head in disgust.

"Efficient. The Nazi's were fucking efficient!"

"What? So Corbyn's the answer?"

"A good dose of socialisms' exactly what this country needs right now."

"You'll pay more taxes, dude."

I continue shaking my head, wondering what has happened to my mate.

"You know what the most brutal fucking tax is?"

"What?"

"Austerity!"

He stares at me, confused.

"That's not a tax."

"'Course it fucking is! A tax on the most vulnerable. That's the political ideology you've signed up to."

"For fucks sake, dude!" Tigger snorts.

"How can you listen to the music you do, we do, then vote fucking Tory, it doesn't make any sense?"

He doesn't really have an answer and after a while, I found it hard to maintain my anger. It wasn't like I was arguing against some hard-line Tory philosophy. There was nothing to debate and I couldn't reason with him; not because he had strong views – more like *no* views. As with most Tory voters, he was politically unschooled and just went along with the mainstream media narrative.

This all changed when he met Sadie. A hardcore lefty from Lancashire and she was having none of it. So, Tigger, encouraged by copious amounts of raucous sex, literally changed political direction overnight. He even went canvassing for Corbyn with Zsa Zsa during the run-up to the last election. So, even if it was driven by carnal desire, at least he saw the light – the political light, that is.

29*TH* JULY 2017, BRIXTON HILL

hatting, smoking, slurping on our tinnies, Zsa Zsa and me are ambling our way down Brixton Hill towards the Academy. Zsa Zsa has three modes: introspective, moany or mischief-making. He habitually writes new songs in his head. I think the rhythm of walking acts as a percussive aid, so you get used to him drifting off.

"You all right, mate?"

"Yeah, just a bit stressed."

"What's up?"

"I'm firsty." He heads towards a Food and Wine along the route.

"Wanna beer?"

"Do we have time? Moonlandingz are on soon," I look at my phone. "Now even."

Zsa Zsa looks at me puzzled, not seeing what the issue is. I smile.

"I'll have a Guinness, mate."

He reaches for the tinned draft version.

"Do the widgets work without a glass?" "Yeah, fink so."

And it did. So, we slurp our beers and continue our journey as I press him further over the cause of his stress.

"I'm all right now, got a beer."

Zsa Zsa, like many people, suffers from bouts of existential angst, but rarely opens up about it. I suspect on this occasion, the cause of his stress is his broken phone, but he would never admit that something so cultural, so material, so utterly *worldly* could be the cause of his discontent. No, not Zsa Zsa the revolutionary.

I haven't really told you how we met, have I?

Chapter Seven

Herding Meerkats, Marketing Marxism and the Last Cultural Taboo

Don't be sod, give a nod, give a nod
Give a nod, to the Sleaford Mods
Leave your job, shut your gob
Be a yob to the Salford snob
"It's All Free" – I, Ludicrous

Meatraffle are a big favourite on the live circuit, one of the unlikeliest yet coolest bands to have emerged from all this. Fat White Family posted a tweet about them in 2015 "*The greatest band in the country right now, bar none*". A statement they have literally milked the fuck out of ever since.

I first met Zsa Zsa at one of their gigs when out with Tigger and Sadie a year ago. The venue was closing but we wanted to continue partying, my gaff was the nearest, so it started there.

5TH AUGUST 2016, KITCHEN TABLE, HOME

Tigger, Sadie, Zsa Zsa, Madame HiFi and me are sitting around the table drinking, smoking and playing each other all sorts of shite into the wee hours. Zsa Zsa and me dominating the choices, lots of dub from him, Au Pairs and Jeffrey Lewis Crass covers from me. And on it went, like a musical flirting match, until Zsa Zsa locks onto me with a serious expression.

"Dave, I got somfin' serious to ask you."

He's either about to sell me drugs or offer me protection. "Should I be worried?"

He smiles gently, exposing his gold front teeth as he shakes his head. I strap myself in, no clue what's coming.

"Would you be our manager?"

I nearly spit out my beer – wasn't expecting that. I guess he liked my choices during our DJ clash/musical foreplay.

"Wow! Fuck!"

I'm shaking my head, perplexed, off balance, drunk. "Meatraffle?"

"Yeah."

"Really?"

"I fink you'd be good."

"Oh man" I laugh, embarrassed. "I'm well flattered, mate."

Of course, I am. Who wouldn't be? Yet through the fog of intoxication, a vaguely more sensible, less ego-pumped voice begins to emerge. I stare at him again, trying to read Zsa Zsa's face, then he cracks a smile and we both simultaneously burst out laughing.

"Is this a wind-up?"

"No, I'm fackin' serious." I think he might be.

"Mate, I'm well interested, but I reckon we should have this conversation sober."

Zsa Zsa agrees, so we exchange numbers and arrange a meetup with the band. He's a democratic band leader after all.

26TH SEPTEMBER 2016, CROWN & SCEPTRE, SW2

A few weeks on and we're sitting round a table for our scheduled band meeting. They all came: Chris OC, Fats, Cloudy Truffles, Tingle Lungfish and (of course) Zsa Zsa Sapien. No, I have not made these names up and this is not a children's book, they're all real people. Okay, their names *are* made up, but not by me.

It was awkward at first, all of us unsure how to kick things off. Fats, a beardy beefcake with intense mania behind his eyes, like he could turn when pissed. Tingle, their lead guitarist; short, shaven, self-contained and *very* hard to read. Chris OC, their keyboardist, with the look of a Cuban revolutionary, complete with moustache and wavy black hair, a cool look, no question. All of them are staring, boring into me with poker-faced suspicion. Their bass player Cloudy has a soft natural beauty and an aura of tranquillity about her, almost counterbalancing the tension from the men. All the while, Zsa Zsa just sits there calmly observing it all, waiting for events to unfold, for the show to begin. I have a few questions prepared, so to cut through the awkward tension, I scan my notes and launch straight in.

"How would you square any commercial financial success with your obvious Marxist leanings?"

They laugh, some of them nearly spitting out their beer. Fats leans in, slightly confrontationally, his eyes darting around as he speaks.

"Why d'you say that?"

"Well, I mean. . . your lyrics?" They all laugh again.

What's funny? They all play in a band whose album cover art is a portrait of Vladimir Lenin, whose mosh pit favourite is an ominous anthem calling on us to collect up all the bankers, stuff them inside a modern-day Wicker Man and burn them alive.

"It's a fair question," interjects Cloudy.

I am instantly grateful for her presence. She has such a warm open face and for that quality alone she could undoubtedly be an excellent therapist. The guys continue frowning, stony-eyed, viewing me through a lens of suspicion. I get it. Who the fuck *am* I?

I can't answer that one.

"What experience do you have?"

"None." I laugh, but it hangs in the air like a bad smell and now they look even more tense and uncomfortable. I look at my pad, but all my pre-prepared questions feel stupid.

Fuck it, time to clear the air, let them know where I'm at.

I chuck my notes on the table.

"Look, I'm flattered to be asked - well considered - to manage you guys, but I'm not sure I can even do this, that's why I wanted to meet you. Find out what's involved, see if it's even feasible. Equally, you need to have confidence in me. So, let's just have a chat and see where we end up?"

"Seems reasonable," says Chris, relaxing.

"Fair enough," adds Tingle, his first comment since our initial greeting.

I continue and for every question pitched, five different answers come back and as the evening goes on, it feels more like they want me to shove a broom up my arse and do all the shite they hate doing. I quickly realise, there's no way on earth I can manage this band, or *any* band for that matter, my life is already too crazy-manic and it's becoming increasingly apparent, managing this lot will be like herding meerkats.

Don't get me wrong, I love Meatraffle. Most of all, I love the fact they exist. They're at the coalface of the last taboo in this woke-driven campaign to strike out all prejudice. That taboo is ageism. I mean, let's be brutally frank here, no A&R person will want to bring this disparate bunch to their next record company meeting. They'd be a hard fucking sell, no question, probably get laughed out the boardroom. They would sooner go for bands like Cabbage, Shame or Goat Girl, with bucket loads of youth on their side, less complicated lives, less logistical issues, less kids and spouses through which to navigate a rock and roll lifestyle and, most importantly, much more saleable to the masses.

There is no denying Cabbage, Shame and Goat Girl are all great bands, their very existence represents a cultural shift, audiences demanding more than just mere entertainment. Anger is back in the mix, politics is cool again, the times are most definitely a-changing, but that's not really my point. Meatraffle are not young, Zsa Zsa least so. Yet, in defiance of these biological setbacks and cultural boundaries, Zsa Zsa is a man on a mission, energetically making up for lost time, prolifically knocking out song after song, all different, all laced with politics, wry humour and a sense of mischief. The only unifying element in Meatraffle's eclectic body of work is Zsa Zsa's trademark trumpet. It would be natural to assume he'd been at it for years, writing his prose, creating his samples, peddling his wares, but no, he only started six years ago at the less-than-tender age of 42, as a non-musician. He ticks all the boxes of an "I'm gonna be a rock star" midlife crisis. Yet, Zsa Zsa wears his age with swagger and carries it off with such stoic confidence, he's become one of the coolest characters within this whole south London collective. Something magical happens with Meatraffle and they keep on surprising, continually outsmarting us, the band collectively lifting Zsa Zsa's musings into cinemas cope. Musically, lyrically and visually, Meatraffle are unpigeonholeable.

***

Some weeks later, in a long, rambling, heartfelt email to Zsa Zsa, I politely decline the job of band manager, which may well have saved him from an awkward conversation. I do offer to help in small ways though, offering to approach some labels on their behalf.

Let's give Rough Trade a go, I thought, they've just signed Goat Girl, a superb Country Teasers/Au Pairs/Bill Hicks inspired band, who hit the ground running with their excellent double A-side single, "Country Sleaze/Scum", released through Rough Trade last year and includes more than just a musical nod to their hero Ben Wallers of Country Teasers.

After a bit of Duckduckgoing I found Jeannette Lee's and Geoff Travis's contact details, so employed the same tactic they'd recently used to snarl Sleaford Mods – an email.

Now, I love Sleaford Mods and as a live experience they're magnificently intense. Quite how two old blokes and a laptop can fill the entire Roundhouse with such frenzied hysteria is a triumph in itself. Andrew Fearn hits play and then just stands around sipping on a tinny, like the Wizard of Oz with the curtain pulled back, holding a mirror to other electronic acts and their so-called *live* shows. Fearn's domain is the studio, so onstage it's Jason Williamson's turn to shine and he doesn't disappoint, spitting out rhymes with machine gun fury, shouting, swearing, saying all the things you would love to say out loud but hold back for fear of being a social outcast or arrested for disturbing the peace. He prowls the stage with manic energy, cutting shapes belonging *only* to him as he repeatedly hits the back of his head, summoning up communal frustration over government corruption, austerity, Brexit, shit wages and whatever else finds itself in Williamson's crosshairs, reflecting back the nation's shattered psyche for anyone not a Tory.

So, I dispatched a cheeky, upbeat missive to Roughtrade, embedded with Meatraffle song links and reviews. Geoff responds almost instantly, friendly too, saying he'd really enjoyed them play Montague Arms in New Cross. I became momentarily excited, until he went on to politely say "I am afraid it's not something we want to get involved in." I pressed him for a reason why, but he failed to provide one.

I'm not saying Geoff is being ageist, but let's just say Goat Girl are young, attractive and way more packageable. This band formed in a Meatraffle mosh pit, now they're regular Guardian favourites and Dan Carey's producing their debut, their trajectory to bigger things seemingly unstoppable. I spoke with their lead singer Clottie Cream one night in The Shed where she told me of the pressures they'd endured to sex themselves up, become an indie Spice Girls. They resolutely refused and for this they must be respected. So, not a pop at younger bands, but ageism in A&R, because it exists for sure. Certainly, Sleaford's were an anomaly, but they'd already made their mark well before their email from Roughtrade.

Nevertheless, in defiance of these cultural setbacks, it's an exciting time for Meatraffle. 6 Music latched on to their feminist post-punk anthem, "The Bird Song", raucously sung by Cloudy, challenging misogynistic labels for women. A double A-side with Warmduscher's "The Sweet Smell of Florida," both produced by Dan Carey and released through his label Speedy Wunderground for Record Store Day in 2016. Now, hot on the heels of Fat White Family and Moonlandingz, Marc Riley has just invited them in for a session. Meatraffle on the radio. Woo!

Chapter Eight

Boiled Frogs, Indie Music and the Big Idea that Totally Fucked the World

Talk about rubbing your face in it
With the trickledown effect
Well, that's just the point isn't it?
It's only just an ickle trickle
A drip in a cell that goes drip drip drip
Caught by a mouth with cracked up lips
"Mannaggia la Miseria" – Meatraffle

When I was younger, I remember gigs being more visceral, dangerous and unpredictable, but somewhere along the way I'd been pummelled into musical numbness by all the bland and predictable shite coming at me from every direction.

It was troubling. What on earth had happened in those intervening years?

Was it just me or a general malaise?

Had I done a James Murphy and lost my edge?

When did musicians become assets and bands become brands, referring to their output as 'product'?

When did music become so safe and predictable?

Punk had long since become a parody of itself and indie sucked so far into the mainstream, the line between "Boy" and "Indie" Band has finally blurred – a wet dream for all those major label A&R knobheads.

Indie? Even the word's been subverted.

It stands for *independent*, what it says on the tin: independently created and produced, independent of shareholder's demanding a return. It was a spirit, an ethos, not a fucking *genre*.

Are we really so idiotic that we allow our art to be reduced to this?

Seems we are, judging by the plethora of lightweight bullshit from a never-ending stream of so-called "indie bands" and their anthemic whiny bollocks, carrying with it all the cultural significance of a wet fart.

Yet, you lot bought it all, hook line and fucking sinker. I mean Bastille, The 1975, Blossoms, Panic at the Disco, Catfish and the Bottlemen. Really?

The indie rot had begun years before with bands like Kasabian, most definitely not what they say on their tin. For all their anti-Establishment imagery and rebellious-sounding noise, they have absolutely nothing to say. NOTHING. Artistically bland, musically derivative and intellectually barren, just empty, meaningless football terrace chanting with as much political insight as the air inside a fucking football. Yet, despite all this, they were massively popular.

Much like with Coldplay, trying so hard to bridge the gap between Radiohead and Jeff Buckley but ending up in a shallow river of wank from which Chris Martin whined about everything being yellow, like it was somehow profound. I mean, unless he has an eye condition, it is totally meaningless cock-cheese with as much depth and authenticity as a Theresa May election slogan.

Since their indie-lite beginnings, Coldplay have been sucking long and hard on Satan's cock, selling what little they had left of their souls to become another empty vacuous shiny auto-tune reliant pop band, which no amount of free trade posturing or coloured tape on Chris Martin's hand can disguise. This man cannot even split up from his wife normally, no, they have a *"conscious uncoupling"*, like every other fucker's asleep when their marriages fall apart, like we're all lesser, unenlightened beings. And to cap it all, he endorsed that pig fucker, Cameron. Seriously, what a cunt.

Are you old enough to remember when festivals were counterculture? I mean, they should be counterculture, that is their point. I remember the days when entering a festival was like stepping into a parallel universe. No cops, no rules – just beautiful, peaceful anarchy.

What are they now? Corporate investments sold on the AIM market, titillating the more adventurous investors looking to get hard over their edgy portfolio choices. It's true, you get 30% immediate tax relief on any lump sum into specific tax-efficient financial instruments, all with innocuous acronyms (VCTs, EIS, BPR). Some of these are specifically designed around music festivals – and have no doubt, these investors *expect* a return. This is why you can't bring your own beer. Shit, you can't even bring your own water, you know, that basic human requirement to stay alive. No, for the privilege of remaining hydrated, be prepared to cough up a fiver a bottle. Rock and *fucking* roll . . .

***

It was innocuously named acronyms for financial instruments that caused the entire international financial system to go down the shitter in 2008. It has never recovered, despite some sleight of hand, media misdirection and, well, just rigging the game hoping no one will notice. The world is in collective denial, but Friedrich Hayek's "Big Idea" is over; neoliberalism is dead. The so-called "free market" fell to its knees and begged the State for help and in that moment negated its entire ideological premise. All we have now is an over bloated facsimile of its former self, a zombie economy pumping out ghost currencies, with nothing but collective belief keeping it going, like a mass suicide cult.

I know the term "neoliberalism" is bandied about a lot these days, but let's just be clear on this, EVERYTHING we are living with now; all the social issues, the homelessness, the debt slavery, the unpoliceable globalised corporate goliaths that have literally hijacked the planet and everyone on it, ALL exist because of it. We now have fewer than 40 people with as much wealth as half the population of the planet. The best evidence there is that neoliberalism is THE reason for the total clusterfuck the world is today and at its core lies a dark, brutal philosophy.

Thatcher idolised Hayek's "Big Idea", intent on giving it life with a Victorian value twist. You may be old enough to remember her taking on the unions, causing pit closures, factory shutdowns and destroying the lives of millions. We all thought she was just cruel and heartless. She was, but moreover these actions were lifted directly from the neoliberal implementation handbook, the first phase of which was to weaken the Welfare State, cut taxes, deregulate, remove the dignity of labour and most importantly crush the souls of the unions. All considered necessary in securing its primary aim of removing *anything* that might distort the market's determination of value, all seen as unnecessary external forces that, in their mind (Hayek, et all), create an unfair market.

In the name of ideology, workers were bullied and national industries privatised, with many dismantled and destroyed, along with the entire industrial base of the UK – except of course weaponry.

Thatcher succeeded, as did Reagan in the States and since then we've seen wages stagnate across both continents, the resulting financial hole in the family budget filled with access to easy credit. We went from being a country of savers – no consumption without the cash – to a nation of having everything now, on the knock, the never-never and like lambs to the slaughter we all became debt slaves.

Very quickly this insane system mushroomed into existence across the globe, accelerated by the fervour at which Western governments fell under the spell of its philosophy: the market decides everything, supply–demand maintains value and everything, *everyone*, is commoditised. The new game in town was deregulation, red tape cut, rule books torn up, the market set free. Over time, this system was fully adopted across the world, whilst its evil twin "globalisation" exploited the rest of it.

Despite its seemingly heartless premise Hayek's 'Big Idea' may well work in its purest theoretical form, but it's based on the premise we're all driven by material ambition. It truly failed because Hayek and his Mont Pelerin Society did not account for the divisive impact of unrestrained monopolies and the unequal complexity globalisation brought to the table, all of which caused the gulf between the rich and poor to accelerate at a truly absurd rate and the reason this whole Ponzi scheme - our financial system - collapsed in on itself. It was Capitalism on steroids and much like the impact of real steroids, it gave the entire system a cardiac arrest. It has never recovered and it is hard to see how it ever will. Okay, they keep trying to convince us it's alive and kicking, that its business as usual, but it's not. A smokescreen, pretending to be running along the same free market rules, merely the appearance of a functioning system.

Let's be clear on this; if we really believed in a true free market economic system, then the banks that failed should have been allowed to *fail* and any government rescue package directed towards all the savers who'd watched their hard-earned cash go up in a puff of derivative fuelled smoke. The "*Too big to fail*" mantra was too convenient; decisions made by politicians either too ignorant, too shell shocked or too concerned about their stock options. If they'd had the balls to allow the banking empire to crumble, it would not have been the Armageddon they sold us. Naturally, it would have led to some chaos, but the system would have adapted. Admittedly, easier to say than do, but my point is nothing disappears, only this ghost currency we've all wrapped our lives around, unable to conceive of anything else.

There is an emerging threat to the current financial system which is becoming increasingly harder for them to laugh off and that's the pure philosophy of crypto currency. An incredible affront to the mainstream financial system, exposing all its weaknesses to anyone who cared to look and cutting out the requirement for banks to even exist. The other reason Crypto is a threat is much like cash, it is anonymous, in fact *more* anonymous – and they definitely don't like that. Crypto is without doubt a glimpse of our future, for the question is not *if* the current system will fail? But *when*? And arguably it already has.

In stark contrast to everyone else, the Icelandic government allowed their three largest banks to crumble into dust, then jailed all the crooked bankers and, here's the best bit, gave billions of Icelandic króna to householders to help them reduce their own debts or compensate for lost savings. They bailed out the people *not* the banks.

Furthermore, Iceland's first female prime minister, Jóhanna Sigurðardóttir, followed Norway's lead and ushered in new rules ensuring the make-up of boardrooms was at least 40% women.

This makes total sense when you consider how, for example, Royal Bank of Scotland (RBS) had a dick-swinging battle with Barclays over the takeover of toxic bank ABN AMRO. Both boardrooms, chocked to the brim with brainless testosterone, pumped up the value to unrealisable levels. RBS won the battle which precipitated their near collapse and subsequent nationalisation, in other words, they threw the problem over the wall to us, the trusty taxpayers.

So, Iceland bailed out the people. An idea briefly considered here but dismissed as a "moral hazard." Seriously? The

UK and the rest of the Western banking system all received government bailouts, corrupt bankers were protected and they made *us* all pay for their fuck-up with austerity cuts. Now, there's your moral hazard right there!

Throughout the last 10 years, they've continued to throw money at this debt powered runaway train by any means possible. Need £40 billion? Switch on the printing press. To starkly illustrate this point, since the global bank meltdown, governments around the world continued creating new money, expanding it further through fractional reserve banking (i.e., debt) and now there's THREE times the amount of money in the global financial system than there was 10 years ago. Yup, it's that fucked.

The system's on life support whilst the rich just get richer, because all the extra money pumped into the system floats to the top. There's only enough socialism in their hearts for the banks, not the rest of us whose debts are real, no government bailouts, no debt forgiveness, we're just going to have to wait for the fucking trickle down.

Ever get the feeling you've been cheated?

Chapter Nine

Tofu Love Frogs, Chanting Hippies, Noel's Breakfast Party

Laced with fame, faux socialism
Fair Trade cocaine in your system
Put it in the bin, let the children fish it out
Shaking both hands, the rebel brand
"Human Baby" – The Phobophobes

Glastonbury was once counterculture and if you went, you were immediately considered *suspect* by normal folk. There was a time I would religiously go, regardless of how traumatic the last one had been.

Over the years I witnessed it morph from counterculture to the sponsored corporatised colossus it is today. Yet, despite its popularity, Michael and Emily Eavis have never been in it for the money, only the love of it and the charities they support, surrendering large sections of the site to the imagination of others. This is what makes *Glastonbury* special, for whilst there are undoubtedly pockets of wrong-headed capitalism within, the overall ethos of the festival is driven by something way beyond share dividends. In the festival world, the Eavis's are the good guys.

Back in the day, my real bro – my brother from the *same* mother – was my main gig buddy. He has long since gone west to the tippy tip of Cornwall, practically in the sea.

Glastonbury was our alternative annual health farm, an excursion from the hard, cold, serious real world. And like with Tigger, whenever we got together anything could happen. The "Glastonbury magic" they call it and we found some back in '97.

29TH JUNE 1997, WORTHY FARM, SOMERSET

It's around 9 a.m. Sunday morning, after what has been a long and eventful Saturday night. Most of our mates peeled away about half an hour ago to crash at our camp, but stalwarts that we are, me and my bro still have one final ritual to complete before retiring to our individual canvas sanctuaries. We are to reach the Stone Circle just before dawn, just before all the hippies and nut-jobs welcome the first slither of sun as it peeps over the Tor-dominated horizon – and they do welcome it, with pagan-infused abandon. Didgeridoos booming, tom-toms clattering, hippies chanting, revellers whooping, cheering, dancing. It really is quite fantastic. Well, it is when you're amongst it, but we're about four hours too late, so not this time, the sun wouldn't wait for us. Still, we've made our pilgrimage now, so we just need a place to park our tired bony arses.

It's another muddy one, which has significantly slowed down our efforts as we tromp and squelch through that special festival mud, the consistency of whipped cream, the colour of shite.

Some of it is shite, mainly cows, sometimes human, especially the following year if you happened to have ventured near the dance tent, for it had been sprayed with human excrement after the shit sucking toilet machine was mistakenly switched to blow. I'm sure you must know that story, so I'll continue with this one.

"Where're we gonna fucking sit?" asks my bro, looking somewhat defeated.

He had a point. Even at this higher altitude the ground around the stones is just a slimy quagmire, the grass long since given up even trying to hang on and every possible space, every stone, all 20-odd, dripping with humans. No room at the Stone Circle Inn and a distinct lack of "we're all one" hippie love. I wasn't giving up, though, it'd taken all night to get here, what with all the various distractions and pockets of weirdness *Glastonbury* constantly offers up. I trudge ahead through the slime, looking for something remotely mud free.

Then I see it. A bed of fresh straw occupied by just one guy in a beanie, deep in slumber. Most definitely room for more. I turn to my bro, nodding at the sleeping man. He squelches over to me.

"Someone's asleep on it."

"Ah, there's plenty of room for us."

To illustrate the point, I walk over and unsteadily plonk myself down on the straw, but my aim is tragically misguided and one of my arse cheeks is now on top of this poor chap's head. I quickly slide off and, in the process, pull his beanie clean off his head.

"Oh, mate, I'm really sorry."

He wakes up, dazed and confused. Sits up and rubs his eyes.

"No problem, pal," he says in a soft Mancunian accent. "I needed to wek up. I'm waitin' on sum maytes."

He replaces his beanie and looks around the site, curiously unperturbed by his interrupted sleep, which hopefully means he's not gonna to hit me.

"Is it okay to sit here, then?"

"I sincerely hope so," pipes up my bro, observing the whipped cream shite encircling this oasis of straw.

The Manc lad smiles warmly.

"Yer sound, fellas, make your sens at home."

We introduce each other. He gave his name, but I forgot it the instant he told me, always do. He likes our hats and the fact we're brothers. We share a few smokes, chat about all kinds of stuff, mainly music.

"What's the best thing you've seen so far?" he asks.

Me and my bro think hard and then answer, almost in harmony, "Tofu Love Frogs!"

"Never fookin' heard of 'em."

"Imagine the Pogues, but on acid," explains my bro.

"Yeah, the whole tent was mental, it was fucking brilliant."

Manc Lad laughs.

"I'll 'ave to check 'em out. Are you gonna go see. . . ?" He trails off, interrupted by a minor rumpus piercing through the morning tranquillity.

A security guard nearby appears to be having some kind of mental breakdown, shouting to anyone who'll listen, retelling a rumour of how the (now banned) travelling community, previously allowed in for free, were planning on breaking in. His version of this particular festival rumour was that they were to achieve this by pushing down part of the large metal perimeter fencing along the edge of this particular field.

"If they push that fence over, all those people sat there will be killed!"

This is probably true, if the rumour's true, as there are indeed many people taking advantage of the grass that still exists by the perimeter fence. But why is he telling *us* this? Does he expect us to just rock up and forcibly reposition them all? As my condition dictates, I feel the urge to intervene.

"Mate, I think you're telling all the wrong people."

He looks over to me, as do many others, so I point to the people all camped down by the perimeter fence.

"You should be telling it to that lot."

Others agree. Laughter ensues, causing the security chap's meltdown to step up a gear.

"Fuck it! Fuck it! I didn't want to do this anyway! I only agreed so I could get in free."

"You shoulda broke in, dude, it's easy!" someone shouts.

It's true, it is.

"I can't even have a toke on a fucking joint!"

Sensing the man's distress, my bro offers up an alternative.

"Release your shackles my friend, remove your uniform and come join us. We have one rolled and ready."

Manc Lad, clearly amused, is chuckling away at all this.

"You two are fookin' mad."

The broken-down security chap wanders off in resignation and we sit back down, Manc Lad still chuckling.

"I thought I was high, but you two are fookin' flyin'. What ya bin on?"

My bro takes this one.

"Shrooms. Mainly."

"Mainly. . . eh?" he laughs.

We continue chattering on about music and stuff until he looks up, distracted. There's a presence behind me from which emanates a way more serious voice.

"Who's this?" the voice asks.

It was subtle, but I saw Manc Lad give him a look and a knowing nod.

"They're okay."

I look around to find this proper heavy-looking dude towering above me, pretty relieved we'd been branded *okay*. The big guy sits down, the circle expands, more people arrive. Manc Lad introduces us to his posse, which apart from Big Guy were all girls, attractive girls, freshly applied make-up; all well out of place here, way too clean. Big Guy gets to work and begins rolling joint after joint in succession, like it was his job. They're neat, too, professional even. Was it his job? One of these delights make its way to me. Tastes peculiar. Chemical. What the fuck? I pass it to my bro, muttering.

"Not sure what's in this. . . "

He takes a draw and moves closer, conspiratorially.

"It's coke."

"In a joint?"

He nods.

Well, that's a first for me, pretty decadent, assuming of course it's not actually crack. I look across at the group. Big Guy's still rolling spliff after spliff, not with cannabis I now observe, as he dips into what appears to be a heavy-duty freezer bag full of coke with a tiny spoon. Manc Lad has since migrated away and is now leaning across to one of the girls opposite, giving her some chat.

I'm not sure what it was, the distance, the angle, the chemicals I'd been smoking or the fact I now saw his profile, but suddenly my brain went fizz, pop, bang and fuck me, the epiphany hit me. We'd just spent the last hour larking around with Noel Gallagher.

I realise this may sound stupid; how could we have not noticed before? Well, in our defence, we'd been up all night, he was wearing a beanie over his monobrow and when you're not expecting it, you just don't see it. He was just this friendly Mancunian lad who'd kindly shared his bed of straw and then invited us to join his breakfast party. I move closer to my bro, feeling the need to share my discovery and to reveal the true identity of our new festival buddy. I speak low and calm.

"Now don't stare or make it obvious. . ."

"What?"

"You know the guy we've been with for the last hour?"

His head begins to turn.

"Don't stare!" I whisper harshly.

"You know who he is? I continue.

He twitches to look. I glare. He controls his impulse.

"Who?"

"Noel Gallagher."

"Fuck off!"

"It is! Have a look, just be natural."

He does, and to be fair, he does it well, casually taking in the scenery without pausing on Noel before returning back to me.

He stares, speechless, visibly upset by the realisation.

I try not to laugh.

"Fucking fuck!"

"Just be normal – he's the same bloke we met."

"Should we say something?"

"No!" I hiss.

"Why not?"

"Cos he clearly fucking likes that we don't know."

"But we *do* know."

"Pretend you don't!" I press.

"Don't know if I can."

"Just try. He hasn't changed."

"He has to me."

"He's still a bloke."

"Yeah, a humongously famous one."

"Okay, a bloke in a band."

"The biggest band in the fucking country!"

"He's still a bloke for fuck's sake."

"Yeah, a hugely successful international rock star bloke."

"Shut up will ya!"

Right on cue, Manc Lad/Noel shouts over, "You lads okay?"

"Yes, mate, just feeling a bit. . . sideways."

Noel laughs and relays our encounter with the security chap to his posse.

My bro is right, though, for as much as I want it to feel like it did before, it no longer does. I try and talk with him normally, but voices in my head keep shouting things at me: "It's Noel-fucking-Gallagher!" – shit like that. I'm not star-struck or anything, it's just this knowledge has brought with it an internal confusion and the experience has ceased to be enjoyable. At a basic human level it no longer feels authentic, like we're faking it, which we are and have been since the moment of recognition, yet to admit this to Noel would change the whole human connection. Also, I don't want to blow smoke. I care little for Oasis's music, so it could get well awkward. All right, when I first heard "Supersonic", I cannot deny the tingle it sent up my spine and their first album was pretty good, even bits of the second. But let's be frank, the music is plodding and derivative, plus Noel's lyrics can be well dodgy.

It was so much more fun before we knew who he was, for as much as I struggle otherwise, the dynamic *has* changed. I guess it did for Noel with the arrival of his entourage, the anonymity he enjoyed with me and my bro unavoidably kicked aside. No longer another festival geezer. No longer a normal guy. Noel's a star again.

My bro has remained catatonic ever since this revelation. I turn to him, speaking low.

"I think I need to go. I'm spinning out."

My bro nods, clearly relieved. We stand up and make our goodbyes. Noel also stands, then hugs us both and wishes us well. Sincere it was too. Don't believe all the media bollocks, all that rock star swagger, he really is a top bloke. A true gent. It's Liam who's the cunt.

Slowly, purposefully, we walk away and as we look back, Noel smiles and nods. He liked being normal, that was our gift to him, albeit a transient one. We gather pace as we head down the hill towards the main festival. Before long we are running, cackling with laughter, lairy as fuck, not quite believing what has just happened.

A couple of our mates, massive Oasis fans, went back to our camp just half an hour before this chance encounter. Of course, we're gonna wake them up. Very fucking loudly. WOO!

Chapter Ten

Touts, Taxation, Blood and Guts

Send the banksters, the pushers of capital
Slave wages, reactionary principles
And the warmongers, captains of industry
The fancy bourgeois
And the bourgeois mentality
"The Wickerman" – Meatraffle

29TH JULY 2017, STOCKWELL ROAD, BRIXTON

We are approaching the Academy, Zsa Zsa is having a proper moan about stupid shit, nothing worth repeating.

"Mate, you're negging me out. I wanna have fun tonight."

"I'm only happy when I'm moaning."

I laugh and he gives me a smile, perhaps his most endearing feature, for when he does his whole face lights up and his mouth literally sparkles. It really does. He has gold front teeth, like he's been punched in the mouth by Midas. Blingy cunt.

"Ain't that a song?"

"Nah, mate," I reply. "You're thinking of "Only Happy When It Rains", by Garbage."

"Should be a song. . ." muses Zsa Zsa.

We continue walking towards the Academy slurping from our tinnies, me talking bollocks, Zsa Zsa leaving most of it to me, but appearing to agree all the same. Not unusual, though, I can talk for England.

Suddenly, Zsa Zsa pulls Madame HiFi's phone from his pocket, hits the voice memo and just rattles out the skeleton of a song, first the sketch of a verse and then a chorus. The song's about only being happy when you're moaning – of course.

"Should be able to do something with that."

Zsa Zsa stuffs the phone back into his pocket, satisfied.

Whilst giving the appearance of listening, Zsa Zsa's right brain is always on, always up to something, mischief mainly, but sometimes art.

"So, how you gonna follow 'The Bird Song'?"

"Dunno. Margo thinks 'Brother'," he sniffs.

Margo Broom is producing their new stuff, a testament to the faith she has in them as they're currently label-less.

"Yeah, that could work, but it's more a love song. 6 Music latched on to the feminist spirit of 'Bird Song'. What about a double A-side?"

"Yeah, we're finking of putting 'Love Hurts' on the other side."

"Okay, but that's also a love song, mate."

He fixes me with his beady eyes.

"Yeah, but love is the engine of *every* revolution."

He might mean this sincerely, but equally he could be taking the piss. You never know with Zsa Zsa and he plays on it.

"Now you sound like Russell Brand."

He chuckles and we pass under the railway bridge. Nearly there now.

"So, where's Tigger?" Zsa Zsa enquires.

I've not really discussed the small rupture in our friendship, it would only complicate things further, though I get a sense he knows something's amiss.

"Him and Sadie got an Uber earlier."

"To where?"

"The Academy."

"From where?"

"The Windmill."

Zsa Zsa screws up his face.

"Fackin' bourgeoisies!"

"What do you expect from a. . ."

I was about to say "Tory" but choke it off, uncertain if Zsa Zsa knows. He's distracted anyway, looking at a text on Madame HiFi's phone.

Tigger and Zsa Zsa are mates so by rights he should have just got it out of the way, confessed his right-wing sins to the Marxist revolutionary preacher that is Zsa Zsa.

But then again. . .

We arrive at the Academy and weave through the thronging crowd milling around the entrance: unofficial merchandisers, hip-hop CD sellers, the tout cartel and those without tickets, waiting for the cartel to agree a price drop, or hoping that someone will appear with a spare they're ready to exchange at face value. You cannot really blame the touts, they're just at the sleazier end of the supply-demand neoliberal economic wank-fest. They reside within the untaxed fringes, the black economy, or, as the EU refer to it when calculating our Brexit bill, *The Underground Economy*. There's a strongly held left-wing view that we have a moral duty to pay our taxes, to make our contribution to society. Now I get that I really do. Not that there's a choice, as they take it from us before we even get it, or if you're self-employed you risk a jail sentence, because HMRC have more power than *any* police or bailiffs. Oh yes, they're the Establishments rubber-stamped Mafiosi. No court order required, they can enter your home, arrest you, freeze your assets and turn your life inside out, upside-down. A moral duty perhaps, but most certainly a legal one. The conflict I have is where and upon what they spend our money to keep this whole merry-go-round spinning.

In principle, I have no issues at all with my tax being spent on the NHS. Despite the unhelpful interference of various governments, it remains an incredible institution and, I shit you not, the fifth biggest employer in the world. It is unquestionably one of *the* most amazing success stories of the last century, yet a forgotten truism is that it's also a working model of successful socialism. Admittedly, it is currently held together with Blu-Tack and string, a direct consequence of this Tory government's obsession with austerity, which has reached new lows. People literally dying over it – collateral damage in the name of political ideology.

The last Labour government also made a dog's dinner of it when they were in charge, creating Private Funding Initiatives (PFI), which means the NHS (i.e., *us*) are legally obligated to repay private companies more than £80 billion over the next 30 years for an investment in hospitals of just 15%

this amount, because some government tosser thought an £11.5 billion Wonga loan would be a terrific idea.

We also have second-rate outsourced services hiding behind the NHS logo, as it slowly morphs into a marketing brand, giving private providers a badge of respectability to hide behind, like the barely regulated Care sector.

Moreover, the NHS has to deal with these ginormous pharmaceutical conglomerates monopolising the drug market, hiding behind patents charging stupendous amounts for life-saving medication and hoovering up our taxes to line shareholders' pockets. Like that smarmy, spunk-rag Martin Shkreli, who put up the price of HIV drugs by 5000% and not one piece of legislation could stop him. As Richard Butler once said, *"It's sick, the price of medicine."*

Then we have the industrial military complex and all the arms companies it supports. Just follow the money and tell me that we are not being collectively mugged in the name of mass murder. The UK is the sixth biggest exporter of arms in the world. That's weapons, planes, tanks, landmines, drones, nuclear missile parts – you name it, we export it. Makes you feel proud.

So, who buys these weapons? Well, roughly two thirds of them are bought by Middle Eastern countries, mainly Saudi Arabia. Since 2010, we have sold arms to 39 of the 51 countries branded "not free" by the government's own think tank – a think tank *we* pay for and *they* ignore. Window dressing to democracy. And 22 of these countries are listed on the government's own *human rights watch list*. I mean why do they even bother compiling a list?

Some of these countries we sell weapons of mass destruction to have no intention of ever paying their bill when the invoice lands on their desk or cave floor. So, who does?

Well, of this you can be sure, these private companies ain't taking no risk. They're on the winning side of what is the biggest Ponzi scheme to have ever existed, our tax system the main financial artery feeding the beating heart of what is nothing more than a large-scale killing machine. Because if any of these warmongering lunatics refuse to pay their bill, the company who sold them simply calls on the "Export Credit Guarantee Scheme" and the unpaid bill is settled. And who underwrites this multibillion insurance risk? That's right, we do. With our taxes. So yes, we very often pay for weapons sold to these deranged despotic murdering lunatics, a win-win for these arms manufacturers, no downside at all, because like fucking idiots *we* all collectively pay the bill, obediently complicit in funding terrorism, because we have no choice, our liberty's at stake.

Al-Qaeda, ISIS, Daesh, or whatever we call them nowadays have been fighting the various Allied forces in the Middle East with weapons made in Britain. It should come as no surprise that the executive board of these arms companies include ex-UK ministers. Like, for example, ex-Labour Defence Secretary Geoff Hoon, gratitude for enabling these violent corporate leviathans to pump out shareholder dividends by cutting more red tape so they can sell any weaponry to any mad dictator they want. No financial due diligence required; no risk to consider. Socialist? Really, Geoff? Nope, just another paid up member of the neoliberal gangbang and another cunt to add to the list.

The other, more cynical reason is that by creating conflicts around the world, we create more need for product. Who cares who kills who or for what reason? So long as they do so with our Britain sold weapons.

It's easy: just send in some NGOs, a few off-book spooks to stir up a rebellion and before you know it there's a government coup, that is inevitably followed by civil war – what a surprise!

All the West has to do is decide which side to back, but even that matters not, because if they can get away with it (and the scummy fuckers *do* get away with it), they'll supply all sides of a conflict. I mean, let's not be picky here; business is business.

So, there you have it, we are up to our necks in blood, guts and human tragedy on a gargantuan scale. And we wonder why we have terrorism?

***

Okay, that economic diversion was longer than expected, but perspective is necessary when slagging off touts. Also, on the flip side, if it weren't for them, I would have missed plenty of decent gigs.

Way worse than touts are all the online bots the large corporate scalpers employ, hoovering up swathes of prime tickets, so they can triple their money on Get Me In, Seatwave, StubHub, or Viagogo; the first two actually *owned* by Ticketmaster, which let's be frank, is very fucking suspect.

As usual, Zsa Zsa is on the triple-A guest list. I'm on a guest list, too, just not *the* guest list, the mecca of all passes, but I have to admit its sheer fluke I'm on *any* list. A bizarre chain of events, a random act of kindness, a sprinkling of blag and some instant karma; sometimes the universe just delivers!

My wristband is the next level down from Zsa Zsa's, but being on *any* list means I'm not up in the balcony, which has to be the worst way to experience a gig. It's like you're not actually there, just vicariously observing every other fucker have a good time.

You might be wondering why I'm on The Moonlandingz guest list? Well, this may take a while, so strap yourself in. .
.

Photos: Batch One

Windmill Pre-Facelift, 2017
Photograph origin undetermined (copied from the Windmill's Facebook page)

Windmill Mosh Pit, 2019
Photograph origin undetermined (copied from the Windmill's Instagram feed)

Ella Harris (PVA) & Tim Perry (Events Manager), Windmill, 2020
Photograph by Holly Whitaker

Piotr (Bar Manager), Windmill, Independent Venue Week, 2018
Photograph by La Staunton

Nasos (Chief Doorman), Windmill, Independent Venue Week, 2018
Photograph by La Staunton

Toby (of the bar), Windmill, Independent Venue Week, 2018
Photograph by La Staunton

Nathan Saoudi (FWF) & Kathleen (Landlady), Windmill, 2019
Photograph by Lou Smith

Seamus (Landlord), Windmill Beer Garden, 2020
Photograph by Cat Yong

Patrick Lyons (MeU), Windmill Stage, 2020
Photograph by Lou Smith

The Rebel (Ben Wallers), supporting Goat Girl, The Garage, Islington, 2018
Photograph by Dave Thomson

Honkies (L to R): Robin McCready, Ollie Cookson, James Sutcliffe, Tara B and Lincoln Barrett, Windmill Shed, Independent Venue Week, 2018
Photograph by La Staunton

Sex Cells: Matt Kilda & Willow Vincent, performing at Madonnatron's debut album launch, Windmill Stage, 2017
Photograph by Lou Smith

Madonnatron with La (L to R): Charlotte Aggett, Beth Soan, La Staunton,
Stefania Cardenas and Joanie Myburgh, Windmill Garden, Independent
Venue Week, 2018
Photograph by Lou Smith

No Friendz frontman, Angus Knight being introduced by Patrick Lyons at
Madonnatron's Debut Album Launch, Windmill Stage, 2017
Photograph by Lou Smith

Goat Girl: L.E.D., Clottie Cream, Rosy Bones (somewhere in the shadows) &
Naima Jelly, Windmill Stage, Independent Venue Week, 2018
Photograph by La Staunton

Phobophobes (L to R): Chris OC, Elliot Nash, Dan Lyons, Jamie Taylor &
George Russell, Windmill Stage, Independent Venue Week, 2016
Photograph by Lou Smith

Meatraffle (L to R): Dan GB, Tingle Lungfish, Cloudy Truffles, Zsa Zsa Sapien
& Chris OC (in the shadows), Windmill Stage, SXSW Fundraiser, 2020
Photograph by Anna Yorke

Warmduscher (L to R): The Saulcano, Mr Salt Fingers Lovecraft, Clams
Baker III, The Witherer & Special Guest of the Band, Windmill Stage, 2015
Photograph by Lou Smith

Fat White Family (version): Adam Brennan, Dante Traynor, Lias Saoudi &
various revellers, The Railway Tavern, Tulse Hill, 2019
Photograph by Anna Yorke

Saul Adamczewski and Alex Sebley, Backstage, The Forum, 2019
Photograph by Lou Smith

Patrick Lyons (MeU), Dylan Jones (Pixx) & Josh Baxter (PVA), Five Bells Beer
Garden, New Cross, 2019
Photograph by Dave Thomson

Lou Smith & Stefania Cardenas (Madonnatron), Windmill Shed, 2018
Photograph by Dave Thomson

Revellers in the Windmill Shed, including (L to R): Tim Perry, Jack Medley, James Sutcliffe, Robin McCready, Joanie Myburgh, La Staunton (mostly hidden), Lincoln Barrett, Finn Whitehead & Ed Kingpin, 2018
Photograph by Lou Smith

More Revellers in The Shed, including La Staunton, Sally Jones & My Bro, Windmill, 2018
Photograph by Lou Smith

Random shot, including Beth Soan, La Staunton, Ed Kingpin & Herman Noel, Windmill Shed, 2019
Photograph by Lou Smith

Chapter Eleven

Life-Changing, Conscious-Shifting Musical Epiphany

Hell, hath no fury like a failed artist
Or a successful communist
But that ain't no excuse to treat my purple fury
Quite like a big black abyss
"Is It Raining in Your Mouth?" – Fat White Family

Fat White Family, one of the key musical protagonists in all this, played an unexpected gig last Wednesday at the 100 Club in Oxford Street. It was announced only days before the gig and sold out in minutes. I love the Fat Whites most of all. They're the reason I'm even here. Witnessing them play the Electric Ballroom in 2014 with Tigger changed my musical landscape overnight – one of those life-changing, conscious-shifting epiphany moments. An utterly insane concoction of stolen influences from the grimiest corners of our musical heritage: The Fall, The Cramps, The Gun Club, The Stooges, The Birthday Party, Virgin Prunes, Fad Gadget, Gallon Drunk, Country Teasers, Neu!, Throbbing Gristle, Alien Sex Fiend, all blended with lyrics so unsavoury, if *Daily Mail* readers were able to decipher them they'd be locking up their daughters until every single member of the band had been safely incarcerated.

Fat White Family began in 2011 after various south London bands, musicians and performers played, jammed and coagulated together at the now legendary "Slide In" sessions, originally held at the Tulse Hill Tavern. Barely noticed at first, like bacteria left to fester within a neglected Petri dish, something alien, unwholesome and seriously strange took form. What emerged was far greater than the sum of its constituent parts – something hygiene deficient, malnourished, feral and gloriously sleazy. Something very fucking special.

Trading under various names, including Nagasaki Dust Patrol and Champagne Holocaust – the latter becoming their debut album title – they eventually settled upon the clearly ironic moniker Fat White Family. None of them are fat. In fact, quite the opposite, but it was always part of a lyric in "Bomb Disneyland", or perhaps a cheeky nod to the thickness of the lines they were hoovering?

Their first proper gig was in 2011 to a small, disinterested audience at one of the 'Easycome' sessions that continue to this day, hosted by south London's grizzliest mover and shaker: Andy Hank Dog.

Someone in attendance *did* take note and that someone was Lou Smith.

The Tulse Hill Tavern was predictably gentrified, so the Fat Whites relocated to The Queen's Head in Brixton where the "Slide In" sessions continued. They also lived there for much of the time, paid their keep by helping out, so there was a period when you could have had your pint pulled by a Fat White.

The Queen's Head is also the place where they draped a handmade banner boldly proclaiming, "THE BITCH IS DEAD" in celebration of Thatcher's passing and via the magic of social media, pictures of this quickly made their way straight into the pages of *The Guardian*, that condescending broadsheet of the centre-left. This was the moment the Fat Whites began making waves amongst the wider culture and not just because of their weird twisted musical offerings, or insane live performances.

Quietus Editor, John Doran, witnessed them playing a "Slide In For Gaza" benefit gig at The Queen's Head just a month before they tore up the Electric Ballroom. He likened the experience to *"being in a lava lamp full of serotonin and adrenaline that's being shaken violently by a hot-handed giant."*

These special times sadly ended when this iconic pub abruptly closed its doors as a venue just a year later in 2015, receiving a gentrified makeover for a gastropub future, leaving the Fat White lads homeless once again. The struggle is real. . .

Simon Tickner, the last manager of The Queen's Head (as a venue), has since retired to the fjords of Norway, miles from anyone and anything. Perhaps, being host *and* landlord to the Fat Whites was enough excitement and mayhem for one lifetime. Or maybe it was the result of an ill-advised Halloween costume idea. An edgy, clearly insane concept cooked up with his black colleague Chris, in which Simon blacked up and dressed as an African witch doctor, whilst Chris decided to mirror this by donning a Ku Klux Klan outfit. Clearly the joke was in the reversal of roles because Simon, whilst arguably not *fully* woke, is no racist. This is evidently clear to anyone who knows him, indeed, his pub attracted one of the most diverse crowds in Brixton, as he tried explaining to BBC news, which is where this story ended up.

Nevertheless, the very thin ice upon which Simon and Chris were skating completely gave way following their direct, hare-brained response to the lady complainant on Facebook.

"*Yo bitch. Ask my black clientele what they think and suck my dick*" went the post.

Clearly, one of those moments that required a few deep breaths and a minute of calm reflection before hitting *send*.

This, of course, did not happen and somewhat inevitably a media storm ensued, upon which anyone and everyone jumped on board, including all the tabloids, engulfing Simon in righteous outrage. In everyway it became a Brixton-style *Bonfire of the Vanities* culminating in a politically motivated investigation by Lambeth Council into whether to remove his alcohol licence and perhaps the real reason why he now lives in Norway.

That night in 2014 at the Electric Ballroom, the Fat Whites were not technically perfect, their influences writ large, but I'd never witnessed anything quite like it. They prowled the stage, erratic, volatile, feral and like moths to a flame the crowd drew in tight until the entire place was a heaving, sweaty, beer-soaked mosh pit. It was dirty, sleazy, repulsive, yet incredibly liberating. Their frontman

Lias Saoudi, a mad-haired shaman fitting onstage like a psychotic in dire need of medication, who might spontaneously combust at any moment. His co-conspirator Saul Adamczewski is alongside him, shouting, screaming, both jerking erratically, the entire band throwing all they've got into every song.

During "Wild American Prairie" Lias piles into the mosh pit screaming like a banshee, slithering his sweaty torso through all the reaching hands. Holding his weird oblong guitar, Saul looks on from the stage, his hooded eyes not quite hiding an intensely deranged stare, managing to simultaneously look incredibly cool and just one overambitious hit away from curling up his toes. Adam Harmer's on guitar, skinny and drawn like one of Lowry's matchstick men, sporting a big mop of messy black hair. He's one mean guitarist, banging out classic riffs in the Cramps/Velvets/Teasers range. Lias's brother Nathan Saoudi stares from behind his keyboard, mouth open and a faraway look in his eyes, as if coexisting in another dimension. Finally, there's Jack Everett, ferociously hammering on his kit managing to keep the chaotic Fat Whites train moving. The least thin Fat White, in that he looks almost normal, albeit a little pasty, yet a truly terrific drummer, quite possibly the best I've ever seen close up. Just about everything the late, great Bill Hicks would want from a band, with bells on.

We had not yet met, but Zsa Zsa also joined the Fat Whites onstage that night adding trumpet to their finale, though he had his work cut out to be heard above the aural melee. He later told me Lias only invited him that same evening with no rehearsal time, so he winged it. This haphazard attitude is what makes this band so raw and precarious, because when it all hangs together it taps into a part of your brain you'd forgotten even existed. It was akin to a religious experience and like newly enlightened disciples of the Sufi mystic Gurdjieff, Tigger and me were wide awake again, because that night the Fat Whites shifted our musical axis and it has never been the same since.

Since then we've seen pretty much all their London gigs, none of which are ever the same, only adding to their shambolic allure. The Fat Whites were *our* band, we discovered them together, though argued plenty over who introduced them to who. It was a shared obsession, we ordered vinyl, consumed live footage and it soon became apparent there was more going on in this corner of London than just the Fat Whites. So, we went exploring and it wasn't long before we ended up at the Windmill, gate-crashing a party full of gate-crashers.

Chapter Twelve

Dickensian London, Broken Britain, Media Grooming, Oh Jeremy Corbyn

There are homeless living on the street
When there's a thousand empty homes
Going through bins to find a lunch
Millions spent on military drones
And I think to myself What a horrible fucking world
"The Other Side of a Wonderful World" – Meatraffle

Much like Tigger, Fat White Family have been worryingly quiet this past year. Various members who frequent the Windmill vaguely mention how they're "working on new stuff", but not a squeak since their Black Lips/Sean Lennon co-written/produced single "Breaking into Aldi" (which, al-legedly, is not how it began, having since been talked out of the songs earlier title "Breaking into Auschwitz").

There are questions asked, theories exchanged, all in hushed tones. Had the beautiful tension between Saul and Lias finally reached breaking point? Had it all gone too far? A seemingly toxic dynamic yet essential to the band's twisted chemistry. Saul a wayward genius, a musical tour de force with riffs to match the dark, disreputable, Daily Mail bating lyrics Lias has no difficulty spewing up.

Apart from their Brixton Academy gig last year, Saul has stopped touring with them, having been thrown out the band whilst in Paris on the night of the Bataclan terrorist attack. Their venue had been evacuated, but Saul refused to leave. Entirely reasonable from his point of view as he was waiting for his dealer, but this turned out to be one hit too far for the rest of the band and to be thrown out of the Fat Whites for bad behaviour is one fuck of an achievement. Nevertheless, this rather drastic action quite possibly ex-tended Saul's time on the planet and if you need any con-vincing, try watching the promo video for "Whitest Boy on the Beach" shot during Saul's physical nadir, without gen-uine concern for the man's survival.

I have since been reliably informed that Saul is back in the fold, though since that gig I've only seen him in his more recent project Insecure Men; formed with his old schoolmate, the sweet multitalented Ben Romans-Hopcraft of Childhood and Warmduscher. Motivated by a desire to stay off the drugs, having recently ended a spell in rehab, it's a more melodic, plaintive and sober affair with a Syd Barret simplicity and dark lyrical prose provided by Lias Saoudi, most certainly a promising sign. Still, whatever their relationship status, the truth is, it wouldn't be Fat White Family if they weren't utterly dysfunctional, full of psychosis and perpetually falling apart. And it certainly wouldn't be the Fat Whites without Saul.

So, when, with only a week's notice, the band sent out a tweet announcing a one-off gig at the legendary 100 Club, the 90 minutes it took for me to be notified was 88 minutes too sodding late. It is, after all, a miniscule venue, capacity a mere 350, only 200 more than the Windmill. How big can a guest list be at such a small venue? Not very, 70 people would be 20% of capacity. Shit fuck bollocks! I'd already left it too late to get tickets to see The Moonlandingz play the Academy the following Saturday.

I try calling Tigger, he doesn't answer, which has become the new normal. From constantly sending each other links to tracks we'd just heard or abusive messages (you know the way men like to express their love for each other), it can now take two weeks for Tigger to respond to a text, if at all. Things changed in our dynamic; a schism occurred some time ago. I can pinpoint it now, I just hadn't noticed the hairline crack appear. Over the course of the last year this crack has grown and it's now an unignorable, quite possibly unbridgeable, gulf. At least it feels that way. I wish it were different, but it is what it is and there's fuck all I can do about it, the world still turns. . .

Okay, so Tigger's not answering. I expect he and Sadie will sort themselves out, the Fat Whites solidarity that once bound us having long since waned. Fuck Tigger, fuck 'em both. I will secure my own entry to this one-off Fat Whites spectacle. Somehow. I *have* to be there.

I make some calls but everyone else is doing the same and all my best efforts fail. Zsa Zsa can't even get himself on the list and Lias is his mate.

There's only one thing for it, my standard default position in life: wing it. Just hoof up on the night and see what occurs. The fall-back position would be the touts, so long as they're not greedy wankers it'll be worth a shot.

***

The day before the gig, Tigger unexpectedly calls.

"Dude, Fat Whites are playing 100 Club tomorrow!"

"I know."

"Are you going?"

"Not sure, I couldn't get a ticket."

"Yeah, we've tried but it ain't happening."

Wonder if he was thinking of me then?

"Can't get on the list either," I reply.

"Yeah, the list is super-tight."

Looks like this call was borne out of desperation.

"So, what we gonna do?" continues Tigger.

Oh, so it's "we" now is it?

"I was just gonna turn up. It'll have to be a tout or something."

"Yeah, that's what I was thinking. You never know, dude, there might be some returns on the door or some plus-ones we can blag."

And so, a plan is vaguely hatched and I'm cautiously excited. Feels a bit like the old days; me and Tigger, odds stacked against us but kings of blag we will get in, of that I have no doubt.

26TH JULY 2017, OXFORD STREET, WEST END

It's a warm summer's evening as I walk towards the 100 Club from Oxford Circus station, dodging consumers carrying their spoils, keeping this consumption-based, planet-destroying, soul-crushing economy going, nonchalantly careening by the many homeless adorning various shop doorways. Along my route I give money to a few, generally the ones who have given up even asking, but there are so many on this relatively short walk it overloads my senses. Still, I would sooner give it to them directly than any of those rattling charity boxes. Who can be unequivocally certain these donations find their way through the corporate machinery and its wall of salaries to the intended recipients?

I am not suggesting all these organisations are suspect, because the desperate truth is there are far too many people now dependent on grassroot charities to deliver support the state once provided. It's the other end of the charity sector I struggle with, the industry networking and corporate virtue signalling, not to mention all the tax breaks. The mere fact politicians and royals are often patrons should be a fucking warning.

Oxford Street's not a proud landmark for all these tourists to witness and hardly emblematic of a supposed First World economy. Not since the days of Charles Dickens have we lived with such chronic levels of poverty. Unemployment is low, GDP is rising, but at the other end of this economic seesaw, we have more poverty, more homelessness, more food banks and soup kitchens since the days Dickens wrote his books. We have less job security, stagnating wages and zero-hours contracts, which helps the unemployment stats massively, but is hardly committed employment unless you consider "*be ready to work when WE need you, or we won't call you next time*" actual employment.

We even have workhouses for kids again. Okay, it's not on our doorstep; not even in our country, but we're certainly the beneficiaries of child labour sweatshops. One of the convenient benefits of globalisation: manufacturing goods in poorer countries where exploitation laws do not exist, so long as it ain't happening under our noses and our clothes are cheap, who gives a toss? All you shoppers don't, that's clear, fingers in your ears, pretending your consumption plays no role in modern-day slavery, la la fucking la. Well, here's an inconvenient truth you won't want to live with, nearly every purchase you make is not just the end of an ugly trade chain profiteering from exploitation but the entire reason it exists.

Are you really so blind to the symbolic meaning of the tape on Chris Martin's hands and the massive dermatological risk he is taking in his effort to enlighten us all?

Theresa May was recently defending the Tory record, rattling out stats like a robot reading an autocue, boasting about how they had taken four million people out of income tax altogether. Boasting. The naïve conceit of this, as if it is somehow a proud achievement to have this many working people earning less than £11,000 a year.

I was a tad disappointed Corbyn missed this in his reply, but his inability to think on the fly is perhaps one of his more disappointing characteristics.

Don't get me wrong, Corbyn is the best thing that has happened to politics in my lifetime. We were so used to slimy, corporate careerists that we'd forgotten what a conviction politician looked like. Of course, it hasn't helped that all the vested interest groups – basically the entire Establishment – portray him as weak, wobbly and somewhat conversely a terrorist.

It also didn't help that many of you, in fact most of you, including Labour supporters, followed this narrative like brainless sheep. Throughout 2016, if you showed any admiration for Corbyn, people would literally laugh, saying "Okay, I like what he says, but he's not a leader". The media groomed you all into believing he was useless, pathetic, a joke and, above all else, not a leader.

In January this year I met Falco, main man in Future of the Left at *Club the Mammoth* one-day festival in London and couldn't resist asking the obvious:

"So, Falco, what *is* the Future of the Left?"

"I can tell you one thing, it's not Jeremy Corbyn."

I was stunned.

"Why d'you say that?"

"He's just not a leader."

See how powerful media grooming is? This guy fronts a band whose very name celebrates socialism, who'd just come offstage playing support to the almighty Fall, yet it could just have easily been neoliberal blairite Owen Smith answering my question, complete with Welsh lilt. *"He's not a leader"* was the mantra. Mass hypnosis. And yes, the political news media is very good at this, as Chomsky eloquently explains in his book *Manufacturing Consent*, as does documentary maker Adam Curtis in *HyperNormalisation*.

The Left need to get their shit together, stop bickering, explain why immigrants are *not* the problem and give us a cohesive vision of a better world. We're living with the result of the Remainers total failure to project any positives that staying in the EU would provide, whilst the Brexiteers just made shit up. Racism is borne out of ignorance and fear, these alien cultures frightening the very same little Englanders who get bladdered on foreign beer and top the night off with a kebab or an Indian.

If they had their way, the NHS would be even more knackered, vegetables would stay in the ground, supermarket shelves would be empty, operations would be cancelled and taxis would, once again, become the domain of fat white bald drivers in overpriced black cabs, pumping out their toxic diesel and toxic opinions.

Between the lines, a dangerous narrative has taken root – a whispering campaign, an entire religion demonised and set apart from the rest. We've been here before and it did not end well.

Still, it was good to see the tide of opinion turn for Corbyn when May made her electoral gamble last month, not enough for an outright win, but watching the results roll in was still worth the sleep deprivation, just to see the Tories squirm and slither as their majority government evaporated before their eyes.

Even more satisfying was watching the disloyal wankers in the Labour party eat their own words and hearing the distant creak of Mandelson's coffin lid closing shut again; for now at least.

Since this election, Corbyn has not stopped smiling, vindicated, confident, the cat with the cream, for despite a hostile mainstream media he changed the conversation, altered the narrative and took back the party.

After decades of mistrust, confusion and apathy, politics is exciting again, finally we have a clear ideological difference: voting *means* something.

I'm trying hard not to get too overexcited, but it's beginning to feel like the balance of power is shifting back to the people and we should always keep in mind that above all else, governments fear their own people. And they *should* be fucking afraid.

Chapter Thirteen

Thin Fat White, Karmic Coincidence, Friends Ununited

Down in the mouth, north and south
London's all the same to me
Here and there with Ian Sinclair
And the Fat White Family, to boot.
"It's All Free" – I, Ludicrous

26TH JULY 2017, OXFORD STREET

I arrive at the 100 Club. You know the place that managed to have ten times the number of attendees than its actual capacity at their legendary *Punk Festival* in 1976 when the Pistols played. If, that is, you believe every fucker

who claims they were there. There is a small gathering outside the entrance and some very friendly bouncers on the
door, a rare thing north of the river. I phone Tigger, only to
discover the pisshead's already taken refuge within a local
hostelry, having already tried to get tickets for an hour without success.

I look around for a recognisable face. No one. I call again,
try and gee him along which is when he informs me he's
also waiting for Sadie. Whilst this news does not surprise
me, a grain of disappointment is released into my otherwise
hyped-up demeanour. No longer the *friends reunited* gig
part of me had hoped for. Fat White Family is *our* band,
we've always done these gigs together, *all* of them. Don't
get me wrong, I have no issue with their relationship per se,
despite the social awkwardness it has created for our families, it's just the whole and exclusive nature of it all, the
perceived threat to their equilibrium I now appear to represent. Plus, the task has just become 50% harder: we now
need *three* bloody tickets.

I look up and as I do, Fat Whites' guitarist Adam Harmer
steps out of the venue's entrance onto Oxford Street.
Hmmm, is this a sign? The universe at work? My flashing
beacon of need causing cosmic coincidence? You make
your own luck, they say. Shall I just rock up and ask him?
Could be well awkward. He's only a few steps away and not
for long, he's just working out which direction to go. Remember the objective; I'm here to see Fat White Family and
one of them is standing right before me. I promised myself
I'd get in at all costs, but what if that cost is my dignity?

Oh, what the fuck. I march up, politely accost him and
ask if he could get any of us in. To my surprise he doesn't
brush me off and ponders my request.

"Actually, there is a possibility."

This is promising, just the mere fact Adam is even entertaining the idea. I mean, I'm sure it's a busy night for the dude.

"A mate of mine might not make it," Adam continues.

Then, with precision timing, his phone pings. A text. He opens the message and smiles.

"There you go, you're now Gerry O'Reilly, plus one."

(Fellow liggers take note: that wasn't really the name he gave, it'd be stupid to give the real one, he might *always* be on Adam's list. Everything else is true.)

"You're a fucking star, Adam!"

But I need another. Shall I push it? I've got this far, two in the bag. I know I'm being pushy and tarnishing the gift already given, but I have to, don't I?

I brace myself, internally cringing.

"Any chance of one more for Tigger's girlfriend?"

See how mature and charitable I'm being?

Adam scratches his head and sucks his lips, like an old-school mechanic when you ask what's wrong with your car. He then looks up at me and smiles.

"I'll see what I can do."

"Thanks a million, mate, you've made my night anyway."

I give him a quick hug, then he trots off down Oxford Street, disappearing into the stream of late-night consumers for a pre-gig drink with his bandmates.

Adam is arguably the least complicated and thinnest Fat White of them all. Not that he doesn't have any issues of his own, battling with personal demons is a CV requirement for joining the band, but he carries them well.

Adam wasn't quite there from the beginning, but throughout all the dysfunction and turmoil, he's remained a reliable constant, a rock in a very hard place. He's a genuinely top bloke, always polite, always friendly and fuck me, I was in. Nice one, Adam!

Still, we need *another* ticket and whilst I believe Adam is sincere, just on sheer logistics alone I feel it is not something we should rely on. I expect the next time we see him will be onstage.

I look around, suddenly aware I am not the only blagger here, that someone else may have been within earshot and taken note of the absent guest's name. After assessing the situation, I satisfy myself that my intel, my new ID, is safe. Tigger's right, I'm a paranoid cunt. I call him.

"Hello, Daaave!" he rasps in his well-practised Papa Lazarou; a terrifyingly dark character creation that would not survive today's level of scrutiny. Probably be chased out of town by an army of woke-enlightened millennials.

"Hey, Tigger. Listen."

"I'm all ears, Daaave!"

"I got good news and I got bad news."

"Okaaay. . ."

"Two of us are in."

In no time at all Tigger is bouncing down Oxford Street towards the 100 Club, filled to his over excitable brim with renewed optimism. There is now only one entry to organise. What once felt futile no longer does. Sadie arrives sometime later, not one for bouncing. Tigger wants me to help get one more and, slightly begrudgingly, I agree to wait with them, pacing up and down as we try out various options, including accosting Taishi Nagasaka, the Fat Whites' bassist. He joined the band only two months before they tore up the Letterman show back in 2015 (minus Saul who'd somehow lost his passport). Next to Lias's blood-curdling primal screams, the look on Taishi's face is my favourite thing about that performance. It is the moment he realises the band he's joined is totally insane. Sadly, this Fat White is unable to assist on the guest list front and we're running out of options, the clock is ticking. . .

Chapter Fourteen

Corporate Subculture, Three Musketeers, Punk Rock Disorders, Superstar DJ's

Honey, it was not me who said that
It must have been that devil on my back
Lawyer man, I don't think I wrote that
That script belongs to the devil on my back
"Devil on My Back" – Country Teasers

Perhaps I should explain my condition better, I owe you that at least. I have ADHD. Attention Deficit Hyperactivity Disorder, to give its full title. Adult ADHD to be even more precise, on account of me being an adult, physically at least. I kind of knew I wasn't normal, never quite fitting in, out of step, out of synch, not functioning like the others. I cannot sit still or wait around, my mind's everywhere at once but never where it should be and as a boy I found it tough making or keeping friends. Still do. I've lived with this all my life but only discovered it recently when my 10-year-old son was diagnosed, the genetic dots led back to me. My wife knew the instant the symptoms were explained, always suspecting something was amiss. She's a wonderful human being, incredibly tolerant and partially deaf, which I'm sure has helped our marriage enormously. I know one thing; I couldn't live with me.

People assume ADHD means mischievous or hyperactive and it can be both in spades, but it's just alternative wiring, a different modus operandi for life. We now live in an age of enlightenment, with names for every condition, more labels than you can shake a stick at. I've no idea what normal is. I love my boy, the way his mind works and through him I've begun to understand what being around me must be like. He's not academically brilliant, yet he has a reasonable understanding of quantum physics. Not because he's some child genius, it just engages him in a way classic education fails to. Their methods are boring causing his mind to over-compensate, so he seeks stimuli, dopamine hits, something to liven things up and this will often involve mischief.

What is odd about ADHD in these politically correct times is that they still call it a *disorder* – not a syndrome, or a condition, but a disorder. I kinda like that. Gives the condition a punk bent.

The attention deficit part of this *disorder* is a major issue for me. Literally anything can distract me from whatever

I'm doing, wherever I'm heading, whatever's being said. Listening to someone without wandering off takes incredible concentration. It can get well awkward. Like, for example, a friend is pouring their heart out over some personal crisis, then in the middle of all this Marc Riley inconsiderately plays something amazing on the radio, then without thinking I blurt out, "I love this!" and turn the volume up. It doesn't go down well. This I've learnt, but never actually learn.

The hyperactive part of this disorder is the reason someone of my advancing years has the urge to go piling into these south London dives week in, week out. I've found the perfect outlet and it's re-awoken a part of me I thought had long since left the building.

Even before I understood this, I had come to realise I'm a small doses kinda guy. I'm fun at first, eccentric some would say, but over time I will wear you out. I will not notice you yawning or checking the time. No, let's crack open the whiskey, there's more shit to discuss, more songs to play, more fun to have. Over the years, I've learnt to limit my exposure to friends, so I have more chance of keeping them.

This is the section of the spectrum me and my son occupy. A spectrum *most* of us seem to be on, well, at least everyone I know. And whilst he has not a single shred of awareness, in fact, he's in total denial, Tigger has some kind of condition. I think that's why I make allowances for him. I think that's why we became mates.

***

And here we are, pacing around the entrance of the 100 Club, still hanging on to the hope of a third golden ticket, another guest list miracle. My head is now spasming with pent-up impatience, the adrenaline buzz from my earlier success dissipating fast, on top of which a worm of doubt has buried its way into my jumbled thoughts. Adam's a straight-up guy, no question, but he's not always *straight*. What if he forgets about our chat and inadvertently offers up this guest list intel to someone else? This thought began as a faint paranoid whisper, but has since become a megaphone in my head that won't shut the fuck up. I'm pacing back and forth, I can't do this anymore, it's sending me insane. What if someone else is Gerry O'Reilly plus one?

"I'm going in," I inform Tigger and Sadie.

Tigger protests loudly, insisting I should stay until we're all in, like all of sudden we're the three musketeers. Fuck that. Time to be assertive. I walk over to the entrance and holler back to them both.

"Whose name should I leave as my plus-one?"

Tigger glares at me with a puzzled, pained expression, like I'm not a team player. He can fucking talk. When Insecure Men played their debut performance at the Windmill earlier this year, I only found out about it because Tigger called me the next day telling me how fucking great it was. Yet he now has the gall to glare at me as though I've broken some kind of secret code. I hold his gaze. Sorry, mate, it ain't gonna wash.

"Well?" I persist.

Tigger visibly deflates, resigned, turning to Sadie to debate the issue. He's trying to be chivalrous, but Sadie ain't happy going in with me, not without a guarantee Tigger will make it too and you can be sure of one thing, I'm not going to offer up *both* of my recently hustled guest list places for these two lovebirds. No no no, fuck that.

"Give them my name then." Tigger shrugs, clearly disappointed in me.

I approach the ticket desk and give them my new name. I'm handed a couple of Fred Perry badges by one of the many hired-in representatives; branding trinkets, for this event had been put on by 'Fred Perry Subculture.'

I enter the belly of the club, it's filling up fast, but after a quick recce of the room draw a blank, I cannot see any of the Windmill gang, at least no one recognisable to me. So where are they all?

The vibe's a bit weird, a corporate edge, like an industry event, all very un-Fat Whites. I go to the bar to the right of the stage and order a stout, not the Irish one, a hipster version, but it'll have to do.

Fred Perry? Have the Fat Whites sold out? I can't hold it against them as despite all the attention and plaudits, they're all still broke. So much so, they've moved out of south London for a five-bedroom house in Sheffield, a snip at £700 a month: Stella Street Fat Whites stylee. Maybe they'll just phone it in tonight? Now that would be a first. I brush these fears aside, I mean, it's not like their adverting McDonalds or luxury fucking cars.

As I return with my drink towards the area in front of the stage, a couple of recognisable faces appear: Finn Whitehead and La Staunton. Now that's better, now I don't feel quite so lost.

They are both tall, lean and handsome, indeed, you could easily mistake them for siblings. Finn is a flamboyant dresser with a great mop of wayward blond hair sticking out in all directions, mainly upwards, making him taller still. La is undeniably striking, with angular features, large blue intelligent eyes and short spiky, currently pink, but forever changing hair. One of those annoying people who'd look cool wearing nothing but an old sack. Yet La is far from annoying, she exudes an excitable energy and possesses a wicked tongue. I've met her at the Windmill a number of times, occasionally accompanied by Finn or Margo Broom but also on her own. I remember the first time we spoke. It was in The Shed after the bands had finished, she came in as I was rolling a fag, so I struck up a conversation. She was a tad wary, perhaps understandably, some random bloke randomly chatting, so I clumsily attempted to defuse the tension.

"Just to be clear, I'm not trying to pull. I'm happily married."

"Don't worry, I've made it a rule never to fuck anyone old enough to be my dad," retorts La.

She got me good, right where it hurts, but it very much cleared the air. I kinda knew we'd get on: we smoke the same tobacco, enjoy the same music, our go-to beverage is the black stuff and we like to watch bands from the mosh pit. I found out much later that she is a presenter on Reprezent FM, not from her, but Zsa Zsa. He sent me a SoundCloud link of him guesting on her show in which they chatted about Meatraffle, interspersed with songs Zsa Zsa chose. A "takeover" they call it in radioland. Until that moment I was unaware, but then I have this rule not to ask anyone what their day job is, partly because I don't want to spoil the mystique, but also because I hate that social game, where people are pigeonholed by whatever it is they do to put bread on the table. It's a rare and precious thing if your hobby also becomes your means of income, yet still this question is used to define us. It's the wrong question; we should ask what people *choose* to do, not *have* to do simply to survive. For most of these folks being a band member is a spare-time activity, unless they've crossed over and are already living the dream.

I remember one band member explaining to me how expensive their scent was after I'd remarked upon its odour.

"Woo! Aren't you living the rock star life!"

"Oh no, I got this with money from my day job."

"Really?"

"Yeah, I'm. . ."

I interrupt, "Please don't tell me, I really don't need to. . ."

"I'm a stripper," they continue.

It caught me a little off guard, but I try and act casual, style it out, be relaxed and without missing a beat, I ask, "Oh really? So, where d'you do that?"

As the words left my mouth, the stupidity of the question became immediately apparent.

"Well, I'm not going to tell you, am I?"

I laugh, shaking my head.

"I don't know why I even asked. I don't wanna know!"

We both giggled and have never spoken about it since.

I never asked La about her day job either, neither did she proffer the information. It's not La's only job I've since learnt, for she is a fully paid-up member of what has come to be known as 'the gig economy'. Much like Zsa Zsa, La knows pretty much everyone there is to know in this musical collective. On her Reprezent show, she gets to play all sorts of weird and wonderful stuff, interviewing all her favourite artists, mainly south London bands, the key players involved in all this. And why not? It is after all a rich vein to mine. Finn is her producer, but also participates and is a great straight man to La's informative, upbeat streams of consciousness accompanying everything she plays.

In/Tro with La is like my own private radio show. She reviews gigs I went to, plays all the stuff I like and interviews bands I know from the Windmill. She has a natural, engaging style with a larger-than-life radio personality, which you discover, when you get to know her, *is* her personality. Check it out on SoundCloud where you'll find many of her old shows, including interviews with many of the characters I'm describing here. If nothing else, it'll help you appreciate that I'm not making this shit up.

Reprezent FM broadcasts from three converted shipping containers within Pop Brixton, a start-up community project involved in all kinds of home-grown issues. Not a commercial station, so no monotonous ads breaking up the flow and killing the vibe, but a youth-led Brixton community-based station. Apart from La's show, they chiefly play UK rap, hip-hop, grime and house, instrumental in shining a light on local talent, like Stormzy and Novelist. And if all this sounds like a plug, it is – and why not? Reprezent FM is an all-round force for good in the world.

There are of course other DJs who play this stuff on a pretty regular basis, mainly on 6 Music. Marc Riley has championed many a Windmill band, along with Gideon Coe. Even Steve Lamacq's latched on, currently championing Phobophobes and Goat Girl; bands who honed their craft at the Windmill, so at least he's finally playing newer stuff instead of all that 90s Britpop shite he's *still* obsessed with. He's even sampled Phobophobes single "The Never Never" for background music on his regular *music news* spot, cleverly looping the clip to keep it below the 30 second threshold, thus avoiding any royalty payments to the band.

Lamacq has also latched onto Shame, another south London band who began life at the Windmill. A lovely bunch of lads and a proper gang whose live shows bristle with energy. Their singer, Charlie Steen, a mild-mannered gent off stage, morphs into a primal sweaty shaman once onstage.

I met Lamacq (or Lammo if you prefer) a couple of times. The first time was during the Belle & Sebastian hosted *Bowlie Weekender* at Camber Sands back in '99, a glorious precursor to all the *ATP* chalet bungalow festivals that followed. Our encounter was pretty affable back then. Not so much the second time, as I somewhat stupidly managed to get right up his pointy hooter.

2ND FEBRUARY 2017, THE LEXINGTON, ISLINGTON

I approach the venue from the other side of the road, already delirious and can just about make out a vaguely familiar profile in the smoking pen. Too impatient to wait for the green man, preferring instead to dodge through the traffic, despite my current state, perhaps because of it. A car honks as I approach the pavement and I can now make out who the profile belongs to. It's Steve Lamacq and he's chatting with someone over a fag. As I close in further, I begin to see who that someone is. Of all the people in all the smoking pens in all the world, Lamacq just happens to be chatting with Tigger. I'm already alcohol ravaged thanks to some overenthusiastic mates in the pub earlier. They were just buying round after round like it was a race, so the alcohol is hitting me after the fact and the image of these two chatting takes on a surreal quality. Time has not been kind to Lamacq, though, to be fair he only really ever had a face for radio. Tigger clocks me approaching.

"Oy, ya cunt!"

Tigger has two volume settings: loud when he's just chatting and when he's about to say something inappropriate or antisocial, an inbuilt megaphone clicks in. Social Tourette's I call it. I approach the cord barrier and Tigger introduces me.

"This is my mate Dave."

I shake Lamacq's hand.

"Well, if it isn't Mr Lamarr."

That's right, in my alcoholic delirium I have somehow managed to mix his name up with that 50s throwback ex-comedian: so, in cultural terms, a C-list celebratory faux pas. Lamacq didn't correct my error. Tigger thought it was hilarious and didn't hide it.

I hop over the barrier, we discuss music for a while, mention a few Windmill bands, he knew some, pretended to know others. He was here tonight to introduce Cabbage as part of *BBC Introducing* where young bands are embraced by the music establishment, given a taste of what success *could* feel like, bring them into line, dampen their fire, quell their anger, make them more marketable to the masses.

Lamacq takes his leave, marching off purposefully to do his BBC DJ bit: introducing, rubber-stamping, taking possession, like a butterfly collector and his latest specimen is Cabbage, a socialist power-punk band from Manchester, their trajectory already in motion.

I turn to Tigger, who's still giggling his tits off.

"That was fackin' priceless."

"Aw God, I'm so pissed."

"I know, dude and proper early for you. How many you had?"

"Er. . . five pints and a couple of tequilas."

Tigger gives me a big hug. "How come?"

"It's a long and complicated story."

"You fackin' nutter, Dave."

"I feel a bit of a cunt about getting. . . what's his name?"

"Lamacq!" splutters Tigger.

"Yeah him."

"Did you see his face, dude? He was proper fucking narked!"

"Ah well, he'll get over it."

"He reckons he's always at the Windmill."

"I've never seen him there."

"On his show he makes like he's a fackin' regular."

"He's full of shit."

"Yeah, he is a bit."

"And he has one of those '*I know more than you*' voices."

"Yeah. Fack him, Daaave!"

We meet each other's gaze and burst into fits of giggles, just like a couple of kids. We are a couple of kids. The smoking area's thinned out. Tigger checks the time.

"Come on, we're gonna miss Cabbage."

"Hopefully, we'll miss Lamacq's bit."

We didn't and like a nerdy uncle trying to sound down with the kids, he confirmed what we'd already figured. He's a cunt.

Chapter Fifteen

Magic Badges, Saul-Less Gigs and the Hardest Round in the World in the World

Baby can you tell me how the universe began?
It started with a whimper
And then there came a bang
"Whitest Boy On The Beach" – Fat White Family

26th JULY 2017, 100 CLUB, OXFORD ST.

I'm still chatting with La and Finn, explaining to them how I managed to get on the list.

"Tigger's on the list, too and he's trying to get his girl-friend in." I lean in conspiratorially. "To be honest, I'm kinda hoping they fail."

"Bit harsh." La laughs.

"He's way more fun on his own. Is that selfish?" I ponder.

Before they have chance to respond Tigger bounces in with Sadie, crashing straight into me, buzzed up on their obvious success.

"You did it. That's brilliant!"

La and Finn smirk at me, knowingly. Okay, I'm being insincere, I'm just trying my best to be decent and sometimes that means pretending. I could blame her for hogging his time, owning his choices, that voice in his ear telling him not to trust me and for basically fucking up our friendship, but I don't. I get how my Mrs and his ex being mates could be an issue for her, a threat even, but Tigger should manage it better, so I blame him for not standing up for our friend-ship and being so fucking weak.

Tigger is laughing, still high on gaining entry to this rarest of gigs.

"How d'you get Sadie in?"

"I just kept fucking badgering 'em dude. They eventually caved in."

If you knew Tigger, you would understand their position. He jerks into action.

"I'm fackin' parched." He turns to Sadie. "Let's go spend these beer tokens."

"You've got beer tokens?" I quiz, somewhat puzzled.

He holds out his hands and reveals a bunch of Fred Perry badges.

"You're kidding me? They're beer tokens?"

Tigger looks at me like I'm mad.

"Yeah, 'course."

The Fred Perry girl probably told me, but as you know, listening's not my strong point.

"I thought it was just promotional shit."

La turns to Finn.

"How did we miss out on them? You're clearly not pulling the right strings."

I was already holding a full pint so I hand her my tokens.

"Here, you two have them. Have a drink on me." I smile. "Well, technically, Adam Harmer."

Profoundly grateful, they head to the bar to exchange Fred Perry badges for beer. And that was the aforementioned random act of kindness. I know it's not much, but it's the small things that count.

Tigger looks at me, puzzled.

"What d'ya go and do that for?"

"Just spreading the love," I shrug.

Tigger cocks his head and gives me one of his "Oh yeah?" looks, as if to suggest giving away beer tokens that were free anyway somehow translates to a sexual come-on.

"Fuck off, Tigger!"

Undeterred, he raises an eyebrow, hanging onto his position.

"I got in free, what's the issue?" I continue.

To him, the issue's simple: La's cool, attractive, a bit of a celebrity within this particular corner of the music world and given half the chance he would probably fuck her. Tigger's just like that, horny as a tomcat, the light always green. Maybe he enjoys the game, the thrill, the chase, the capture. I mean, he seems to know no boundaries. He's never really tried it on with my Mrs; well, nothing beyond some mild flirting and a lingering kiss on the neck which she just put down to overexuberance. I like to believe it was because he valued our friendship too much, but I can't discount the fact that my wife, in her own way, would have made it abundantly clear there wasn't a prayer. I would also like to think this is not just due to her concerns over his dental hygiene. The truth is, she's also sad over the break-up, we'd all become super tight and she considered Tigger practically family. Now she's cut off, defriended, all modes of communication shut down, no longer permitted in his life, not anymore, for these are the rules he's chosen. It's been tough for us all, witnessing the tight bond between our two families rupture and the little bubble of love we all once occupied go pop. Tigger let it all go, all except me that is, I've been way harder to airbrush away, both indelibly linked by music we like, people we know and gigs we attend. Like tonight, though this one is different. Well, at least so I thought, as when we spoke last night I had the distinct impression he wanted to reconnect and what better occasion than a Fat Whites special at the 100 Club?

Things appear to be happening onstage. PREGOBLIN, the support act, are due to perform. Instruments are checked, musicians appear, guitars strapped on, drum kit tested and the lights slowly dim along with the DJ music. Then we see Alex Sebley, PREGOBLIN's main man, shuffling up to the mic; everything about his appearance a warning to the kids on how not to live your life. Appearances can be deceiving though, for this man is incredibly involved in this whole south London thing, his history intertwined with the Fat Whites, having once been a member of The Saudis with Lias and Nathan. La likens him to Lawrence of Felt/Denim/Go-Kart Mozart notoriety. A pretty good comparison, as Alex is a musical explorer, an experimenter, yet underneath his scruffy demeanour, a showman lurks, itching to entertain.

PREGOBLIN kick off their set and what an unexpectedly delightful funky pop groove it is. Word has it that Alex Sebley is about to sign a publishing deal with a sizeable label and from this you can see why. It's not a big stretch to imagine these songs being polished into nuggets of shiny superficial Capital Radio playlisted shite, sung by the latest vacuous media-constructed pop diva. But here, at the 100 Club, performed by someone who looks like he's just taking a break from his crack pipe, it sounds fucking awesome.

It steps up a gear as Jessica Winter joins him onstage, bringing her own sassy, sexy and very soulful vocal interplay to the whole proceedings. The word is that various labels are currently sniffing around this band so they may well become something. Either way, Alex is undoubtedly destined to be a successful song craftsman in his own right, if he survives his own shit.

Quite unexpectedly, Adam Harmer appears onstage, the man responsible for my presence here this evening. I turn to Tigger.

"Maybe they'll do 'Touch the Leather'?"

"Why would they do that?"

"Cos Alex co-wrote it."

In fact, he co-wrote a few of the early Fat Whites' songs, including this wonderfully sleazy anthem, the song that broke them through to a wider audience and onto 6 Music, when the world took note of this feral bunch of drug-addled lunatics. This information pleases Tigger immensely and he begins calling for it, loudly of course. Some guy nearby ask us why a Fat Whites' song is being requested, so Tigger informs him and the intel quickly spreads through the crowd, along with a new-found respect for this weird geezer standing before them, temporarily subduing their impatience for the main event. In no time, a whole chorus has joined the call for "Touch the Leather" and for the first time since Alex took the stage, he smiles, perhaps enjoying the recognition for the creative part he played in this song's existence, this soundtrack to every fetishist's dungeon. Not a verified fact, but incredibly likely. I mean, there are only so many times you can play "Venus in Furs".

Alex takes the mic.

"I am sure you will be hearing 'Touch the Leather'. . . just a bit later."

The crowd roar and the band launch into a song called "Combustion," a proper disco number, accentuated by Alex and Jessica's vocal interplay. Everyone's dancing. It's like a song you've always known; a timeless classic.

After they leave the stage we all head for the bar. Sadie gets a round in, she insists.

This is looking promising, perhaps an alcohol-based olive branch? Or a thank you for at least getting one of them in? Or probably nothing beyond getting a round in. What do I know? I overthink everything.

We all head up to the 100 Club's smoking area, basically Oxford Street, not even a pen. I'm chatting with La and some friendly random bloke, when Tigger bounces up.

"Fack me, dude, they were fackin' amazing!"

As you've probably noticed, Tigger swears a lot. More than me, in fact.

"What time are Fat Whites on?" I ask.

"Nine thirty, theoretically," replies La, always informed. "Shall we go in?"

Despite our enjoyment of PREGOBLIN, the Fat Whites are the primary reason we're all here. Even with The Moon-landingz promoting "Interplanetary Class Classics" and touring the shit out of it, as good as they are – and they are brilliant live – there was still a large Fat White-shaped hole that no one else could fill, even with Lias out front. The Fat Whites last London gig was when they conquered Brixton Academy. A brilliant show and the only time I've ever seen them perform their single "Breaking into Aldi." This was some 10 months ago, so an unreasonably long break for them, making this small club event all the more exceptional.

I hadn't clocked it, but everyone's since gone in, well everyone except me and the random bloke I'd been chatting shit with/at. I check the time on my phone. 9:43 p.m. Woops. I put my fag out, say goodbye to the friendly random bloke, whose name I was told but obviously wasn't paying attention and make a dash for the stairs off Oxford Street into the throbbing underbelly, where, beneath the traffic and consumers, the 100 Club nestles.

Halfway down the stairs, I bump into Nathan Saoudi, the Fat Whites' keyboardist, looking decidedly dazed and confused.

"Hey, Nathan, when're you guys on?"

He looks at me, eyes glazed, trying to focus, clearly in a bit of a hole. I really shouldn't say this, for it promotes all the wrong values, but I'm actually pretty heartened to find Nathan all fucked up when he should be onstage. A clear sign that despite the corporate bullshit surrounding this event, all is not lost: mayhem still prevails.

"Er. . . what time is it?"

I check my phone again. "Nine forty-five."

I watch as this information works its way to a part of his brain still vaguely functional.

"Er. . . shit, now!"

I follow him in as he slowly but purposefully heads for the stage. The air is charged, the crowd primed and already roaring. I work my way to the front where Tigger, Sadie, La and Finn are in position. The Fat Whites are onstage, well, all except the Saoudi brothers. Where the fuck did Nathan go? Then out of nowhere, he appears and the crowd let out another huge roar as he carefully positions himself behind his keyboard wearing a look of Brian Wilson faraway confusion. No Saul tonight, which does feel odd. I mean, he is such an integral part of it all, both live and in the studio - especially the studio. His looming presence, those hooded eyes, that toothless grin will all be missed, not to mention his masterful guitar strokes. Only one to go. Lias. The band is poised, ready to begin, trying not to look concerned, though clearly wondering. . .

Just before awkwardness sets in, Lias appears like a returning hero, the crowd clapping, whooping, screaming as he surveys the auditorium, staring, blinking, looking unwashed and somewhat slightly dazed. Then, as if emerging from somewhere dank and grimy below the 100 Club, the pulsating beats and throbbing bass of "Tinfoil Deathstar" reverberate through the floor. The already feverish crowd let out a huge primal roar.

From the moment Jack Everett bashes his kit, the stagediving begins and Lias is off, feeding on the frenzied feedback. The crazier he gets, so the crowd follow and before long the mosh pit is a pulsating pile of bodies, torsos and limbs continually passing overhead as the stagediving intensifies. The corporates are in the room, but they're quickly pushed to the back by the multicellular mass of true Fat White fans, chanting along to every line of every song. There is nothing in the way of new material, but it matters not, this is a celebration and the tension they conjure whilst teetering on the brink of chaos is palpable, the entire club a sweaty, heaving, crowd-surfing human mass. Yet, as good as it is, something is still amiss. And that something is a someone. And that someone is Saul.

I'm parched, I need a drink; water, beer. I no longer care, so hard as it is, I prise myself away and squeeze through the revellers behind me, working my way to the bar, accepting I'll have to sacrifice a song or two. But no, not here, as another great thing about this place is the unusual layout means both bars are still close to the action, so I can continue watching whilst my stout is being poured. When the bartender returns, I spontaneously add to my order, despite the logistical challenge this will undoubtedly cause. Beers for Tigger and Sadie.

I work my way back slowly with all three beers out front like precious cargo, helping the packed audience yield more easily to my inconvenient presence. As I weave my way through the throng, the Krautrock beats of "Whitest Boy on The Beach" kick in. Shit, it's gonna go mental. I manage to make it to the post in front of the stage with beers more or less intact, but it's currently way too crazy to attempt transporting them to Tigger and Sadie out front. I settle behind the awkwardly positioned post, an enormous obelisk slap bang in the middle of the mosh pit. My view is significantly diminished but this has to be the best version of this song I've ever heard them perform. When it finally reaches its noisy hypnotic climax, I move in further, but it's so rammed I cannot quite reach. I shout, but just like me,

Tigger's also partially deaf from years of aural abuse. I cannot get any closer without an alcoholic fatality, so I ask the dude in front to tap Tigger's shoulder. He obliges and Tigger lights up when he clocks me and my precious cargo. He reaches over and takes the beers, proper grateful and all. Sadie's equally pleased by this timely liquid gift.

During the set there is a small revealing moment and a hopeful sign of a healed relationship. By this, I mean between Lias and Saul, in case you're getting confused. The crowd are asking them to play "Goodbye Goebbels", a chilling lamentation from the dark twisted communal mind of the Fat Whites, written from the perspective of the Führer himself in the moments before he and Goebbels top themselves, whose lyrics describe a hauntingly tender moment between them, during which they mourn their failure to fully implement the Final Solution and fantasise about a Fourth Reich. So not a band for the squeamish or faint-hearted. When they play this song Saul and Lias usually harmonise together, so when the audience call for it, Lias looks up and with all sincerity addresses the crowd:

"Not without Saul. We can't do Goebbels without Saul."

And that was that, everyone understood, Lias was right, for despite writing the lyrics, the song belongs to Saul. Check out his solo performance at the Windmill supporting The Rebel, sensitively captured by Lou Smith and available on his channel. If you were not paying proper attention to the song's unsettling sentiments, his performance could make you weep. It really is a thing of transcendent beauty.

The Fat Whites round off their set by banging out the most full-on rocked-up version of "Bomb Disneyland" I've heard. Some of you will know this crowd-pleaser in which the lovely Fat White boys tell us of their wish to kill all our children with dirty bombs unleashed onto various leisure parks, along with other even darker images. After this explosive climax, the band casually shuffle offstage as Lias mumbles something about this being the last time they will ever play that set. There is no encore, there rarely is amongst this south London collective, a gig cliché they refuse to adopt.

The revellers slowly disperse, trying to readjust to normality after an hour of utter chaos and madness. They certainly don't want to leave. I mean, Wednesday night or not, how can you just go home after that?

Chapter Sixteen

Wrong Country, Challenging Content, Instant Karma

Young people of today
Don't like the devil's jokes
They do not comprehend irony
They are worse than their folks
Satan has told me privately
That I must stop this trend
To punish non-freethinkers
Satan has come again
"Satan is Real Again" – Country Teasers

I head for the bar which is thankfully still serving; ears ringing, soaked to the skin, mouth dry as sandpaper, much of my previous beer shared with the crowd, some orally but mostly over their backs. On my way, I bump into Finn and behind him is La, both buzzing from the gig and drenched in sweat.

"How good was that?" La shouts, beaming.

"Yeah. I was worried by all that Fred Perry shite, but they smashed it," I reply.

"They certainly did, I mean, wow!" adds Finn.

"Yeah but 'Fred Perry Subculture'. What does that even mean?"

"Free beer is what it meant to us!"

"That's how it starts, Finn, that's how they get us."

"We're all corporate whores now, Dave," laughs La.

"You two okay for drinks, I'm gagging?" I ask.

"I'd love one," says Finn.

"What you having, La?"

"Piss off, Dave, it's *my* round."

We move towards the bar together. La orders beers then turns to me smiling from ear to ear.

"That was so fucking brilliant!"

That's the thing about her, there's no pretence, it's not a career, she goes to see the stuff she plays, it's her life. Unshackled by corporately concocted playlists, panel-based decisions on what we should hear, La just plays whatever the fuck she likes, meaning Finn has the thankless task of bleeping out all the cussing, for her show's on FM radio so Ofcom rules apply. It does not stop her, though. Only recently she played a song by The Rebel, a third of which had to be bleeped out, not just for swearing, but other offences too. Now, you wouldn't hear that on the fucking Beeb.

The man behind The Rebel is Ben Wallers, most renowned for being frontman/songwriter to cult British band Country Teasers, formed in Edinburgh with strong ties to Brixton. The Rebel is effectively Ben's solo vehicle where his former bandmates have been replaced by an outdated, repurposed Nintendo Gameboy to glorious effect. This moniker was inspired by the classic Tony Hancock film of the same name, but unlike the film's protagonist, Ben is no fake. He's a mysterious eccentric individual with a devil on both shoulders. A Leftie who toys with the right in dark and dangerous ways, writing songs about misogynists, racists and fascists from the point of view of his subjects - à la the aforementioned "Goodbye Goebbels" by Fat White Family. Indeed, you'd be hard pressed *not* to hear Country Teasers' influence running through their debut album *Champagne Holocaust*, something they do not deny, but celebrate, so fair play to them.

Ben fearlessly and unapologetically wades into seriously dangerous waters, taunting and challenging the listener to get behind the joke or miss the point. He is quite probably the bravest, boldest musical satirist to have ever existed, because you're never certain where his opinions stop and his satire begins, infusing his lyrics with an unsettling power.

As The Rebel, Ben Wallers often plays the Windmill, quietly enjoying the renewed interest in his work and undoubtedly flattered by the influence he has had on so many of these bands. Ben is incredibly charming and polite, even after informing him once that upon first hearing them I had to stop what I was doing and duckduckgo "Are Country Teasers racist?" He was not at all affronted by this, just massively curious as to what the search results turned up.

So much so, I am sure that was the first thing he did when he returned home that night. Maybe. . .

Ben has also been working on another project with fellow Country Teaser Alastair Mackinven, under the moniker The Stallion, in which they reimagine the entire Pink Floyd opus *The Wall*, renaming their version *The Dark Side of The Wall*. Ben swears he's a massive fan and even though he is prone to fibbing, on this I do believe him, curious as to what the nutter's going to do with it. They also plan to give *The Final Cut* the same treatment. A forgotten gem of an album and the only one I'm still inclined to play, yet pretty much airbrushed from their musical legacy. I couldn't resist asking Ben about it.

"I love that album!" exclaims Ben.

"Me too. It's my favourite Floyd album."

"And mine! Why does nobody like it?"

"I've got a theory. . ." I offer.

He nods for me to continue.

"Well, the album's their most political. It slags off Thatcher, the nuclear arms race and the Falklands War. Most Floyd fans are flag waving, Trident-supporting, Tories."

"Hmm, you could be right," ponders Ben. "Isn't Gilmour a Tory?"

"Wouldn't surprise me. Kinda looks like one."

"All I remember was the album petrified me as a kid, thought we were going to be nuked at any moment," confesses Ben.

The Stallion also claim that a cover of "Purple Rain" is on the cards, but that could just be Ben winding up a journalist, so I don't even ask.

Mr Wallers is in the building tonight, La saw him earlier. I guess after languishing in relative obscurity for 20-odd years it must be pretty amazing for Ben to watch his protégés strut their stuff and witness the delayed impact of his music on south London's country punk emergence in all its various forms.

"Here ya go, Dave," says La, passing me a pint and then Finn his.

"That was amaaazing!" says Finn, smiling. "I canna wait 'til Saturday."

La turns to me.

"Are you going Saturday?"

"What? The Moonlandingz? I thought I'd be away, so didn't get a ticket. It's all sold out now. I'm going to Madonnatron's thing at the Windmill anyway."

"We're doing both!" exclaims Finn, excitedly.

La looks to Finn.

"Have we any spare guest list?"

Finn considers this carefully. . .

"Actually, I think we might."

He looks at his phone. Counts his fingers. I wait, hopeful.

"Yes, we do."

"There you go, Dave. Sorted," adds La.

"Really? You have a spare ticket? I don't mind paying."

"It's guest list, Dave."

"Whose list?"

"Moonlandingz, I think?" says La, uncertain. Finn nods.

"That's brilliant!" I splutter, excitedly.

"Well, you gave us your beer tokens," reasons Finn.

I give them both a hug.

"Woo! Fucking amazing, instant karma!"

Chapter Seventeen

Guest List Hierarchy, Anti-Anthems and The Cunt Wall

Shane MacGowan's tying my shoes
I got Jerry Lee Lewis in a head lock
You spend fingering your ideals
Baby all I ever found's the sweetest spot
"I Am Mark E. Smith" – Fat White Family

29TH JULY 2017, STOCKWELL ROAD, BRIXTON

So, three nights later, I'm queuing with Zsa Zsa for the guest list entrance of the Brixton Academy. We're directed to different windows on account of our guestlist classifications. See, even if you manage to get on one you're still embroiled within a hierarchical system, you just cannot get away from this shit. Who cares anyway, I've been spared the bullshit of haggling with greedy touts or getting shafted on Viagogo.

The muffled sound of "Vessels" reverberates though the wall by the guest list entrance, a delightfully sleazy glam rock stomper. I feel my phone vibrate. A text from Finn.

You in yet?

The Moonlandingz have begun and I should be in there, not out here, queuing. I'm already feeling a sense of prima donna entitlement. I mean, this is not how you treat guests. I reply to Finn.

Nearly. . .

Finally, I'm wristbanded and vaguely arrange with Zsa Zsa where I might be since he's waiting for Madame HiFi.

I enter the Academy stage left via a door I've never been through before, which in itself feels special. I quickly weave my way to the bar for replenishments before turning around to face the stage. I love the majesty of this venue with its faux-Italian Renaissance interior and the convenient way it slopes to the stage.

The Moonlandingz have just launched into "Sweet Saturn Mine" – their ode to semen mentioned earlier. I do so love this anti-anthem, its hook line the perfect antithesis to all that punch the air, "*ain't life great*" bollocks. Instead, we have Johnny Rocket nihilistically screeching "*I don't feel all right*", which is strangely redemptive and life-affirming.

As the song comes to a fitting banshee-wailing climax, my phone vibrates. It's Finn again.

Well?

Shit, I forgot to text him.

Woo! I'm in! Thanks fellah!

The place is heaving. My phone vibrates again.

Centre middle

It's already rammed. The chances of finding him and La, or Zsa Zsa and Madame HiFi for that matter, are frankly remote. The Academy's a large venue, its capacity almost 5,000, so "Centre middle" is not much to go on. I know who I will find, though – Tigger. Without any shadow of a doubt, he'll be in the mosh pit.

Not sure if Sadie will, she often isn't and at the beginning of their relationship, hardly at all. This made the mosh pit the one remaining space our friendship could still reside. Admittedly, not much discourse could be had, but at least it was ours.

So, off to the front I go, to dig out Tigger.

Firstly, though, I need to navigate the Cunt Wall.

***

I do realise this requires some explanation, so here goes:

The Cunt Wall is generally found at bigger concerts, less often at smaller venues and never at the Windmill. Put simply, if you try reaching the front from any direction, at about the midway point, you will come across a wall of punters who do not possess sufficient metal to go further in but will do all they can to prevent anyone else. Basically, a wall of cunts.

In order to get to the front where all the fun folk are, the Cunt Wall must be breached and there's a number of tactics one can employ. Here's just a few:

People Train: A particularly popular and often effective strategy. Quite simply, when a people train comes your way, you just hop on board, as it's those at the front who get to deal with any flak and once the Cunt Wall is breached you just stick tight and follow. This generally works best if those at the front of the train are female. I'm not being sexist, it's the men that make up the Cunt Wall who are, as they're more inclined to give way to women. Though, it has to be said and not just in the interest of balance, but because it's true – the Cunt Wall is also made up of women.

Cunt Deception: Much like The Moonlandingz did, though far less elaborate, you act out a fictitious backstory and make like you're going *back* to your mates. This requires a degree of confidence and some acting skills, all the more convincing if you are carrying several beers. Cunts don't see themselves as cunts, just righteous, so if you appear to be heading somewhere specific and ask them politely to pass, it confuses them. Nevertheless, with this method there is still no guarantee your drinks will survive the journey – cunts will be cunts.

Cunt Skittles: A more aggressive way of breaking through the Cunt Wall – a system I neither practice nor condone – is to just charge at it with such force, the cunts break apart like skittles. This is based on the principle, to take on a cunt, you must *be* a cunt – a worse cunt. This is also how fights often start, which is fine by me because it is generally cunt on cunt in beautiful symmetry.

And finally. . .

Cunt Circumvention: My own particular favourite, where you cut down one side of the venue, working your way along one of the outer walls towards the stage. When you can go no further you cut into the audience from the side, thus encountering less resistance. You still need to pierce the Cunt Wall for it is shaped like a horseshoe around the stage, but the trajectory makes it easier as you're technically heading away from the stage, albeit at an odd angle and much like a chalk line in front of a chicken this confuses cunts, subduing their irritation.

When you finally breach the Cunt Wall, things begin to loosen up. People are no longer territorial, full of that "we've been here longer" mentality, like we're all queuing for a Black Friday sale – it's a gig, you morons.

On the other side of the Cunt Wall people are friendlier, looser, more forgiving. Closer to the stage they're bouncing, smiling, singing along.

And when you finally arrive, everyone's like "Hey, come join the party!" Because it's always a party at the front and isn't this why we're all here?

Chapter Eighteen

Glory Holes, Singing Librarians, Slimy Friends and Turkey Necks

I found myself in a leather bar
There was sweat dripping off'a my wurst
"Hey boy" said the man to my right
"Do you need something to quench your thirst?"
"Glory Hole" – The Moonlandingz

Woo! I've made it and as I suspected, Tigger's amongst the throng, shirtless, sweaty, excitable, like a puppy after being cooped up indoors far longer than is healthy. He is swept back and forth by the sea of perspiring bodies, so I move in closer and when the human tide rolls back, I slap my hand on his back. He spins around, fire in his eyes, then upon seeing me, his whole face lights up into a mad wide-eyed grin and almost bowls me over as he throws his semi-naked slimy body over mine. No longer a puppy, more an oversized dog after swimming in the grimy Thames, yet my general disgust does not outweigh the sentiment of the gesture, for there's no denying this feeling. The double drum beats of "Glory Hole" reverberate around the room bringing the simmering mosh pit back to the boil, Tigger and me out front, arms around each other pogoing in unison, sharing a moment.

If you are not familiar with the song, it appears to be a touching anthem describing how Johnny Rocket visited a German leather bar, where he was effectively drug raped and in the process, with some friendly leathered assistance, discovers his own G spot. By the song's climax Johnny is revelling in this new-found knowledge, proclaiming that everyone from Kanye West to Sleaford Mods, even his own dad, has a glory hole. I mean, what more could you want from a song?

In many ways, Tigger is a great gig buddy. He appears so batshit crazy that people just leave us alone; most of the time at least. He's not aggressive, in fact quite the opposite, he's full of brattish love, as loud as he is tactile with no off button. This can be intimidating to some and just plain annoying to others with the occasional punter not yielding so readily, so preventing a fight is part of my role within our strange relationship dynamic.

I'm alone again. I didn't notice Tigger leave, but it's not unusual, probably thrown himself back into the throng, always drawn to the centre of the action.

Tonight, The Moonlandingz strut their stuff, put on a good show, but something's amiss. Is it the larger stage? All their previous gigs have been in much smaller venues, though it's not new territory for Lias, when the Fat Whites played here they completely owned the stage. Maybe it's the absence of Rebecca Taylor who usually moonlights from Slow Club to tour with them. She and Lias have developed this overtly sleazy sexual stage routine, the perfect visual accompaniment to their squalid lyrics and the whole Moonlandingz schtick. Tonight, though, it's considerably restrained. Rebecca's replacement's a librarian. Literally. Maybe. Nevertheless, Johnny (Lias) tries getting frisky at one point but it comes over as awkward and he has the good sense to wind his turkey neck in. Perhaps the indifference of the Goat *only* fans has permeated the stage, but Johnny and the band struggle to prime the atmosphere. He even keeps his trousers on for the entire set. A first, surely?

I look around and there amongst all the sweaty human limbs I recognise Sadie's face amongst the crowd. So, she *is* here. I then notice Tigger enveloping her protectively from behind, a human shield against the feisty pulsating human mass surrounding them. The image is both primal and romantic. They seem happy together, they really do.

I remember when they first met, two years back now, at a benefit gig in Brixton. . .

Chapter Nineteen

Bots, Algorithms, Voluntary Profiling and the Economics of Gentrification

I found myself in a leather bar
There was sweat dripping off'a my wurst
"Hey boy" said the man to my right
"Do you need something to quench your thirst?"
"Glory Hole" – The Moonlandingz

28ᵀᴴ MAY 2015, HOME

Tigger appears at my door all excited and pregnant with news. He has the Fat Whites on Facebook, keeping him in the loop, whilst I stubbornly refuse to surrender my life on-line. This does not mean I'm a tinfoil-hat-wearing-nut-job, just the recognition that a darkness lurks within the heart of Facebook, a sinister side that's up to all sorts of skulduggery with your data.

All you Facebookers and tweeters have made it so easy for them, willingly giving up your personalities, your core values, as they hoover up your "likes", your shares, your retweets, your activities, your associations, your purchases – *all* your digital footprints.

When I say "they", I'm not talking about some sinister men in black, or the illuminati, or some sad pasty spooks masturbating over compromising pictures hidden in the creases of your hard drive. It's all moved way beyond Snowdon's revelations. No need for human intervention, just bots and algorithms, way more efficient and always there, never sleeping, skulking in the shadows of your digital world, deciphering your keystrokes, where your mouse hovers.

This profiling's not just for later use, but a specific you, the one online in that given moment, analysing your state of mind as you inadvertently shine a light on your innermost world: your emotional state; upset, happy, drunk, high, more susceptible to purchase, donate, gamble, masturbate. It's all in real time, hitting you up with an opinion, an issue, a product, a horny neighbour, whatever, whoever, for they already know your predilections, what bait to dangle. Go on, hit the link, click the PayPal button, tap in your password, what have you got to lose?

We now live in a virtual society, collecting, friending, following people we do not even know and never will. Filtered photos, cropped images, airbrushed versions of ourselves, out there for all to see, the glass always half full, rose-tinted slices of the good bits, "ain't our lives just peachy". Don't get me wrong, tragedy is discussed. Well, retweeted, commented on, liked, not liked, an emoji for every emotion, the impression of giving a shit, adding our bit to this unreal reality, pushing truth aside as we continue fleshing out our own algorithmic avatar, until nothing means anything anymore.

Why is privacy no longer a basic human right? *"I don't care if they're monitoring me, I've got nothing to hide"* is the usual refrain. If you are one of these people lazily justifying the surrender of your privacy, there are two points I'd like to make:

Firstly, as Orwell's protagonist effectively illustrated in his dystopian novel *1984*, the human monkey will alter its behaviour when observed, even if it's just the mere possibility of being observed. An accepted fact amongst behavioural scientists, because Winston was never certain the telescreens were watching and listening at all, yet moderated his outward behaviour regardless, simply because they *could* be. Do we really want to be living like this? We *are* living like this.

Secondly, to surrender such freedoms and give up on privacy is not just to the advantage of the current government, but any future government. And just look at the state of the world – can any one of you predict anything anymore? Who knows, things are so upside-down back-to-front, that as weird as it may sound, Donald Trump *could* end up becoming the US President. Fucking hell, imagine that!

Tigger likes his Facebook and thinks I'm just a paranoid cunt. He's right; I am.

"You never guess what, dude?"

"Er, I dunno? Fat Whites are playing somewhere?"

"Yeah, at Brixton Electric, in a couple of weeks."

"Fantastic!"

"With Alabama 3."

"Wow. Who's supporting who?"

"Not sure, Facebook says they're both headlining. Some kind of benefit thing."

"What's it in aid of?"

"Fuck knows."

"Does that bit not matter?"

Tigger shrugs, screwing up his face. I grab my phone to search it up.

"So, it doesn't matter if it's. . . I dunno. . . an EDL fundraiser?"

Tigger rolls his eyes. My duckduckgoing yields results.

"Okay, it's to raise money to help local residents keep their homes."

Tigger looks at me blankly.

"Shall we go, then?" he asks.

I ignore him.

"You know, those black-hearted fuckers you voted for?"

"Oh, fuck off!"

I continue, just to annoy him.

"Gentrification."

He looks confused so I friendsplain some more.

"Councils getting rid of poor people from inner cities."

Tigger feigns interest, just to humour me.

"It's all about the fucking money. Your lot have stacked the cards that way," I add.

"It's not my fucking lot!" protests Tigger, as if he can somehow divorce his vote from the government it helped install.

Though to be fair, it wasn't just his lot, Blair picked up the neoliberal baton with glee and a little too much gusto.

A system that turned world leaders into salesmen for their respective nation's corporate interests. The only diplomacy that mattered for Blair was that regarding trade, particularly one of our main trades – weaponry. Blair was an excellent salesman. That we know, because armed with nothing but a sexed-up student dissertation, he managed to convince both the US and UK government to go to war in Iraq, murdering tens of thousands of innocent civilians, not to mention all the soldiers dying, not for any glory or noble human purpose, but an imperial whim in this international game of geopolitical Monopoly.

"They treat everything like it's a business."

Tigger's eyes glaze over and he shakes his head like a dog drying himself.

"What the fuck? I just want to see the bands, dude!" he complains.

"Ignorant twat."

"Fuck off."

The gig has been put together by *Brixton Buzz*, a local issue online magazine that is raising a fighting fund to stem the tide of Brixton's gentrification. This entire event was driven by the plight of residents occupying Cressingham Gardens in Brixton, facing eviction because Lambeth Council believe it would be better to demolish their homes and sell the land to a private developer, who plan to fill the space with luxury apartments. The issue is far more complex and the council do their best to make it sound like the opposite, but it's not.

This system is not wrapped around people, but budgets, cost centres and financial efficiency. Everything's for sale, people no longer figure beyond how much and of what they are driven to consume. Councils can no longer serve their communities, they have to make the books balance and people are an inconvenience, especially poor people. They are forced into functioning like companies, austerity cutbacks creating the perfect "divide and rule" toxic environment, fighting each other for crappy jobs, shitty money and affordable housing.

"So, we going then?" asks Tigger again.

"Course we fucking are!"

Chapter Twenty

Industry Pimps, The Rage Factor and the British Terrorist Unit

And I'm down with the kids
'Cause my facts are alternative
And I won Strictly Come Dancing
Without even trying
And I've got a nasty coke habit
Good thing you know nothing about it
"Cardboard Man" – The Cool Greenhouse

Now, I do accept that social media can also have an upside. The mere fact that Corbyn confounded the political Establishment by removing Theresa May's parliamentary majority is evidence of its power. The unfortunate reverse side of this coin is that we get things like Brexit or Trump.

Another positive example of its power was when Simon Cowell received a right royal kicking from a Facebook campaign. What began life as an idea, a prank, once let loose on to social media by Jon and Tracy Morter, took on a super-virus life all of its own. Not their first attempt, but that song by Rage Against the Machine and its *"Fuck you, I won't do what you tell me"* refrain quickly gestated, multiplying as the contagion exponentially spread throughout various social media platforms, even good old-fashioned word-of-mouth. It really was a thing of beauty.

Cowell was dismissive, no concept of failure, thought he could control it all. But no one could; not even that omnipotent industry pimp. Once the genie was out the bottle and word was out, the downloads increased and the mainstream media clambered on board with classic tabloid hype injecting the entire campaign with steroids. In the final week it went crazy, overtaking Cowell's latest *X Factor* meat-puppet winner and pummelling the soulless shite into the ground where it belonged. Woo! It was fucking special.

Gaining entry to "The Rage Factor" had taken some serious organising: registrations completed, photos uploaded and then a lottery. The gig was free, as Rage Against the Machine were thanking us for propelling their anti-authority anthem "Killing in The Name" to the 2009 Xmas number one spot and finally breaking Cowell's *X Factor* dominance which had ruined the previous four Christmases for anyone with a morsel of taste.

Yeah, yeah, all you naysayers, I'm aware that Cowell benefited financially from the Rage song's success due to his involvement in their label, but it wasn't about the money, it was a modern-day Aesop's fable about a manipulative, megalomaniac control freak and how his fevered ego took on the entire record-buying, downloading public and lost. His God complex faltered. He pretended he was cool with it, but no matter how hard he tried, he couldn't force that smarmy smile of his to reach his eyes. We all saw it, Cowell, your face betrayed you. You fucking lost.

6TH JUNE 2010, MY BRO'S WHITE VAN, LONDON

Careening through the middle of London in my bro's dodgy white van, smoking, drinking, music blaring, having a party, stoked on the success of securing tickets for this rarest of events. Also, one of our ever more infrequent re-unions, always underestimating how much we've missed each other and always overcompensating.

We're about halfway there, my bro's driving, there's no satnav and it's becoming increasingly hard to focus on the ancient *A to Z* my bro still possesses, it must be a dozen mayors old. We're at some lights on Brompton Road waiting for them to go green. My bro turns to me.

"Straight on?"

I focus on the map.

"Shit, no, left."

This is technically correct, so my bro pulls the van left, but we're met with blaring horns and faced with a line of cars. Whatever the map says, this is clearly a one-way street.

"Fuck no. Straight!"

My bro yanks the steering the opposite way, dramatically jerking the van back on course. More horns blare, different cars, different reasons. I don't know why, but with hyped exuberance, I stick my head out of the window.

"Fack off!" I shout before settling back in my seat. "Sorry about that."

He looks at me, raising his eyebrows.

"This fucking *A to Z*'s an antique!" I proclaim.

We both crease up.

"Take the *next* left," I instruct.

I pick up a music rag from the floor of his van, rest it on my lap and begin rolling another as we sing along to Carter USM, just for old times' sake.

Suddenly my bro stops singing. Something in his wing mirror has caught his eye. His brow furrows with concern.

"You okay?" I query.

"What's that?" he asks.

"What?"

He turns the music down to reveal a siren wailing. I did hear it but managed to blend it in with the music – I mean, it was Carter USM after all. I try looking behind but have no visuals since we're in a white van with no windows at the rear and wing mirrors angled for the driver.

"Fuck!" says my bro, staring directly ahead, face hardening with fear. "Pigs!"

"Shit!" I reply as I clock the all-too-familiar blue light reflecting off the chrome wing mirrors.

"I have to stop."

"Shit, fuck, bollocks!"

The van is full of spliff smoke, I'm halfway through rolling another and we're both drinking. Rather than embarking on a high-speed car chase through London, my bro reacts as you should in such situations and brings us to a grinding halt. He stares ominously at the wing mirror.

"What's happening?"

"They're getting out.

"Okay"

"Now they're walking over."

He turns to me.

"You need to lose that shit!"

Referring to the half-rolled spiff and all the necessary ingredients on a magazine nestled upon my lap.

I hastily try to hide it under my seat, but there is no such place in this very basic van and my legs fail to provide adequate cover. We are fucked.

A second later cops simultaneously appear at each of our windows, obviously choreographed. I clumsily try to wind mine down, but it keeps jamming. My bro has less difficulty and I overhear his cop's opening line.

"You're a long way from home?"

Seems they've already wired in my bro's number plate. I finally wrestle my window down and my cop addresses me.

"You lost, sir?"

"Er, no."

"Well, you looked it earlier."

"Yeah sorry, I didn't realise it was one-way, It wasn't clear on the map."

"The signs were."

"Yeah, well. . ."

"Have you been drinking?"

"Er, yes. Not him, just me. I'm only map reading."

"Not very well it seems."

"Er. . . yeah. . . no."

I hear the other cop asking my bro for his driving licence. My cop continues with me.

"So, where're you heading?"

"Finsbury Park."

"What's happening there?"

"A concert."

"Really? Who?"

"Rage against the Machine."

A moment of recognition flickers across his face.

"So, you have tickets?"

"Er, yeah."

"Can I see them?"

"Sure."

I rifle through my pockets and produce the ticket which very fortunately incorporates my mugshot, so no mistaking who it belongs to. He looks impressed.

"And your friend has one, too?"

"He's my brother."

"Ah, I see."

"He's up from Cornwall."

"Visiting?"

"Well. . . briefly. . . just for this concert really."

My bro produces his ticket. Then my cop looks at me, amused.

"Have we done something wrong?"

He laughs and nods to his colleague in silent agreement over something or other.

"We're from the British Terrorist Unit."

Terrorist Unit? What the fuck? This is getting worryingly serious and very surreal.

"So, what do you want with us?" I enquire timidly.

He laughs again, shaking his head. I wish he'd stop laughing, he's just making things worse. He signals to his partner and they walk off for a conflab. I turn to my bro.

"Terrorist unit?"

He looks ashen and stares straight ahead.

"I know."

"The van stinks of weed."

"I know."

"Are we fucked?"

"Maybe."

"Fuck. Fuck. Fuck."

"It's worse for me, I'm fucking driving!"

They approach our respective windows. My cop addresses us both.

"Look, we can see that you two are. . ."

I visibly gulp. Why *does* that always happen? He smiles.

". . . having a bit of a party."

"Yes but. . ."

He raises his hand to close me down.

"Whilst my colleagues in traffic might be interested in you, we're not."

"So, what's gonna happen to us?" I enquire, pathetically.

"You're going to *carefully* continue your journey to your concert."

"What?" I blurt.

My bro glares at me to shut the fuck up – a glare I know well.

"Yep. To be honest we're quite jealous."

"Really?"

"Yeah, we'd love to be coming, too."

The other one chips in.

"Yeah, I love Rage. Wish I'd known before."

Am I tripping? These coppers are Rage fans? My cop turns to me.

"Just one thing you can do for us. . ."

Here's the rub. I thought this was too easy.

"What?" enquires my bro, suspicious.

"Would you consent to completing a survey?"

"A survey?"

"Yes."

"What for?"

"Your background and ethnicity."

"What's it used for, though?" queries my bro.

"Just stats"

"For what purpose?" Asks my bro.

"Nothing really. Just logging the ethnic backgrounds of all the people we question," explains the cop.

"And nothing else?" I ask.

"So, we're the token whites to build up the Caucasian quota," snipes my bro.

A bit too cockily for my liking, given the situation we're in.

They respond with blank stares before turning to each other, communicating telepathically. Okay, they may not be professionally interested in us but they have made it pretty fucking clear there are other divisions just a call away. We're most definitely *not* in a position of strength and they're offering us a way out. I can no longer hold back.

"Yeah, no problem, we'll do the survey."

My bro looks at me sternly. I return his gaze with a *"we have no fucking choice, you fucking idiot"* glare.

We complete the survey, which was inane and everything my bro had said it would be, because in our own small way we were complicit in helping the British Terrorist Unit rebalance their racist books, all because we're white.

Then they left, wishing us a great concert, almost like normal people. Almost. They even gave us a receipt. I mean seriously, the British Terrorist Unit ignore our felonies, conduct a roadside survey and then give us a receipt before sending us on our way as if nothing had ever happened.

Craning my neck, I watch them walk back until they step inside their van, still trying to get my head around what's just happened.

"Weird."

My bro looks at me in baffled relief.

"Just a bit." He looks into his wing mirror. "Jesus!"

"What?"

"There's two vans and their both full of cops!"

"Really?"

"And I bet they're all armed like fucking Rambo!"

I turn to my bro.

"Perhaps we should go."

My bro turns and meets my gaze and we crease up in tension relief. We quickly pull ourselves together as we're not yet out of danger. He turns the key and pulls the van away merging into the busy traffic. Then, for reasons unclear my bro begins wrestling his window back down.

"What are you doing?"

He flashes me a smile then sticks his head out.

"FUCK YOU, I WON'T DO WHAT YOU TELL ME!" he hollers, before turning his attention back to the road, clearly still pumped on adrenaline after our brush with the law.

"Except, we just did." I remind him.

"I know. I feel dirty now," he replies, clearly irritated. "How about you finish building that spliff?"

I look at him curiously, shrug my shoulders and reach for the magazine under my legs.

Chapter Twenty-One

Science, Charity, Love and Letterman

Lies make my world a happy place to be
I lie to the women and I lie to the men
And I don't mind if they lie to me
I lie in bed and I lie standing up
And I lie when I'm sitting down
If I had a penny for every lie I told
I would have 100 pounds
"Lies" – Country Teasers

11TH JUNE 2015, EN ROUTE, ELECTRIC, BRIXTON
It's the night of the benefit gig featuring the Fat Whites and Alabama 3. A Thursday night, so almost the weekend, just need to slide through Friday with mild tinnitus and

an empty head. I meet Tigger by the station, both already stoked with excitement, he grabs my shoulders.

"Dude, we're supporting a great cause and seeing some great bands. Charity with benefits!"

"You've changed your tune. Let's hope they don't sniff you out, this lot have a nose for Tory scum."

"Fuck off," hisses Tigger.

Whilst our prime reason for going tonight is the Fat Whites, we both have some history with Alabama 3, albeit separately. They would often play support to Primal Scream, including a legendary all-nighter at Brixton Academy featuring a surprise 3 a.m. performance from Spiritualized.

I'd like to say I can remember this historic happening, but a friend of mine had procured some Hawaiian magic mushrooms from a stall in Portobello Road market before it was outlawed and we tried some on the way, just for science. They came with no instructions, so our portion control was driven by ignorance. I only managed half of Alabama 3's set before losing my grip on reality and my ability to stand. My strongest memory of the evening was Neil Hannon (of Divine Comedy) stepping over me as I lay on the sticky carpet, grimacing at my semi-paralysed state.

Tigger and I are yakking on the train, talking shite, guzzling warm beer on this very pleasant June evening, alive with possibility. Tigger wants to party. He's on day release from the demands of his kids, moaning clients, needy workers, unpaid bills, hostile in-laws, unwelcome guests wearing suits and a far from functioning marriage. Basically, his life. This was his escape, his *me time*.

The Electric, it is rammed. Everywhere you turn there's posters and literature detailing various housing issues across Brixton: Cressingham Gardens, Guinness Trust residents and behind the stage a large "Save Brixton Arches" banner. An action group formed in response to Network Rail's attempts to evict 30 local businesses from their trading units within Brixton's railway arches. Why? So, they can bring in an architect to wank fairy dust all over them, then triple the rent for the likes of Nando's, Starbucks and all the rest of the globalised retail shite we see on every high street, everywhere we fucking go. So yes, a very political gig and the atmosphere is charged. Well it is the Electric.

As we head for the bar I turn to Tigger.

"They're definitely gonna fucking sniff you out, mate."

"You can be such a cunt," he replies, shaking his head.

I turn to respond, but a young skinhead girl has just brushed by, taking his attention with her. She has the air of a young Sinéad O'Connor, all angry and vulnerable. Tigger's transfixed.

I order beers and try chatting with him but he clearly has other things on his mind, fortunately, one of them is the Fat Whites and the DJ music has already faded. The crowd begin cheering as band members stride onstage and assume their positions, all of which thankfully diverts Tigger's attention. Saul looms over the audience, already shirtless, donning a large Stetson, giving him the look of an undernourished extra from *Brokeback Mountain*.

Lias, also shirtless, stares vacantly at the mass of revellers like his unofficial rider was a little too much. There's a crackle in the air and the throbbing bass of "Auto Neutron" echoes around the room as the two semi-naked frontmen stand there grinning, deranged, like Nurse Ratched's meds are beginning to wear off. It's not what you'd consider a moshing track, but it doesn't matter to this audience, they're going to party anyway.

Tigger bounces straight into the action and like his heroes, quickly peels off his shirt. The music slowly builds, Lias has already gone feral and I feel myself drawn into the multilimbed mayhem until I'm pogoing with Tigger to the best live band in the UK. Possibly the world.

They were in celebratory mood, having just conquered America. Not by gigging until they shat blood or self-destructed, as so many have before, but as a result of a simple twist of fate that secured them a live appearance on David Letterman in which they were allowed to perform "Is it Raining in Your Mouth?"

From this side of the pond this seemed like programming madness. And yes, it is about what it sounds like it might be. The entire song structure is sexual, building to a musical climax as Lias maniacally screams *"C'mon baby, shoot your load. . . shoot it in my face"*, leaving no room for doubt, but what a way to make an impact, it really was perfect television. Conversely, Bill Hicks had his final performance axed from the very same show, all because he poked fun at pro-lifers. What a twisted moral compass these Yanks possess.

Tigger nudges me, nodding towards the skinhead girl who is now standing nearby.

"Fucking hell, dude, I like her."

"Come on, man, you got a lovely Mrs at home."

"Yeah, I know. . . just saying. Wanna beer?"

"Don't you wanna wait for them to finish?"

"I do, but I'm fucking parched, dude."

Tigger heads for the bar and the bass line of their single "Cream of the Young" kicks in, a slow lament to underage sex, calming down the mosh pit a little. You could hear this song on 6 Music for a time, until (I assume), someone clocked on to the lyrics. I retrieve my phone from my pocket and hit record, but part way in my battery gives up the ghost. Fucking smartphones, draining unnecessary juice just so they can monitor my movements and listen to my conversations.

Tigger returns with beers, whilst chatting to the skinhead girl along the way. She then slides away and burrows into the mosh pit. Tigger passes my beer.

"I *really* like her, dude."

"Steady now," I warn.

"What do you mean?"

"I mean, don't be a cunt."

"Fuck off. Everything's cool, dude."

Undeterred, he moves into the mosh pit clutching his beer, splashing and moshing as he goes.

I note the skinhead girl is now talking to this guy. As it happens, a brick shithouse of a guy and they kiss, a proper kiss. This could get well dangerous and I really don't fancy Tigger's chances.

Where is he?

I look around for his bobbing shabby strawberry blond head.

Then I see him, he's already clocked the skinhead girl and is working his way towards her. It's too late for me to intercept and before I know it, he's trying to chat with her, not an easy feat in a Fat Whites mosh pit. I look at the big guy nearby, he isn't happy, so I move in closer on my mission to avert disaster, well, at least a black eye. I finally reach Tigger, grab his arm and pull him towards me. He protests like a guilty toddler, still feigning innocence after being caught red-handed.

"What?"

I pull him in tighter, placing my mouth over his ear.

"See that guy over there? That big fucker?"

Tigger looks over.

"Yeah?"

"That's her fucking boyfriend!"

"Fuck off!"

"It is!"

He looks again.

"You sure?"

I nod and as I do the skinhead girl intimately embraces the big guy. Surely it's obvious to him now? It is and a look of disappointment spreads over Tigger's face. I'm not sure why, but in this moment I feel strangely sorry for him. He shrugs his shoulders, quickly brushing it off, a meaningless fleeting fascination, his disappointment transitory. We both laugh, for as physical as Tigger is, he's a lover not a fighter.

The Fat Whites turn in another brilliant performance and we continue moshing right through to their "Bomb Disneyland" crescendo.

We then go outside for a smoke and a debrief, before returning to catch the country acid house music of Alabama 3, but mainly from the bar. We'd already agreed to head back to mine afterwards and continue partying. Well, that was the plan, but now Tigger's disappeared. I look around the Electric and eventually find him chatting with a girl, a different girl. I head over with the intention of encouraging our departure, but as I approach, they launch into a full-on snog. Oh blimey. I decide to wait it out a while, so retrieve my phone just for something to do. Fuck, I forgot my battery's dead, the crutch that helps get me though these moments temporarily removed. They're talking intensely, intimately, exchanging numbers and shit. Now they're snogging again. Jesus fuck, I can't stand around waiting, I just can't. I'll leave, Tigger's a big boy, he can get himself home.

I head for the exit and just as I reach the door, I hear him shouting.

"Oy, ya cunt! Wait for me!"

He bounces up from behind and hurls himself at me.

"Fuck, man, what was I supposed to do?"

In the Uber ride home we discuss the gig, as it was one of those instances where the main act had difficulty following the support. No criticism of Alabama 3, the Fat Whites are a tough act for anyone to follow.

The truth is, I have a massive soft spot for Alabama 3, my old man was mad for them, introduced to him not by me or my bro, but his TV, for he loved *The Sopranos*. The theme tune led him to their albums, which he'd play relentlessly, until that is, cancer reared its unwelcome ugly head and eventually took my old man away. I remember how blown away he was when I alerted him to the fact that Alabama 3 were not from the US, but Brixton.

Tigger mentions the girl he had met, how it was just a bit of flirtatious fun, nothing serious. He had some attention, some ego feedback and was happy with that. My wife believes flirting is important for this reason, to desire and be desired is all you really need. Still, I'm pretty sure a full-on snog crossed the flirting boundary.

"Mate, be careful. . ."

"Just a bit of fun, dude. Innocent fun."

It wasn't.

"I'd delete her number if I were you."

"Already have, dude."

He hadn't.

I paid little attention at the time, Tigger was unhappy in his marriage, permanently on heat, always on the hunt, but this was *way* more serious. He was about to unleash a slow-motion dirty bomb and the closer to the epicentre you happened to be, the greater the impact. . .

Chapter Twenty-Two

Collective, Subjective Experience and Unfriendly Friends

I wanna be a hedgehog
Spikes, all over my back
"I Wanna be a Hedgehog" – No Friendz

29TH JULY 2017, BRIXTON ACADEMY,

The Moonlandingz have just ended their set with krautrock crowd-pleaser "Man in Me Lyfe." There's no encore, they're not headlining and don't do encores anyway.

Tigger bounces into me still sweaty. Sadie catches up and tugs his arm.

"I'm off tut loo, wait 'ere fer me."

He nods, then turns back to me.

"That was fucking wicked, dude."

"Yeah, they were good, but it wasn't their best."

Tigger's disappointed by my appraisal, he'd clearly enjoyed it and why shouldn't he? Whilst a gig is a communal experience, it's also a collection of individual ones and they can be staggeringly diverse. We all hear, see and feel something different, so this Moonlandingz gig went through every human filter in attendance: their audience position, the people around them, whatever baggage they brought in, whatever shit they'd thrown down their neck, whatever pain, grief or sorrow they're battling with, whatever hormones are flowing through them, whatever enzymes their stomach microbes are releasing, whatever, whatever, whatever. My point is, what happens onstage is not *just* a collective experience but one that is entirely unique to each and every fleshy pod of consciousness in the room. What a killjoy I'm being. One of those "I saw them at the beginning" wankers, but then again so had Tigger.

Yet, this is also the point I have been attempting to illustrate, the exhilaration of a band in their ascendance, full of wide-eyed excitement and primal energy. In that respect Angus had a point because I have no doubt that No Friendz would have been a more visceral gig and in many ways I regret coming to this monstrous space. Don't get me wrong, I have enormous affection for Brixton Academy, always was one of my favourite venues but nowadays I'm hooked on the smaller ones, they're more honest, communal, exciting and well, just way more fun.

"Sorry, mate, it's probably just me." I conclude.

He stares at me, unsure how to respond before animating back to life.

"We're getting beers, dude. What're you doing?"

Now, that is a question. What to do? Goat or Madonnatron? Should I stay or should I go now? It really is not an easy decision. Obvious, if a simple quality measure's applied, it would have to be Goat. As good as Madonnatron might be tonight (which I'm yet to be convinced of), as a live spectacle they could not come close to Goat at this point in their career, not even in the same league and would never claim otherwise. Angus would, though. Still, tonight's a special one. Madonnatron's album launch, so more of a happening than just a mere gig and a happening at the Windmill is always a party. And I really like parties.

Tigger was still waiting on an answer, but I'd forgotten the question.

"What?"

"What's the plan, dude?" he reminds me.

"Ah yeah. I think I'm gonna head off to the Windmill."

"What?" his face contorts. "Why?"

"Gonna catch Madonnatron."

"Fuck Madonnatron. Goat are gonna be awesome, dude!"

"I expect they will. . . I dunno, it all feels too big here."

Tigger rolls his eyes. I punch him playfully on the shoulder and rough up his shaggy hair some more.

"Gonna go for a smoke first, ya coming?"

"Yeah, just waiting on Sadie. I'll be out in a bit."

I head towards the smoking pen outside of the venue and as I do, my phone vibrates. Madame HiFi's calling.

"You still here?" she asks.

"Yeah, just going for a smoke."

"You staying here, then?"

"Nah, I'm off back to the Windmill."

Madame HiFi talks to someone in the background, inaudible, then comes back on the phone.

"Can you wait for Zsa Zsa? He says he'll walk back with you."

It seems poor Madame HiFi's become Zsa Zsa's PA since his phone curled up its toes.

I arrive at the smoking pen outside the venue. La and Finn are here already with a bunch of Windmill regulars. They welcome me into their cluster and we all chat, hyped up, the night still young. I take out some gum and offer out the pack.

La stamps out her cigarette, smiling, before theatrically popping a piece in her mouth. Her face contorts.

"What the fuck is this?" she splutters.

My gum of choice, black Airwaves with liquorice overtones and, as La has just discovered, good for clearing your head. I show her the pack.

"Gives you dragon breath." I chuckle.

La continues chewing, pondering.

"Actually, I could get quite into these."

"Once you do, La, you can never go back."

La smirks at my dodgy pun.

"What did you think?" enquires Finn.

"Are we still talking about gum?" I query.

"Of The Moonlandingz," Finn clarifies.

"Ah. Well. . ." I should probably be diplomatic. "Hard to say, really. It wasn't *their* gig."

"Yeah. And..?" presses La.

It feels like they're rounding on me for an opinion, a verdict.

"Well, it lacked energy and it just wasn't sexy. In fact, where was Rebecca tonight?"

Finn looks to La.

"Did I hear she'd left the band?" he says.

"Not from me." La shrugs. "I thought she was just guesting anyway."

"So, who else *is* here tonight?" asks Finn.

"Yeah, did your cunt mate come, Dave?" asks La, having previously found herself on the rough end of Tigger's mosh pit shenanigans.

Then, from nowhere, Tigger chips in, "Maybe Lias puking all over the stage at *Glastonbury* was too fackin' much for her."

Everyone laughs at this image, simultaneously grimacing, but also curious as to how long he and Sadie have been standing there. La shoots me a glance and succeeds in saying "*yikes!*" with her face.

"I didn't know that." Finn laughs.

"Yeah, he came onstage and before he'd even begun, spewed up everywhere but still did the gig." Tigger cackles.

There is a ripple of laughter.

"She looked fackin' disgusted," he elaborates, though I am sensing people want to move the conversation on, away from puke.

"The Academy's too big for their thing," I say.

"That's cos you've spent too much time at the Windmill, Dave!" teases La, playfully.

"Small and sleazy innit," adds Finn.

"Yeah, my kinda place." I chuckle. "In fact, I'm going back in a sec, just waiting on Zsa Zsa."

La looks confused.

"But you'll miss Goat!"

"I know. . ." I shrug.

"Dave, they're fucking awesome!"

"Yeah, stay for a bit," adds Finn.

As much as their loveliness makes me want to stay, a voice in my head is telling me to go. Maybe my condition makes it hard for me to change my mind. Maybe it's not a condition, it's just who I am. Or maybe the Windmill has brought me back, full circle and it just *feels* good.

***

I spent my formative years in the once industrialised, now fossilised town of Gainsborough, set within the bleak flatlands of rural Lincolnshire, monstrous pylons and clusters of cooling towers dominating the skyline in every direction. It wasn't quite the North but it *was* fucking grim and a bit too far from anywhere, meaning a good night out required some serious organisation and a mate who had access to a car.

The nearest place for our gang was not a city but a small market town where once existed the legendary Retford Porterhouse, owned and run by the late Sammy Jackson, co-founder of Nottingham's Rock City and by all accounts, including his own daughters, a bit of a dodgy geezer. Pretty much everyone scrambling up the greasy post-punk pole played The Porterhouse, including The Fall, Wire, Gang of Four, New Order, Fad Gadget, The Mekons, Prefab Sprout, you name it, even U2 back in the day when Bono was shy and nervous, before he got lost in his own reflection, the messianic impact a stadium full of adoring fans seems to have on some folk.

The Porterhouse was dark, seedy and woefully unloved. Marc Almond was so taken with its overall sleaziness he brought Soft Cell's non-stop erotic cabaret there twice, *after* "Tainted Love" had barged its way into the mainstream and unexpectedly assumed the number one slot. It was also edgy, unpredictable and occasionally violent, but the sense of danger was part of its draw. I worked there for a time, DJing between acts, oblivious to the historical importance these bands would ultimately come to represent, their influences still ricocheting decades later.

The Porterhouse is where it all began for me, my musical underpinning and if it weren't for the Sammy's, Seamus's and Kathleen's of this world, what a dull world it would be.

***

"He's a Windmill whore, that's why," adds Tigger, with barely concealed aggression.

He seems to have developed some unspoken issues with me. I've challenged him on it several times, but he always ducks the issue and shuts me down. Right now, all I want to say is "*What's your fucking beef*"?, but there's too many onlookers, so decide to ignore it, just rise above it.

"I'm going there cos you're staying here, ya fucking spunk rag."

Okay, not necessarily *above* it.

"He's going cos he's Windmill Dave, innit," asserts La.

"I like that! Windmill Dave!" hollers Finn.

Tigger looks momentarily confused, then his face fills with excitement as he looks over my shoulder.

"Zsa Zsa!"

He bounces past me and hurls his sweat soaked body at Zsa Zsa, who, ordinally would love a good hug. He grimaces and turns to me.

"You ready?"

"Yeah, sure."

We make our goodbyes and off we trot, to the best fleapit in this whole metropolis. I turn back to the Academy, Tigger and Sadie staring, muttering to each other. Am I imagining shit? What's their beef?

As we're walking across the entrance to Stockwell Road, La Hollers after us:

"See you later Zsa Zsa! Windmill Dave! We're heading down after!"

"Woo!" Zsa Zsa shouts in response.

"Windmill Dave? I like that." Zsa Zsa sniggers.

Not so sure myself. I change the subject.

"So, what's the deal with the Fat Whites nowadays?"

"They're back in the studio," replies Zsa Zsa.

"Saul too?"

"Yeah, he's back and guess who's producing?"

"Sean Lennon?"

"John Cale."

"Fuck off – really?"

"Yeah, not sure if it's the whole album. I fink Sean might still be involved."

"That is so fucking cool!"

"Wanna meet him?"

"Who? John Cale? Fuck yeah!"

"I'll 'ave a word with Lias, find out when he's next in town."

I guess this collaboration began after Lias sang "Heroin" some months back during John Cale's Velvets tour. It was good too, once Lias really got into his stride. In fact, way better than seeing The Velvet Underground perform it when they briefly reformed the original line-up and gave us a matinee appearance at *Glastonbury Festival* in 1993. How excited I was, having obsessed over them in my teens, woven into the musical fabric of my life ever since, but anticipation has the habit to set you up for disappointment and as it turns out they were pretty unexciting. I'm sure back in the day, spangled on acid in Warhol's Factory would have been a very different experience than mid-afternoon in a cow field, with the sun blazing down.

It is all looking very promising for the Fat Whites: Saul and Lias back in the studio, differences resolved, love renewed, hope restored, John Cale producing. Zsa Zsa interrupts my tangential thoughts.

"Shall we get a beer?"

This is becoming a habit.

"Sure, but it's my round."

So, into another Food and Wine we go, then tinnies in hand we stroll past the Electric. Zsa Zsa turns to me.

"So, what's the fackin' deal with Tigger?"

"What do you mean?"

"What's his problem?"

"Me, I think."

"Why?"

"Dunno? I guess it's because I'm linked to his pre-Sadie life. I represent some kind of threat to their equilibrium?"

"That's fackin' stupid."

"Well, I still see his ex."

Zsa Zsa looks at me, like I've broken a code of honour.

"She and my Mrs are best mates, it's impossible not to," I clarify.

"How d'ya cope with that?"

"As best I can, in the circumstances."

Zsa Zsa nods.

"I've heard his ex is abitova nutta."

I splutter out my stout.

"From who? Tigger? That bastion of sanity?"

"Yeah, but ain't she makin' it 'ard for 'im?"

"They're making it hard for each other. It's a fucking divorce."

"Fair point."

"It's just noise. *He said – she said* bollocks."

Zsa Zsa nods, thoughtfully.

"Yeah. I guess I only 'ave one side ovit."

We continue chatting and before we know it we've arrived back at the Windmill. Angus is outside by the picnic tables, smoking, drinking, gobbing off as usual. He clocks us approaching.

"You total cunts! You missed our best ever gig!"

Zsa Zsa laughs and gives him a hug.

"They're always the best." Zsa Zsa chuckles.

Angus rests his head on his shoulder, turning to face me, sneering campily.

"It's the same shit every time, Angus," I taunt.

He cocks his head with the look of a dog trying to comprehend the human language.

"You just need to stop being a diva and write some new fucking songs," I continue.

His bandmates snigger: they like it when we spar. Angus lets go of Zsa Zsa. and walks over to me threateningly, boring into me with his strange cuckoo nest stare. I return his gaze, smirking, refusing to yield.

"How very fucking dare you! We are the best band here, even with our old rinsed out shitty songs, we can still kick the piss out of everyone else!"

"Even Meatraffle?" I ask, playfully.

"Especially fucking Meatraffle!" booms Angus.

Zsa Zsa smiles, totally unruffled.

"Come, comrade, let's get beer." I say, grabbing his arm.

I turn back to Angus.

"And you never saw Nirvana at *Reading*."

"Fuck off, Dave. I totally fucking did, you cunt!"

All ham theatrics of course, or Angus is indeed a sociopath.

Chapter Twenty-Three

Towed by a Butterfly to Nirvana

And I cry crystallised tears
And I wanna be blind
So I stare up to the sky
And flood myself in the light
"As the Sun Sets" – Sorry

When we had our Nirvana debate I never told Angus that I *had* witnessed their *Reading* performance. I did not really get the chance and I expect the self-obsessed fucker cared even less. I'd not planned to go, it was a dilemma for sure. I loved Nirvana but hated *Reading* and hate won out, at least initially. In the light of what happened next it seems ridiculous to allow the boozy studenty soullessness of *Reading*

Festival to get in the way of witnessing one of the greatest rock bands to have ever graced this planet, but the context was different back then and at the time the conversation went something like this:

"You going to *Reading*?"

"Nah."

"Nirvana's headlining Sunday."

"Yeah, but fucking *Reading*? They shoulda done Glasto."

"Yeah, know what you mean."

And so, it was decided. Fuck *Reading*.

Of course, things would've been a whole lot different had I been asked:

"Shall we go to *Reading* and witness Nirvana's last ever UK performance, because Kurt or Courtney (whichever theory you subscribe to), will soon blow Kurt's brains out with a twenty-gauge shotgun."

Or even:

"Seventeen years into the future, this concert, over which we are pointlessly deliberating, will be immortalised within a best-selling video (well, a multi-formattable digital file, but let's not go there). Eight years later, a free online organic encyclopaedia will explode onto the internet and display a 93% meta-critic rating for *Nirvana, Live at Reading*."

Okay, that would have made little sense at the time. Let's just say, this performance will be chiselled deep into the coalface of rock and roll legend.

30TH AUGUST 1992, PENGE, SOUTH LONDON

It's bank holiday weekend and a typically miserable Sunday morning; putrid grey, pissing rain, gusting wind. I'm still in bed, relieved we hadn't wasted money on sodding *Reading* tickets.

The phone in the hall starts ringing. I throw back the quilt and head towards the shrill, bone-chilling noise. No caller ID back then, so yes, a risk, but there was no other form of immediate communication available, so friend or foe, salesman or bank, mother or ex, you took the fucking call.

I was relieved to find my mate James Dowdall on the other end of the line.

"Hey, James!"

James was lateral, ambitious, Dublin smart and just the right side of crazy, working in A&R at Island Records, tasked with looking after Julian Cope who'd released the epic "Peggy Suicide" last year and was working on his follow up "Jehovakill". It was a truly impossible job yet one that gave him immense joy. We'd become good friends over the years and he has the dubious honour of giving me my first ever ecstasy tablet when he got us on the list for The Orb at Brixton Academy earlier this year. It was a Double Dove and blew my tiny mind to pieces leaving me with no actual memory of the gig itself, just a vague recollection of being there and the sound of a pulsating electronic bass.

"You got plans today?"

"Er. . . nothing special. Why?"

"I got a couple of triple-A passes for *Reading* going begging. Would ya like 'em? Feckin' Nirvana tonight!"

"I know. Shit. How come you got spares?"

"They're L7's, but a lot of their entourage have fucked off already. These feckin' Yanks can't cope with weather."

Some of you may be old enough to recall American grungers L7, particularly their infamous and quite brilliant live appearance on that ridiculous 80's car-crash TV show *The Word*. They performed their single "Pretend We're

Dead" and as their finale, unexpectedly revealed all from the waist down whilst continuing to play. It was very in your face, very punk and caused a minor stir at the time.

Almost as much as the time *The Word* producers thought it'd be a real hoot to invite acting legend and long-suffering alcoholic Oliver Reed to guest on the show. They thought it would be even more fun to cram his dressing room with all manner of free alcoholic delights and in a particularly vile move, planted hidden cameras throughout.

Oh, how we laughed at this gratuitous invasion of privacy when they revealed edited footage of poor Ollie, believing he was alone getting steamed off his nuts. When he was totally bladdered to the point of insanity, like a Victorian freak show, they offered him up to the live TV audience, where he frothed at the mouth like a deranged orangutan. Oh, how we continued to laugh, especially when a mic was thrust into the poor drunken wretch's hand and the band launched into the chords of "Wild Thing". Of course, Ollie goes for it, with inebriated abandon like a drunk you would never want outside your house. It was wrong on so many levels and in so many ways. *The Word* truly was the nadir and ground zero of tabloid TV, a precursor to a format that has since become our norm. Now we have hundreds of channels, thousands of shows, no content, just dumbed-down fodder for the masses to prevent us from thinking. Revolting entertainment to distract us from revolting.

On the plus side, the only plus side, all the bands on *The Word* were live and raw, like they should be.

Having collected our reassigned triple-A passes, my girlfriend and me are driving down the M4 through the wind and rain in an old Fiat 124, with wiper blades long past their prime. A borrowed car. A terrible rust box, so small and light that if the wind whipped up anymore we could be blown across the motorway.

Nirvana and Nick Cave are my only reasons for going. Not my girlfriend, though, the comedy tent is all she cares for; she couldn't give a toss about the music. So, this is the deal: we watch comedy together, then break out for Nick Cave and Nirvana.

Like all best-laid plans, it does not go to plan. We tromp through the waterlogged muddy grass, only to discover there is no longer a comedy tent. Turns out the wind had blown it down, along with my girlfriend's already weather-diminished festival spirit. Comedy is now off the menu and so is any reason for her wanting to stay, yet she's fully aware I'm only here for the bands and it's hours before home time. Nevertheless, she makes a stoic effort, though, it must be said, with utter leaden misery.

I think, somewhat selfishly, how am I going to enjoy Nirvana now? I ponder the options. We both need releasing from this entanglement of differing desires and unworkable compromise. But how? I know fully well she would sooner be spending Sunday evening curled up on the couch with a book or watching TV, not trudging around a quagmire surrounded by pissed, boorish students, waiting for bands to play she cares little for. I need to enjoy Nick Cave and Nirvana, unfettered, unburdened, devoid of relationship responsibility.

Think.

Okay, Nirvana will be onstage in about four hours and whilst I do not relish the thought, there is technically time to drive her home *and* make it back. The round trip without problems is roughly three hours (in this Fiat), plus an hour or so of cushion time for the unexpected, so it is within the realms of possibility. This may mean sacrificing some Bad Seeds. Tragic I know, but collateral damage in the overall plan.

I lay out my slightly insane proposal to my girlfriend and without a moment's hesitation, she accepts.

So, once again, we're in this borrowed tin-pot car rattling down the M4 back towards London through the August summer bank holiday wind and rain. All is going to plan. No delays or disruptions, the only limitation is this car, barely making 60 miles an hour without the feeling it might shake apart or be whipped into the air by a sudden gust of wind. I mean, it's already blown down Reading Festival's comedy tent.

Thankfully, we arrive home safely in good time and my girlfriend literally skips down the path, clearly relieved, looking forward to being back inside on this miserable summer Sunday evening. She opens the flat door and I follow her in, an opportunity to refresh, relieve, grab snacks and a change of clothes.

I fly out of the bedroom, kiss goodbye, sad to be separating but relieved I will no longer feel the pressure of her disenjoyment.

I climb back into the trusty rusty Fiat and set off back to *Reading*. I now have a spare triple-A pass. Seems a waste. . .

Do I have time to try out my mates? See who might be up for it? Maybe, if I'm quick. I don't currently own a car, let alone one with a Motorola car phone installed, so I make a small detour to Surbiton to drop in on my mate Stephen. His flat is currently the general hang-out, the most likely place to take a chance on.

I press the buzzer and hear movement, whispering, I think. I buzz again.

"Who is it?" Stephen shouts, somewhat sheepishly.

"It's me, Dave."

After an unreasonably long time, I hear the door unlock and then open, but just a slither. He peers through the crack for quite some time.

"Stephen? What the fuck?"

He opens it fully and his face melts into a ridiculously happy grin, then flamboyantly welcoming me inside. I follow him into the living room where the usual gang are huddled.

Something feels odd, the room has a strange ambience and they're all staring at me wide eyed. I try and talk with them but they're making little sense, then one of them spontaneously melts into a giggling fit, instantly setting the rest of them off. Hysteria permeates the atmosphere as they try and fight the impulse, but it's clearly too strong.

Are they all spangled?

Eventually, they all calm down so I take the opportunity to explain about the spare backstage pass.

"Yeah, let's go!" Stephen eagerly proclaims.

"Yeah!" they all excitedly agree. "Nirvana! Fuck yeah!"

Too excitedly.

"But I only have one spare," I inform them.

Stephen looks to the floor, momentarily confused, before lifting his head to reveal an unusually intense grin.

"Want some tea?"

With that, they all fall back into helpless giggles as Stephen wanders into his kitchen. He reappears with a teapot which he ceremoniously places before me. We stand there in silence, Stephen still wearing his Cheshire cat grin, nodding in the direction of the teapot. The others just stare wide-eyed, trying to contain their hysteria.

"What is it?" I ask.

"Tea."

"Well, I kind of assumed that."

They all giggle.

"Special tea," clarifies Stephen.

I lift the lid and take a peak to reveal floating organic fungal matter infusing the boiled water with its otherworldly magic. It was indeed special tea. Turns out earlier today they'd been out picking magic mushrooms in Richmond Park. A remarkably successful harvest too and now they're all tripping on their spoils, clearly incapable of leaving the room, let alone embarking on a tortuous journey down the M4 to stand in the rain for a full-on affront of nihilistic rock.

I was almost persuaded to stay and join their psychedelic parallel universe but resolve to remain on plan, stick to my mission, so skip the tea and make for a hasty exit to avoid further temptation.

As I bid farewell, Stephen stares at me, still unnervingly intense, then hands me a small paper bag. I take a peek. Entangled beige stalks of tiny pointy-topped magic mushrooms. He places his arm around my neck.

"These'll lift Nirvana off the stage, buddy."

"Why not? Thanks man."

I smile with genuine appreciation before stuffing them in my coat pocket and stepping out the door.

"You're a top banana, Stephen."

He giggles and I hug him goodbye.

***

Back in the Fiat, battling through the Sunday shopper traffic (which is ironic as shops aren't legally allowed to open; God doesn't approve of rampant consumerism on

Sundays) and for the third time today, I work my way back on to the M4.

It is such a dull and soulless road, made worse by the lack of amenities within this shitty Fiat. No music; the cassette player never worked and the aerial has long since parted company. Just the sound of the road and the rattling of the car. At least the rain has finally stopped.

God, I'm bored. Bored of car noise, bored of this fucking motorway. What am I doing anyway? Kurt Cobain has been pretty unreliable of late. What if I get all the way there and it's a no-show? Kurt blowing the gig for a scag hit. Should have just got spangled with my mates.

I ponder, consider, evaluate. I'm thinking how long do shrooms take to kick in? A good hour at least, so, if I time this right, I'll be coming up just as Nirvana hit the stage. Now, wouldn't that be fucking great?

When did I last eat?

I reach into my coat pocket and grab a handful. They look pretty harmless. I put them to my nose. They smell just like normal mushrooms. I shove a few in my mouth. Hmm, quite a tasty snack. A bit like the raw mushroom pieces in the Pizza Hut salad bars. Only stringier. Earthier.

Psilocybe semilanceata to use their proper name and as hard to eat as they are to pronounce. After a while it's like a stringy clump of mushroom chewing gum. I take a glug from my water bottle and gulp the earthy lump down my throat. When *did* I last eat?

I'm about halfway, the rain and wind has subsided, the motorway almost empty except the odd lorry. There are always lorries. Still, things are looking up. I stop at a service station for petrol and a wee. In the queue, I look around and find my resolution's a little sharper. Must be the country air or the neon lights, but everything's so vivid, pulsating with life.

I climb back into the Fiat feeling a little off, not sure why. I start the engine and make my way along the slip road back onto the M4.

My hands on the steering wheel have caught my attention. They look strange. Are they even *my* hands? Weird, inhuman, almost alien. Something is definitely off. Am I getting ill?

Then it hits me. The shrooms have kicked in. Fuck. Fuck. Shit. Shit. Shit. This wasn't supposed to happen. This is way too quick.

First rule of a psychedelic experience: don't panic. Even when you're driving a tiny tin-pot Fiat down the M4 in the dark. It *is* dark! When did *that* happen? Lights. Put on the lights. The lights? Think. What turns on the lights? This isn't really my car. Try not to panic. Don't crash. It's not a cartoon. Crashes are real. They hurt. They kill. Don't think about death. Stay in the lane. Where is the lane? Lights. Click. Windscreen wipers come to life, squeaking across the now dry, dusty surface, leaving circular road film track marks over the glass. My girlfriend said I should change the wiper blades. I really should have.

I wrestle with the other stalks and buttons. Click. Lights. We have lights.

But the windscreen's a mess. Don't focus on the streaks, look at the road.

They do look cool, though. Beautiful, organic shapes, patterns within patterns fanning out in front of me, rippling with movement as if they're alive. They *are* alive. LOOK AT THE ROAD! Okay, this is real. This *is* real.

Something is coming at me from somewhere. Something big. Behind me, I think. It's going to hit me. An unreasonably bright light in my rear-view. Like a close encounter. It *is* going to hit me. Course it isn't. Just paranoia. Just a lorry.

Second rule: don't let paranoia in.

And don't look in the mirror. Too bright.

Third rule: don't look in mirrors, period. Too weird.

Look at the road. It'll be fine. Put the screen wash on.

Where is it?

Found it. It groans, the water bubbles and splutters as the motor whines, desperate for liquid company. Nothing hits the windscreen, it's empty. Fuck. The light from behind is almost on top of me. Stay in the lane. I cannot see the lane. I hear a growl to my right. All I can see are ginormous wheels. Monster wheels. Really close. Too close. They could crush a fucking bungalow! The car is being sucked in by its gravitational pull. I tighten my knuckles around the small plastic steering wheel as I wrestle with the pull of death. No Nirvana for me. Death is pulling me in. I hang on, pushing the car against the force.

It's passing. Thank fuck. It's passed. Gravity reverses. Shit. I sway onto the hard shoulder, the gigantic wheels kicking up brown spray, gallons of it. The windscreen is covered. Like obscured glass on a bathroom door, only brown. Where's the lane? Where's the road? I have to sort this. Death could occur. I need to fucking see! I wind down my window, stick my head out and gauge the road. There's a hard shoulder. I'm already half on it. I pull in further. Too far, too quick, into the bank, up the bank. I'm losing it. I feel the shadow of death descending. Get a grip! Stay alive! I yank the wheel, roll back down the bank, hit the brake and judder to a stop.

Silent. Stunned. What just happened? Am I alive? I *am* alive! What am I doing? Going to *Reading*. Nirvana. Yes. Right. I need to see. I can't drive when I can't see. I scratch around looking for something. Anything. My bag. I pull out the snacks. Snacks! When did I last eat? A lifetime ago. A universe away. A spare T-shirt. That'll do. Will have to do. I desperately need to clean the window, so crumple the T-shirt which feels so big. So nice and soft. I smell it. Like flowers. FOCUS! I rub the windscreen hard. Nothing changes. It's still covered in brown slime.

It's on the outside, stupid. I melt into giggles. Idiot. I giggle some, until I realise this means I'm gonna have to get out of the car.

Really? Leave this warm cocoon? I got snacks. Drinks. I could just stay here. I could. . .

Nirvana for fucks sake! Get a fucking grip!

I take a deep breath. Grab the door handle. Here we go. . .

I step into the empty void. The motorway wasteland. It's dark. It's cold. Focus. Get this done. It can be done. Stay on plan.

Okay. Here we go. I lean over the bonnet. It's warm. That's comforting. I put my hands on it. Fuck! It's hot. Don't do that. Focus. Clean the slime off the windscreen. Cars whizz by. I duck. I remember someone telling me once the average time to die if a person remains on the hard shoulder is 45 minutes. How long has it been? I have no idea. I could die here. I'm not even moving and I could fucking die! Stop thinking. Fear is talking. Focus. I continue cleaning. And ducking.

It's working. Yes. I can see inside the car from outside. It has to be the same the other way, surely?

I open the door and re-enter the safety of my metal cocoon, throw the mucky T-shirt in the back and shuffle back into my seat. I look up and woo! I can see through the windscreen. It worked! I'm so happy I could cry.

Fucking hell, I *am* crying!

Stop crying.

What's the time? Where am I? The M4. But where?

It's pitch black. I look at my watch. Numbers, patterns, dials. What does it all mean?

Just go. Nirvana will be onstage soon. Drive!

I turn the key. It starts. This is good. I love this car. I need to love it more. Drive. The car and me judder into movement and bounce onto the lane as one. Another car swerves past from behind. Horns blaring. Why are they so angry? So unnecessary. Very distressing.

I build up speed: 20. 30. 40. 50. Touching 60 now. Fast. Rattling. Such a cute rattle. Rhythmic. God, I love this car. I stare ahead. A sign. *Reading* 20 miles. That's good. I think. The road is barren. Dark. Too dark. Shit. Lights. I twist the stem of the stalk (is that what it's called?) to turn them on.

Click.

I look up.

What now?

What the fuck?

This is not real.

It looks real.

It *can't* be real?

It definitely looks real.

A large white butterfly has appeared right in front of my car. When I say large, I mean four feet wide. At least. Seriously. It isn't real. I do know this. But it *is* joined to the car and it certainly *appears* to be towing me, even though it can't be, even though it can't even be there.

No matter how hard I try, I cannot rationalise it away, this huge white utterly beautiful butterfly with delicate wings, gently pulling the Fiat down the M4. A Butterfly? At night? Is it a moth? Nope, it is definitely a butterfly. Of course, this isn't happening, none of this is real, how can it be? I'm arguing with myself over what kind of flying bug my hallucination is, as if this detail actually matters. But right here, right now, it *does* matter. Think normal world. Straight world. Where giant car-towing butterflies do not exist.

Is it my headlights? Maybe. Yes. Light from the head-lamps making shapes on the road. But this butterfly is not on the tarmac. It's right in front of the bonnet, elegantly flapping its delicate wings.

Slowly, a sense of calm envelops my entire being. A trust in whatever is happening here, in this unreal, yet real-look-ing flying bug that appears to be leading the way.

I'm on the M4, in the dark, being towed by a butterfly to Nirvana. I grab another handful of shrooms and stuff them in my mouth. This is gonna be okay. . .

Chapter Twenty-Four

Converse Trainers, Military Coups and Rock Star Bacteria

I take myself down Sisters Avenue
Get an illegal hello, an illegal high
I'm making love to an idea
Well, it's the only thing that's mine
"Free the Naked Rambler" – Phobophobes

29*TH* JULY 2017, WINDMILL, BRIXTON,

As Zsa Zsa and I enter the Windmill, Ghost Car have just hit the stage. We head for the bar, Piotr serves us beer and then move in closer to watch. On the way, we bump into Chris OC, whom you may recall from the Meatraffle band meeting. He's also a member of Phobophobes, purveyors of psychedelic apocalyptic existential pop and currently the

Windmill's true resident band, having built their own rehearsal space in the basement.

There's no gang mentality in these parts, no one owns no one, so they're all involved in other bands, side projects, fuck-a-bouts, or like guns-for-hire, filling a line-up gap whenever needed. So, it's perfectly cool for Chris to play keys for two major bands on the same circuit, unless they both have gigs on the same night, then things can get tense.

The Phobophobes say Wall of Voodoo are a major influence for them, but their organ driven sound puts me in mind of Blue Orchids (formed by Martin Bramah, original guitarist in The Fall). According to La, they're south London's very own boyband on account of them all being pretty hot. They're certainly a mighty force live. On lead guitar, the quick-witted wind-up merchant that is Jack Fussey, (who brings to mind a young John Cale, a comparison he seems to find offensive), on bass the hysterically droll Bede Trillo, on drums former Fat Whites member Dan Lyons, on keys Meatraffle's Chris OC and on vocals and guitar, brooding songwriter (and massive Leonard Cohen fan) Jamie Taylor.

It has been an incredibly painful time for the band, battling to continue in the long shadow of tragedy and grief. Only a year ago they lost their lead guitarist and very good friend George Russell, who, at the tender age of 24, lost his life in that very rock and roll of ways. The poor blighter did not even make the 27 Club.

This shattering event almost tore them apart, so paralysed with grief, unsure if they should or even *could* continue. Thankfully they did, because George's mum encouraged them to, citing the band as one of the happiest periods of his life and for them to give up would be the last thing he'd have wanted. How could they refuse?

The band regrouped and resolved to keep the whole Phobes train moving, compelled to do whatever was required to finish their debut album. Half was already in the can and they have since been rustling through old demos, live recordings, studio cuts; *anywhere* they might find George's guitar work. The whole process a bittersweet experience, a touching memory, yet incredibly painful, for they plan to posthumously immortalise George's guitar work on every track, exorcising their pain and loss as they absorb this devastating tragedy into their work. All except recently departed Elliot, their lap steel player, who was George's best mate. He found it all too much to continue without him, but still remains close to the band, focusing instead on providing illustrations for a hardback book of George's poetry which the band are helping to fund with benefit gigs.

The Phobes' journey has not all been marred with pain and misery. Back in 2015 they put themselves forward for the "Converse Rubber Tracks Studio Takeover" in which Converse (yes, the "All Stars" people) selected 28 bands from the 9,000 that applied, to give free recording time within twelve legendary studios around the world and a legendary producer thrown in for good measure. As luck would have it and against some pretty steep odds (321:1, to be precise), the Phobes became one of the chosen few. If at this point you feel the impulse to bring the calculator up on your phone to check my maths, you should get yourself tested.

The Phobes were offered Abbey Road Studios to work with legendary producer Ken Scott, whose CV is like a Rock and Roll Hall of Fame in its own right, having worked with

The Beatles, Elton John, Bowie, Pink Floyd, even Judy Garland.

Ken was full of anecdotes and showed the band all manner of old recording equipment used by many of these legends, including the oldest microphone in the studio.

Elliot Nash took it upon himself to take swabs from various mics to collect any remnants of dead skin or dried saliva left behind by all the musical giants who've graced these hallowed studios. Elliot later added these samples to various Petri dishes, from which he grew a collection of bacteria, but not just *any* bacteria; Rock Star bacteria. The plan is to use each of these as the cover art for their future releases and one Petri dish has already graced the cover of their tremendous single "Human Baby". I recommend checking out the accompanying video, a fitting homage to George, recorded at the Windmill during a special tribute event held in September 2016, marking what would have been his 25th birthday, for it beautifully captures the occasion and the unhinged magic of this place.

I should tell you more about Chris OC, because the very fact he even exists at all is a dark twisted miracle. OC is short for Olivares Chandler and Chris has the well-groomed appearance of a Cuban revolutionary, complete with Che Guevara hair and tash, yet he's not of Cuban descent, or Argentinian for that matter, but Chilean.

Remember that band management meeting with Meatraffle? Well, that same evening, after we'd finished all the businessy stuff, some of us went outside for a much welcome smoke. I certainly needed one after being the focus of Meatraffle's attention for a good hour, during which the idea of managing them morphed from flattering to fucking terrifying.

26TH SEPTEMBER 2016, CROWN & SCEPTRE, SW2

I'm outside with their lead guitarist, the shaven-headed Tingle, chatting about the band, their plans and potential labels. Tingle is serious, very grounded and impressively switched on to the business side of it all, perhaps more so than the rest. He's still sussing me out, I totally get that, though I had already made my decision, even if he'd come to the same one.

Chris OC is here also, but his mind is on other matters, in fact he's pretty buzzed up. After pressing him, he excitedly explains how tonight marks the eve of his father receiving an official pardon from the Chilean government, for crimes against the Thatcher/Reagan-endorsed, neoliberal-embracing, fascist dictator that was General Augusto Pinochet. If this bit makes it to print, it will mean Chris is cool with its inclusion, but it is a book in its own right and in the right hands, a powerful film. This is just a little teaser.

Chris OC owes his entire existence to Augusto Pinochet. I realise this sounds weird and no I'm not about to reveal he's Pinochet's bastard love child – he's not. Just hear me out.

It was the early 1970s. Chile had a democratically elected left-leaning coalition government, led by socialist President Salvador Allende. Chris's dad, whose full name is José Segundo Olivares-Maturana, was a sergeant in the Chilean Air Force. The context of what happens next is important, because since 1932, Chile had sustained one of the most reformist, representative and stable democracies in the world. The West did not like this one bit. Successful socialism? This must be stopped, we don't want people getting the wrong idea, it might catch on. So, they got to work, providing arms to three right-wing Chilean rebel groups whilst economically isolating the entire country with sanctions. They know the drill, they've, quite literally, written the fucking book.

Chris's dad received intelligence of a military coup being planned against President Allende, so he and 81 others informed their superiors. The military coup regrettably succeeded and in that moment, José and his comrades found themselves on the wrong side. They had, according to their post-coup twisted logic, retrospectively committed treason, even though he was simply doing the honourable thing and serving his then president and country.

Pinochet came to power as a result of this US-backed coup d'état, to take back control from all those democratically elected troublesome Lefties. The US, bastions of so-called democracy, aided and abetted a military dictatorship in a foreign country and then removed sanctions once their man was installed.

This is nothing new to them, the CIA has since confessed to many: Iran in 1953, Guatemala in 1954, Congo in 1960, Dominican Republic in 1961, South Vietnam in 1963, Brazil in 1964 and a whole heap more since, including of course Afghanistan, Iraq, Syria and Libya. Many of which our own poodle government has provided "shoulder-to-shoulder" support, providing weapons, dropping bombs and sending our soldiers to die, not really knowing what for.

Don't get me wrong, the US love democracy, so long as the politics of a country doesn't veer too much to the left; or *at all* even. If it does, they'll fuck you up and put their own man in.

Look around, the Neoliberal Establishment are up to all manner of geopolitical shit every minute of every day all over this anxious world. See what happened when Greece voted in a left-wing government? They rounded on them like a pack of wolves on a broken chicken coop. The most effective way to undermine support and destroy confidence is to prevent people getting to their own money, so they closed the banks and switched off the ATMs. Quite understandably, panic ensued and the populist zeal that lifted the Syriza party from the dust, dissipated as quickly as it had ascended.

Immediately after Pinochet's successful military coup, José and his so-called co-conspirators were rounded up, imprisoned, tortured, some even executed. Chris's dad was incarcerated for two years.

Human rights lawyers and various pressure groups piled in on the Chilean government and José got lucky. He avoided execution and was successfully extradited to the UK, along with many others. Upon arrival, they were allocated places to stay around the UK and José began his new life in Sheffield.

This is where he met Sara, an interpreter who helped José with his legal case and acclimate into UK civilian life. Along the way, a bond developed, a friendship grew and before they knew what had happened they'd fallen in love. Sara had a flat in New Cross in south London, which meant constant travel back and forth to Sheffield for her work, so José travelled South to move in with her. Within the year their love produced a child and that child is Chris OC.

This is why tonight, the eve of José's official pardon, the usually laid-back Chris OC is so animated and understandably emotional as he retells his father's story. It took 45 years for José and his comrades to receive a full official pardon from the Chilean government, but finally Chris's dad is receiving formal recognition for the brutality he endured and the injustice that has tainted his entire adult life; but more importantly and why Chris is so made up, he's still alive to tell the tale.

It is of course a bittersweet tale with a happy ending, in that Chris would not be standing here now telling me all this without the brutal military coup in Chile and the emergence of military dictator Augusto Pinochet. I cannot imagine a world without Chris OC. Meatraffle, Phobophobes, in fact, this whole south London collective would be significantly diminished by his non-existence. As the great man said, there's a crack in everything, that's how the light gets in.

29TH JULY 2017, WINDMILL, BRIXTON

Ghost Car finish their set and Chris OC taps me on the shoulder, clicking his lighter.

"Smoke?"

He isn't playing tonight, he's a punter like me.

"Yeah sure."

We weave our way through the lively, excitable Windmill crowd and head for the beer garden.

Chapter Twenty-Five

Paedo Presenters, Offensive Millennials and the Crackerjack King

If I wanna go to that awards do
Don't get arsey 'cause
The organisers didn't invite you
"Just Like We Do" – Sleaford Mods

As we enter The Shed Chris clocks his bandmate Bede, bass player in Phobophobes and also the mighty SLEAZE, another Windmill mainstay, woven into the fabric of this collective because when they're in the house it's always a stomping knees-up; a band that truly lives up to its name and in all the right ways. Dave Ashby, their terrifically sweet, delightfully barmy singer, transforms onstage into a total sex god, crackling with carnal energy. It is unlikely you'll ever see them on TV or hear them on your radio (apart from La's show), so to really get what makes them so compelling you have to catch them live. "Saturday Matinee," their mosh pit favourite, is a stomping twisted homage to all the paedophile TV presenters of any boomer's childhood, belting out the singalong chorus, "*I'm not a monster, I'm not a nonce, sir, it was the sixties, and she was sixteen*". SLEAZE also have a keyboardist called Deniz, best described by Dave Ashby:

"He's a fucking amazing keyboardist but totally shit at life."

Interestingly, Bede has a connection to Youth (producer, Killing Joke bassist and Paul McCartney collaborator), the nature of which I'm forbidden from divulging for fear of violent repercussions, but I can tell you this: When Youth was roped in to produce Spiritualized's follow-up to their 2012 album *Sweet Heart, Sweet Light*, Bede was invited on to the production team at his studio in southern Spain. The resulting album never saw the light of day as it failed to match the vision of perennial perfectionist Jason Pierce. This mattered not to Bede; he got to hang out with one of his heroes and such random moments in life must be cherished. Now, he and the rest of the Phobophobes are going back there next month to work on their new album, with Youth at the helm.

I look around The Shed and it's quite literally chock-full of musicians. Indeed, right here, right now there must be members of at least eight different bands: Goat Girl, Honkies, Warmduscher, Meatraffle, Phobophobes, Fat White Family, PREGOBLIN, Sex Cells, SLEAZE, No Friendz and of course Madonnatron. Okay eleven bands, possibly more as people are piling in all the time; in fact, you feel out of place *not* being in a band. No one makes you feel that way, to them it's irrelevant, though the contagion is strong and many a band has gestated within the Windmill's mosh pit. And The Shed. And the loos.

Amongst the noisy smoking rabble of future pop/rock stars, I spot living legend Patrick Lyons; beat poet, hustler and MC to the Fat Whites, amongst numerous other projects of his own. He clocks me, his face widening into a smile as he bowls over for a chat and a chat with Patrick is always interesting. Catch him early, he'll enthusiastically offer up some fascinating anecdotes. Catch him late and he still has plenty, they're just less coherent.

"Yo, Patrick, how's it going?"

He grabs my shoulders, gives me a hug and fixes his eyes on mine, demanding connection. He's not young, yet they sparkle with youthful energy.

"All the better for seeing you, Dave!" he booms theatrically in his Irish-American drawl.

During our chat, he gives me a Fat Whites' story I hadn't heard before, telling me of a time their set was unexpectedly cut short at the Purple Turtle in Camden. When I say cut short, I mean switched off halfway through their second song.

It began with a death metal obsessed promoter who already had issues with the band and a T-Shirt donned by Nathan Saoudi. By the time the Fat Whites hit the stage they were pissed in every sense of the word and once Nathan faced the audience, it was impossible not to see emblazoned across his chest the words "Let Me Fuck Your Face."

Okay, it's pretty hardcore, but this is the Fat Whites.

Nevertheless, as you've no doubt already surmised, someone took offence and we live in a culture where it's now an offence to offend. Some would say this is a clever way of diverting the debate from questioning the shitstorm surrounding us. Encouraging arguments over who is offensive to whom, all from the perspective of our virtual bubbles designed to digitally reflect our own views.

Still, we hammer away at our keyboards, liberating our opinions with just a few clicks, sent forth into an ocean of babble, believing what we say actually matters, that it'll somehow make a difference as we preach to our very own choir, some of whom make the effort to hit the "like" button, validating our existence and providing a meaningless transient dopamine hit. Or we find ourselves trolled by arrogant geeky keyboard warriors, drawing us into futile debates no one else will read or give a single sloppy wank about.

Meanwhile, in the real world, offence takes on a whole new significance and things can happen. Actual things.

Is it me, or is there an irony at work here? That someone in the audience consciously decided to go see a band renowned for their antisocial antics, delivering songs about rape, abuse, fascism and underage sex, who regularly strip naked, often throwing their sweaty bodies into the audience, yet the thing they find most offensive are some words on a T-shirt? Seriously? Being offensive is the Fat Whites' raison d'être. According to Patrick Lyons, it was a young millennial lady who took exception to Nathan's T-shirt graphics, complaining to management, so the power was cut and the whole band narrowly avoided a night in a cell. It's pretty assumptive that it was directed towards women in any event, I've met Nathan and I couldn't be 100% certain.

Offence is way too subjective to ever police, it would make for a crazy world.

Oh, I almost forgot; it *is* a crazy world.

Drunk and angry, unplugged but unyielding, the Fat Whites continued to play. Bouncers try to rush the stage igniting instant bedlam as a furious Saul hurls his guitar at their feet before repeatedly whacking the stage with a mic stand. Whilst Lias, now fully naked, dances with the confused bouncers before grabbing his cock and giving the whole shebang a petulant dry wank; and in the very act of embracing his own humiliation, he somehow succeeds in weaponizing it.

Okay, this all may sound criminally insane, but it might also be the most rock and roll *fuck you* imaginable, earning them the NME headline "The Most Dangerous Band in the World".

Young Millennial, if you're that offendable, don't ever listen to Bill Hicks, Doug Stanhope, Stewart Lee, or Country Teasers and certainly don't listen to Fat White Family, let alone come to one of their gigs. In fact, stay the fuck indoors if coming out means you'll ruin it for the rest and cause the plug to be pulled on a Fat Whites gig, because *that's* offensive.

According to Patrick, he single-handedly talked the police out of throwing the boys in a cell, pointing out to the cops how unmanly they all were:

"I know they're called Fat White Family, but just look at 'em officer, they're all so scrawny, man. Do they look dangerous to you?"

Apparently, this did the trick.

Nathan still wears this infamous T-shirt, but never on-stage.

"*Rolling Stone* magazine are interested in putting that story out next year," explains Patrick.

I hope this is true, but thought it was worth a mention all the same.

"I love that poem you did with Meatraffle."

"Ah yeah, man, 'Serve and Obey'. That was cool."

"Works really well. Sort of happy, yet sinister."

His face lights up.

"Yeah, man, it was real fun doing that."

"You got more stuff?"

"Sure man. You not heard 'Crackerjack King'?"

"Don't think so?"

"Okay, then I'll perform it."

"What? Now?"

"Sure man, just for you."

And off he goes, the full performance, theatrics an' all, oblivious to everyone surrounding us.

Patrick is perhaps best known for providing the world with one of the weirdest NME acceptance speeches ever when Fat White Family won the Philip Hall Radar Award. You can see it on YouTube, entitled: "Weirdest Speech at NME Awards 2014".

Patrick steps up to the podium alongside Lias to introduce his acceptance speech and after a suitably surreal meandering introduction, he gives way so Lias can take the mic. Things do not stay on script, however, because earlier that evening (perhaps an ill advised way to calm his nerves), Lias devoured way too many magic mushrooms. So, instead of charming the audience with witty anecdotes, he just stands there grinning fatuously, blissed out on psilocin and utterly disconnected from the reality around him - not to mention the 8 million viewers watching on TV.

As it turns out, Patrick had also sampled some of these earthly delicacies, though his portion control was way more sensible, if, that is, having *any* amount of hallucinogens before collecting an award could be considered sensible. Fortunately, Patrick has the wherewithal to appreciate it was now on him and him alone to fill the acceptance-speech-shaped hole. Nevertheless, despite his condition – and you have to watch closely – Lias summons up sufficient mental capacity to pick Patrick's pockets, successfully removing his keys and wallet, whilst Patrick - consummate professional that he is - carries on regardless before bringing things to a close, using the NME award as a visual aid to give all Fat White Family critics the middle finger, proclaiming:

"You gotta see 'em live! I'm Patrick Lyons, telling it like it is."

Patrick had to go straight from this award ceremony to his daughter's wedding where he delivered yet another speech, though, rather disappointingly, this footage has not yet found its way onto YouTube.

Back in The Shed, Patrick's finishing his poem:

"The Crackerjack King needs money for bling
Power, fame, fortune, glory
And your life don't mean a thing
No, your life don't mean a thing."

He holds his trilby to his head as he bows and I applaud the mad fucker.

"That was great! You should get Meatraffle on it. Get it out there."

"I got some plans Dave, don't you worry. Just you watch this space."

"I sure will."

I can hear the noise of a band tuning up rumble through the walls of the Windmill.

"Hey, Patrick, I'm gonna go in now, don't wanna miss Madonnatron," I continue.

He looks momentarily startled.

"Shit, man, I gotta go do my thing, y'know."

And off he trots, to do his thing. I follow him out The Shed and bump into Lou Smith, the other south London videographer mentioned earlier.

"Hey, Lou, how's things?"

"Hey, Dave. Yeah, good thanks."

Lou is tall and lean, his lined face still handsome. He has the look of a filmmaker or Boy Scout leader. Khaki jacket, black hair tied into a ponytail tucked under a patrol cap, always a camera in hand and a rucksack of accessories over his shoulder. He can be socially awkward, unable to give you much eye contact until he feels safe, but when he does you will find a true gent, sensitive and passionate about his art.

"You filming tonight?"

"Not much, John has, though."

"Yeah, I saw him earlier."

"I'm gonna try and get some of Madonnatron's set."

"Sounds like they're getting started."

"Yeah, they're just tuning up,"

Lou was one of the first to get on board with what is happening here. For him it began when he saw the Fat Whites play live and felt the impulse to document them in their infancy. He saw early on how special they were and it was his recording of them playing the Windmill in 2011, under the moniker Champagne Holocaust, that kicked it all off. Lou uploaded the video onto YouTube, this caught the attention of Liam and Luke May, who at that time had set up Trash-mouth Records, though, up until that point only for their own musical output, mainly Black Daniel with Clams Baker, the Stetson-wearing frontman of Warmduscher.

The May brothers were immediately smitten by the footage, instantly signing them to Trashmouth, coercing them into the studio for a haphazard, tumultuous recording session in which they nailed down their stunning debut album *Champagne Holocaust*, having since switched their band name to Meat Divine & the Fat White Family, short-ening it further before the album release. So, Lou Smith's recording of their Windmill performance in 2011 became a small yet hugely significant link in the chain that kicked this whole beautiful thing off. He went on to film their early promos for both "Cream of the Young" and "Special Ape", the latter of which he also directed.

Lou is also the go-to man when a band reaches the point where they need merch, having produced some of the most iconic T-shirts within this whole south London collective. Anal perfectionist that he is, what you get with Lou is qual-ity, not iron-on bollocks that peels off in the wash. So, for this and the part you play in documenting all the magic that continues to reveal itself within this small shabby Brixton pub, I salute you, Lou!

Liam and Luke have an interesting backstory, for their band Black Daniel scaled some cultural heights, a couple of tracks appearing on Hollywood film soundtracks and, I shit you not, they landed a support slot for that all-American, air-punching soft rocker Bryan Adams on the European leg of his tour.

Trashmouth quickly expanded their palette further, re-leasing the stupendous and very textured compilation,

*Thinking About Moving to Hasting*s, followed by debut albums from Meatraffle, Warmduscher and now Madonnatron, whose album launch is what tonight is all about.

Chapter Twenty-Six

Headless Children, Horror Movie Teddy Bears and Pagan God Offerings

In my late teens I think
Someone spiked my drinks
I have craved all types of drug
And alcohol ever since
"Spiderman in the Flesh" – Country Teasers

I go back inside the Windmill, working my way through the thronging crowd, swelling by the minute as more pile through the door.

As I head for the bar, I'm physically accosted by Lincoln Barrett, one of the most loveable nutters embroiled in this community and the other 25% of Honkies, whom we met earlier. Lincoln's a busy chap, for his other band Sorry have been touring and he's now in a third band called Midnight Itch, in which he steps away from his drum kit to take the vocals. He has a congenital deformity in his right hand, so gripping a drumstick is quite a challenge for him, yet despite this, perhaps because of it, he's a spectacular drummer, with a style he's clearly aped from Animal out The Muppets.

Tonight, Lincoln is his usual affectionate self, not one who pays much attention to the concept of personal space, but all part of his charm. He looks at me with mad beady eyes before sniggering manically like an acid-infused Muttley.

"Woo! It's gonna be a mad one!" he barks.

Well, it is now, if that was in any doubt. He grabs me again and forces me into another hug. Lincoln's flying high. On what, it's hard to fathom? He's not *acting out* the crazy drummer myth, this *is* who he is; an irresistible ball of infectious madness and you cannot help but love the dude.

"I didn't think you were playing tonight?" I query, trying to ignore the fact that he's constantly moving on the spot to an erratic rhythm all of his own.

"We're not. Haven't. Just here to see the bands mama! And party!"

Then he looks at me seriously, as though he's just realised something.

"Can't go too mad, though, we're hopping down to the south coast."

"When?"

"In the morning."

I laugh and punch his shoulder.

"So, this is you not going *too mad*?"

He cackles.

"I gotta fucking drive. Southampton!"

"What's happening there?"

"A festival."

The word feeds into his mania.

"WOO!" he hollers.

"Who're you seeing?"

"Er. . . well. . . Ket and LSD mainly."

I splutter out my beer, coughing and laughing.

"I was asking who's playing, ya nutter, not your drug regime."

"Oh. . . er. . . can't remember. Doesn't matter."

"Fucking hell man, you'll be spinning out on that combo."

He looks into my eyes with an insane grin, like a horror movie teddy bear.

"Ha! Good!"

I laugh and he gives me another tight hug. Then faces me nose to nose and fixes my gaze.

"Come with us, mama!"

"Oh, man, I can't. . ."

"You can!"

"I got shit to do."

"Fuck the shit, come party."

I really can't, not without chaos ensuing in my life. Thankfully, the lovely Edie Lawrence arrives and saves me from Lincoln's intense man-love. Edie is striking, head shaved, very cool, very bright and an incredibly productive talented artist who creates very dark stop-motion plasticine animations. Like fairy dust, Edie sprinkles her own brand of artistic flourish onto all this, creating promos, providing artwork, flyers, even hosting musical happenings of her own. She is also Lincoln's partner, so on top of everything else, she has to deal with this batshit crazy bundle of love.

Patrick Lyons' disembodied voice booms through the PA system as he launches into his surreal hyperbole. The crowd respond in kind, all stoked and ready to party. The whooping and cheering intensifies further as the Madonnatron ladies take the stage, launching straight into "Tron", their new single, currently enjoying 6 Music attention, particularly from the lovely Gideon Coe whose voice never fails to calm my soul.

I move in closer, not that the stage is far away, but it's hard to see anything when it's this rammed, no sloping floor here. so cut down the side and work my way to the front. There's no Cunt Wall here, it's just easier and more courteous.

Stefania and Charlie are crunching away on their guitars, Beth intensely bashing her kit. And there she is: Joanie, the girl I met watching Zsa Zsa and blimey, she has powerful stage presence, plus she can actually sing, her harmonies actually in harmony and when she takes the lead her voice is strong. Their whole sound has an unsettling, hypnotic, gothic feel, like the four of them might round us all up, seductively sedate us, then present us as sacrificial offerings to some pagan god.

When the riff of their earlier single "Headless Children" kicks in, the mosh pit envelops the entire audience and when surrounded by moshing, you have no choice but to join in, become part of the multicellular organism a good mosh can become. Not in any way violent, just great fun, but if you resist it can be unpleasant. So, if moshing ain't your thing, don't get hostile, just move back. Equally, if you like a good mosh, then go for it, just don't be an aggressive dick about it.

We're all bouncing along to the thumping drums of "Headless Children". I see La amongst the throng, her unmistakable tall frame and pink spiky hair. Clearly Goat ended their set a while ago and judging by how rammed it is now, this place has become the after-party for many. La clocks me and shouts something inaudible before working her way over.

"Woo!"

Still moshing, she gives me a hug.

"Daaave! You should have stayed. Goat were mind-blowing!"

I wince.

"Don't. Please. . ."

"You having a good time?"

"Yeah, I love it here. *Fuck* the Academy."

"But they *were* incredible."

"Enough! I'm getting a drink, let me get you guys one, I owe you that at least."

"Don't be silly!"

"I insist. Where's Finn?"

"At the bar, it's his round."

I work my way back through the throng and spot Finn at the corner of the bar, giving Toby his order.

"Finn!"

He looks up, startled.

"Yo, Dave! You missed Goat and they were fucking *amazing.*"

"Oh God, not you as well."

"That'll be nine pounds," interjects Toby impatiently.

"Let me get this, Finn, I owe you guys."

"No, you don't."

"I insist."

Toby's already hard face hardens further still.

"Can we get on with this, I got other people to serve?" asks Toby, not masking his annoyance.

"Can I have a stout, please?"

"I need to take for these."

"I know, I'm paying. I want to add a stout to the order."

"So, who's paying for these?"

"Me."

"Nine pounds."

"Yeah, but I want a stout too."

"As well as these?"

"Yes."

"Why didn't you just say that?"

Before I had a chance to correct his misunderstanding, which would have been pointless in any event. I look to Finn and we both crack up laughing, no discussion required.

Finn holds up his glass in salute.

"Cheers!"

I show him my empty glass and so he pours a little of his Roofdog into it.

"To guest lists!" I say.

We clink glasses, then La returns from her moshing.

"Guys! I *so* need a drink!"

Finn passes her pint over.

"Having fun?" I ask.

"Yeah, thirsty though!"

She takes a few glugs.

"I cannae believe how good Madonnatron are now," says Finn.

He's been watching them from the bar – another benefit of this microcosm of a venue.

I laugh. "Yeah, when did that happen?"

"Practice innit," says La.

Toby returns with my stout which is gratefully received, then I turn to them both.

"I'm off back in, see you later, guys."

"Thanks for the beer, Dave!" says Finn.

"Yeah cheers, Dave, we'll come find you in a bit," adds La.

Another thing about this Tardis of a venue is the more packed it is, the bigger it feels, mainly on account of how long it takes to get anywhere, but as I've already said, no Cunt Wall exists here providing you're not a dick about it. Just don't knock anyone's drink, don't stand in front of short people, don't yabber through the gig and above all else, don't be a cunt.

Photos: Batch Two

Ben Wallers as The Rebel as Spiderman, The Five Bells, Newcross, 2018
Photograph by Lou Smith

Meatraffle's Chris OC, Windmill Stage, 2015
Photograph by Lou Smith

Warmduscher's Jack Everett & Clams Baker, Windmill, 2018
Photograph by La Staunton

Beth Soan (Madonnatron) & Jack Medley (Jack Medley's Secure Men),
SLEAZE Afterparty, 2018
Photograph by Lou Smith

Lincoln Barrett (Sorry) during filming of Goat Girl video, "Scum", 2016
Photograph by Holly Whitaker

Scud FM: Gavin Mysterion & Zsa Zsa Sapien, Hideaway, Streatham, 2019
Photograph by Lou Smith

John Clay & Stefania Cardenas, Windmill Shed, 2017
Photograph by Lou Smith

Simon Adamczewski, Windmill Beer Garden, Jack Medley's Megarave, 2019
Photograph by Lou Smith

Meatraffle's Cloudy Truffles & Zsa Zsa Sapien, Windmill Beer Garden, 'Jack Medley's Megarave', 2019
Photograph by Lou Smith

Jack Medley & Lias Saoudi, Backstage of The Dome, Tufnell Park, 2018
Photograph by Beth Soan

Jarvis Cocker & Patrick Lyons, 100 Club, Oxford Street, 2018
Photograph by Dave Thomson

Shame, The Railway Tavern, Tulse Hill, 2019
Photograph by Anna Yorke

Nuha Ruby Ra, Windmill Stage, 2019
Photograph by Lou Smith

Kae Tempest, Windmill Stage, 2018
Photograph by Holly Whitaker

Peeping Drexels, Venue MOT Unit 18, South Bermondsey, 2020
Photograph by Lou Smith

Sleepeaters, Peckham Audio, 2019
Photograph by Lou Smith

Fontaines D.C., Windmill Stage, 2018
Photograph by Dave Thomson

No Friendz: Angus Knight & Adam Brennan, Windmill Stage, 2018
Photograph by Lou Smith

PREGOBLIN: Alex Sebley & Jessica Winter, Windmill Stage, 2019
Photograph by Lou Smith

Sleaford Mods: Jason Williamson, The Apollo, Hammersmith, 2019
Photograph by Anna Yorke

Fat White Family: Lias Saoudi & Saul Adamczewski, The Windmill, 2019
Photograph by Lou Smith

Warmduscher, Test Pressings Festival, Hackney Wick, 2019
Photograph by Anna Yorke

The Moonlandingz: Johnny Rocket & Rebecca Taylor, Village Underground,
Shoreditch, 2018
Photograph by Lou Smith

Fat White Family, The Forum, Kentish Town, 2019
Photograph by Anna Yorke

Mosh Pit Crowd Surfer, Windmill Mosh Pit, 2019
Photograph by Anna Yorke

Chapter Twenty-Seven

He's Not Really a Cunt

People make demands
It's hard to understand
Background hum at best, right now
Holding back the light
Put down your batter ram
Calm your shaking hands tonight
"Tinfoil Deathstar" – Fat White Family

Madonnatron finish their set to thunderous applause. I slip away quickly before the throng to grab some fresh air and a ciggy, only to find it's already standing room only. I feel a light punch on my shoulder, which to my surprise and delight was administered by Dominic Hicks. Not in a band, but a director/producer with a penchant for chillingly dark short films – sort of Chris Morris meets Charlie Brooker. He is also talking with Clams Baker and Jack Everett about directing Warmduscher's promo for their next single "I Got Friends".

"Again!" he shouts.

We met when The Moonlandingz played their first London show at The Lexington and became instant friends, vaguely planning to meet up, never actually doing so, yet constantly bumping into each other at various gigs around London, but this is a first at the Windmill..

"This keeps on happening," I reply, laughing.

Dominic is one of those people you sometimes bump into in life where there's an instant chemistry and like a shot of adrenaline, their sheer presence raises your game. We just spark off each other, flying off in various directions, shape-shifting conversational sculptures, erratically changing course and never ever reaching a destination because there's always somewhere else to go. Dominic has ADHD, too. Well, that, or he's taking way too much speed.

A lairy voice from behind interrupts our flow.

"Dave, you old cunt, what a gig you missed!"

It's Tigger. He bowls into me, unhinged and clearly wankered.

"Calm down, you fucker!"

"Fuck me, dude, Goat were fucking legendary."

Funny how every gig you miss always is. Although, I can hardly talk after my humble Nirvana brag. And just in case you harboured any concern over my well-being, I did make it to the gig in one piece. Not the butterfly, though. It disappeared upon arrival. Its work was done. As for Nirvana, they *were* truly incredible, especially when experienced through the supernatural filter of four dozen psychoactive mushrooms. They did not lift Nirvana off the stage as my mate had predicted, they went one better, enabling me to project my consciousness onto the stage, singing along with the band, cackling at the obvious irony of Kurt's rock and roll antics. It was an out-of-body gig experience like no other, so I've given the DVD a swerve, preferring instead the technicolour version etched within my cranium.

"Nearly blew my head off!" continues Tigger, still banging on about Goat's performance.

"Looks like it succeeded, mate."

He looks at me, processing what I've said.

"Fack off, ya cunt!"

Dominic has been observing all this and I become aware of my lack of social etiquette, not that Tigger's made it easy.

"Tigger. Meet Dominic. He's the chap I've been telling you about."

Tigger cocks his head, eyeing him suspiciously.

"All right?" he nods.

Dominic smiles and nods back.

"So, Dom, what shit's he been chewing yer ear off with?" sneers Tigger, with his usual sensitivity towards my condition. Dominic laughs.

"Everything. Pretty much."

"Oh yeah? Like what?"

"Er, films, books."

"Time," I add.

"Space," continues Dominic.

"The multiverse."

"Shit venues."

"Neoliberalism."

"John Lydon."

"Butter."

"Music."

"The unremembered eighties."

"Fucking bastard Thatcher."

"Politics."

"Lots of politics."

I love playing word tennis with Dominic.

"Yeah, let's talk more politics, hey, Tigger?"

Tigger glares at me, a flicker of doubt cutting through his otherwise desensitised state. He surveys the room and turns back to us both, failing to focus on either.

"I'm gonna get a drink."

And off he staggers. Dominic's bemused.

"What the fuck was that about?"

"Ah, that's Tigger. He's just a bit wankered."

"Seems like a proper cunt."

I look at Dominic and consider this for a moment. I guess as introductions go it was not the best impression.

"Nah, he's all right really."

The truth is Tigger is far from all right. Not *because* he's off his tits, but the *reason* he is. He has a lot to escape from: a marriage in meltdown, a business collapsing, finances in reverse and by all accounts – mainly his – a pretty intense new relationship to manage. Who could blame him for wanting to feel good? And in Tigger's case, drink, drugs, music and sex tick all those boxes. We all have our crutches, our addictions, but the real problem is not the things we're addicted to, that's just misdirection, but why we need them, what drives the need to numb the pain and seek out external triggers to release some happier hormones.

Dominic's comment about Tigger continues playing on my mind and I start to wonder if his boyish innocence is blinding me to what is obvious to everyone else. Could it be he actually *is* a cunt?

19TH JULY 2015, MY PLACE

Tigger turns up at my door, unannounced. He's a total mess, but this time it's not a case of 'the fear' from too much partying. No, something has knocked his entire world out of kilter. Another woman.

"This is it, dude. She's *the one*," he gushes.

"What? Who?"

"That girl I met."

"Jesus fuck."

I'd never heard him talk like this, a man possessed, delirious and in every conceivable way, utterly love-struck.

I was sort of pleased for him, but most certainly wary. Plus, there were obvious complications to consider, both practical and emotional.

I usher him into the kitchen.

"Tea?"

"No thanks, dude."

"Whiskey?"

"Fuck yeah. Great idea," he splutters.

"I wasn't serious," I reply.

"I fucking am."

Blimey, it's only midday. I reach up for a bottle of single malt my bro left on his last visit. He loves a good whiskey.

"So, what's her name?" I ask.

"Sadie." He stares into the middle distance. "I'm gonna tell Sally."

Sally is his wife.

"Really?" I implore. This is new and worrying territory.

He looks down at the floor, face sombre and nods.

"When?"

"Tomorrow."

"Fuck!"

I freeze on the spot holding two whiskey tumblers as I assimilate.

"This is heavy duty shit, Tigger," I continue.

"I know. . ."

He takes one of the tumblers, then his face folds into a twisted smile as he raises his glass to mine.

"Cheers!"

"Er, yeah cheers."

We clink glasses in hollow celebration.

"What you gonna tell her?" I probe.

Tigger opens his mouth to speak, but nothing comes out.

"You okay, mate?"

He snaps back, takes a glug of whiskey before fixing me with a face I've never seen before. Is this his whiskey face?

"I'm leaving her. . ."

I also take a big glug, then try not to cough. Fucking hell, what do you say in situations like this? Get into the practical stuff?

"What about Ellie and Dylan?"

Tigger winces, clearly an issue weighing heavy on him. How could it not? He looks up.

"They'll be upset, but they'll be okay. . ."

"You have to make sure they don't think you're leaving them, mate."

"I will, dude. . ."

He looks troubled as he momentarily considers the enormity of what this all means.

"I've not felt like this before, dude."

He wells up. I move to embrace him and he nestles his head in my shoulder, jerking rhythmically as he melts into a sob.

"I. . . I don't know how I'm gonna tell her," he blubbers.

Nor do I. It's certainly not the easiest conversation to have after feeding the kids and washing the pots. Am I supposed to somehow help him find the words? Is there any useful advice one could ever possibly give?

According to my mum's favourite singer, Paul Simon, there's fifty ways to leave your lover. Though, if you count them up, which I have, he only ever mentions five at best; a fact that always annoyed me as a kid. *Come on, Paul, where's the other forty five?* What annoys me about the song as an adult is the total bullshit sentiment imbued within it, trivialising the total rejection of a human being you've shared a very intimate portion of your life with. We all know the reality, Mr Simon, it's profoundly difficult, unless you're an emotional plank. This is why so many parting couples say, "it's mutual", when everyone knows it's just a convenient moniker to maintain the dignity of the one being left and reduce the guilt of the one doing the leaving. Mutual? About as mutual as Chris Martin and Gwyneth Paltrow's New Age-infused alternative to splitting up.

With Tigger and Sally this conversation will be *way* more seismic, they've been together since childhood and have known nothing else, not a casual thing by any stretch; this will be heart-breaking, flesh-tearing, breakdown-inducing nuclear shit.

Within no time ominous dark gathered above our two families. A hard rain was gonna fall. My wife and I tried hard to avoid becoming embroiled in the ensuing acrimony, so came up with some rules, an attempt to outsmart the wider issues whilst supporting them both the best way we could. Our main rule being, anything Sally tells my wife or Tigger tells me, we never *ever* discuss with each other. No compromise, for we both know when the hate levels are turned up to 11, *any* ammunition that can be used, will be used. In fight to the emotional death *nothing* is sacred.

This turned out to be a tough position to maintain, not helped by Tigger and Sally constantly pumping us for intel at every given opportunity, every innocent utterance dissected and interrogated. It's entirely understandable, as up to that point they had shared their lives, their home, their Christmases, their birthdays, their kids' birthdays, finances merged, extended families visited, domestic chores agreed, bodily fluids exchanged, even their music collections merged - surely the final commitment in *any* relationship? Now a veil has gone up between them and neither has a clue what is happening with the other. It's a difficult and disorientating time, for where once they both previously knew the score, there was nothing but silence, an information void with nothing to replace it but fear and the voices in their heads.

A divorce can turn easy-going friends into needy emotional vampires, draining away your joy of life as they feed. Like wildfire, their break-up descended into a paranoia-fuelled emotional warzone, consuming everything in its path and we were slap bang in the epicentre.

There was a selfish expectation we would always put our friendships above our marriage. It wasn't being guardian of their secrets that caused the anguish, but the second-guessing and suspicion within our own relationship, as distrust grew over each other's role in whatever paranoid version of reality our heads had become infected with. We began to see each other as accomplices in the diabolical behaviour of our respective mates and in our naïve attempt to support them through this, we'd taken sides. Opposite sides.

My sympathy was never really with Sally or Tigger, it was with Ellie and Dylan, for they had to live through this and survive it. When you bring kids into this crazy, fucked-up world, your main role is to help them understand it, no mean feat in itself, so to watch the world they've come to rely on unravel before their eyes is devastating.

Remember how acutely sensitive we were as children? The power of our feelings, the intuition we possessed before life chewed us up and pummelled us into detachment. That's why it's a big deal, kids *feel* the trauma, way more than adults *ever* could.

So back to the question: is Tigger a cunt?

I guess on the face of it he is, but arguably people who don't love their partners yet stay with them, are equally cuntish; depriving the other any opportunity to find their own happiness, even if they've convinced themselves otherwise, is an act of selfish cruelty. Too cowardly to leave, too selfish to be honest, stringing the other along whilst holding out for something better.

I would rather be on my own than coexist with someone emotionally ambivalent. A lesson learnt the hard way I hasten to add.

29TH JULY 2017, THE SHED, WINDMILL, BRIXTON

I can't answer the question, I need a change of scene.

I turn to Dominic.

"So good to see you, man."

"And you man."

"I'm gonna see what's occurring inside, catch up later."

"Abba when I came out. That's *why* I came out."

"Ah." I smile, resigned. "Steakhouse is on the decks."

Chapter Twenty-Eight

Soulless Hootenannies, Gurning Rockabillies, Schizoid DJs

All packed out and looking good
Strapped up tight and clean
No mess right now
But late tonight
They'll be dripping glitter dreams
"Disco Peanuts" – Warmduscher

I walk between the bar and the loos somewhat high-spirited, if not a little giddy, but the pleasure of my alcohol buzz is soon overwhelmed by exasperation over Angus's musical selection, for he has the entire room on their feet to Kool and the Gang's "Boogie Nights". For fuck's sake! I march over to the DJ booth.

"NO! NO! NO!" I exclaim.

"YES! YES! OH YES!" he replies, smirking proudly. "Look, they're dancing!"

"That just makes it all the more annoying."

A hand grabs my shoulder.

"There you are!" A voice from behind.

It's La and she's beaming, happy, possibly as drunk as me, she certainly should be.

"Hey, La!"

"What's happening?"

"I was just seeing if I could get this tosser off his irony trip and play something more wholesome, more befitting of this place."

"It's not irony. I love it. I love *all* of it!" declares Angus, with total commitment.

"'Course you do."

"You'll like the next one."

"Yeah, sure we will," I reply snarkily.

"Wait and see," he smirks.

"Right, it's my round," exclaims La. "Stout, Dave?"

I probably shouldn't.

"Ooh yeah, please," says my mouth.

She heads for the bar and I note Angus buried in his laptop studying his playlist, obviously looking for something truly trashy to play, so I head for the loo. Then I hear something familiar, something from my youth. Frenzied computerised guitar and drums jangle through my brain, searching for neuronic connection. Suddenly, it comes to me; it's

"Free Range" by The Fall, a lost gem strangely ignored by many purists, considered too poppy. I hurl myself into the bouncing mass to enjoy a good old fashioned pogo for old times' sake. Angus joins me, hanging off my shoulder pogoing in unison, perhaps happy at my obvious approval, or perhaps not, for Angus cares little of the opinions of others, much preferring the voices in his head.

The song comes to its crescendo before abruptly ending, which I'm secretly pleased about, as I'm close to collapse. At least I can reliably assume the next song will not be one for me, one of the benefits of Steakhouse's erratic choices when you're out of breath or need a wee. I was right. Angus follows The Fall with Bachman-Turner Overdrive's "You Ain't Seen Nothing Yet". He really is taking the piss, which reminds me, I need one. . .

After relieving myself, I walk over to the bar where La, Finn, Zsa Zsa and Chris OC are all chatting together. Zsa Zsa clocks me and opens his tattooed arms for an embrace.

"It's our manager."

Zsa Zsa still has me listed as "Dave the Manager" in his phone, well at least until it broke.

This clearly confuses La, she doesn't know the story.

"Here's your drink."

"Ah cheers, thanks."

I so need one after that brief exertion. Pogoing's fucking hardcore at my age.

"So, *are* you their manager, Dave?"

Zsa Zsa and Chris OC laugh.

"No, La. It's a long story," I explain.

"How long have you two known each other, then?"

I'm trying to think, then Zsa Zsa responds.

"It's like. . . it's like we went to school together."

"Yeah, he used to bully me, La."

"I fink I remember him from the showers."

"I'm hard to forget," I reply, campily.

"This is clearly all bullshit," asserts La.

"Yer not wrong," confirms Chris with a smile, before wandering off with his beer.

Zsa Zsa looks at me with a gooey grin.

"Well, it feels that way, don't it, Dave?"

What a sweet sentiment. I give him a hug.

"I love ya, bruv," I say to Zsa Zsa.

"Me you, man. I love your style."

"Ah, look at you two, having a moment." La smiles.

I should feel embarrassed but I'm way beyond that. "You Ain't Seen Nothing Yet" finally comes to an end and then, rather pleasingly, I hear the familiar xylophone rhythm of "Uncertain Smile" by 80s electronic outfit The The.

"Oh my fucking God, I love this!" exclaims La, grabbing her pint.

I uncouple from Zsa Zsa. "I gotta dance to this, bruv,"

He smiles and I theatrically offer him my hand.

"Fancy a dance?"

"No," he curtly replies.

He rarely does, but when Zsa Zsa does cut some shapes you know it's a special night. I make for the dance floor again, bouncing my way into the throng, La's and Finn's spiky tops dominating the happy human mass which is now spilling onto the stage. The The appear to be having a latent resurgence amongst this crowd, maybe even beyond. Matt Johnson's angsty, politically charged lyrics were not fashionable during the shiny *greed is good* eighties, didn't chime with the times. Yet here at the Windmill they feel strangely relevant. Politics is back in the mix, not obviously, but it's there which is perhaps why The The are enjoying a new-found appreciation amongst a younger, more receptive audience.

I do so love this song, the rhythm, the lyrics, the nostalgia. The alcohol haze obviously helps. I open my eyes, refocus and right in front of me is ex-Phobophobe Elliot Nash, cutting some shapes and despite him being offensively young, he's singing along to every word.

He notices me staring and cracks a smile. I lean in to speak.

"Aw, man, this song brings me right back."

"This might just be my favourite song ever," replies Elliot.

Which is odd considering he probably hadn't even been born in The The's heyday and it wasn't even a big heyday.

"I hope this is the original single version, not the one Jools Holland ruined with his piano jazz."

"Is there another version?"

"Yeah, the original single mix."

The one small but irksome tragedy on The The's otherwise superb debut album *Soul Mining* was the decision to replace the original's sublime sax solo with Jools Holland's derivative jazzy piano riffs. (Okay, for train spotters or spectrum dwellers and to prevent being pulled up on a factual inaccuracy, the original version of this song was put out by Some Bizzare Records entitled "Cold Spell Ahead" - and it's way weirder.)

Something about Jools Holland gets under my skin nowadays, the older he gets the stodgier he becomes and this is reflected in his show. A cloud of depression descends upon me when watching *Later. . . Y*et like the days of *TOTP*, I cling on for the odd morsel of something exciting or truly ground-breaking, now a rare occurrence, dumbed down over the years into a glossy affair, more appealing to an *X Factor* audience. Worse still is the faux, festive, soulless Hootenanny, which if I ever end up watching I know I have utterly failed in my New Year's Eve planning. Not even a *live* show, but a pre-recorded phoney party with a fake countdown.

I remember back in 2005 seeing Arctic Monkeys' first performance on *Later. . .* At the time they seemed edgy, such was the back-slapping apathy within the world of "indie", having to be reminded that music should not just tickle our intellect but punch us in the gut. Arctic Monkeys were never that edgy or particularly innovative, but on that show, that night, they played their tits off. It felt real, committed and was electrifying to watch. It was also clear from the get-go, their adolescent singer was a surprisingly good wordsmith. This was back when he was shy, spotty and kind of endearing.

All of that has since changed and if you need a living example of just how easily fame can turn a nice young lad into a big-mouthed cunt, you need look no further than Alex Turner. And, if you're after tangible proof, then the smoking gun has to be his acceptance speech at the Brit Awards in 2014, where you'll find Alex, all quiffed up, shiny and wet, like he's dropped out of a rockabilly action figure mould and hasn't had chance to dry. It's impossible not to feel second-hand embarrassment as he gurns through his pre-prepared prose, trying to pull off a Jim Morrison but coming over like a coked-up Tetley Tea man in a village hall poetry competition. He even uses glass ceiling imagery to define the pain and struggle this bunch of straight white males have endured. The rest of the Monkeys look on, awkward, embarrassed, like they just want to deck the twat and I reckon they should have, for if nothing else it would have made for great TV. Oh and what was the award? The Mastercard Album of the Year Award; neoliberalism subsuming one of the very art forms it should be challenged by. Turner then drops a wireless mic, as if it were somehow an act of defiance, after first offering to pay for it, which he could do so a squillion times over. Whatever symbology Turner had in mind, this was most definitely not punk, just a pumped-up fevered ego swinging his dick, spouting, "I can afford this. Can you?"

Sorry, Alex, you're probably still a nice lad, but for that and that alone, you're on my cunt list. Don't worry though, you're in highly esteemed company.

Chapter Twenty-Nine

Weird Mates, Fragile Egos, Pissy Floors

Down here in the darkness, we assume the best
Refuse every kindness, swallow your distress
Baby beats his chest so that he can hide
That soaring precipice that he's passing off as pride
"Feet" – Fat White Family

Elliot and me are at the urinal along the wall of the gents, pissing in unison whilst continuing our chat. He has just explained to me how his dear departed friend George Russell introduced him to the album version of The The's aforementioned single, so for Elliot there is a powerful emotional connection etched into the song's grooves. Still, I persist. I can't stop myself.

"All I'm saying is have a listen. How can it hurt?"

"I can't, I love the album version too much, I don't wanna spoil it."

"It won't, trust me, it merely elevates it."

Elliot shakes his head.

"I dunno, man."

I do appreciate Elliot's difficulty and what is driving his stubborn resolve, but I'm on a roll now.

"Why do you want to listen to that Tory-voting Establishment twat playing the same jazzy bluesy shite he plays on every other fucker's songs. All I'm saying is try out the original. I promise from the bottom of my heart, you will not regret it."

I try buttoning up my flies but lose my footing on the piss-soaked floor. Quick as a flash Elliot grabs my shoulder and steadies me, saving me from stupidity, humiliation and a wet stinky floor. I should perhaps mention I'm quite drunk at this juncture. I stumble out the toilet and thank Elliot for ensuring I do not smell of urine for the remainder of the evening. He laughs and heads towards the dance floor area. Not me, though, it's time for some fresh air. Admittedly, most of it will be sucked through some burning leaves, but the nicotine buzz might clear my head a little. I turn into the leafy beer garden and spot Joanie sitting at a table with the rest of Madonnatron. She clocks me and smiles as I approach.

"You're a dark horse, aren't you?!" I say.

She laughs, coyly.

"You were great!"

Seems to me that getting Joanie on board was a smart move. They're a different band now and a force to be reckoned with.

"It was fucking brilliant."

Joanie smiles bashfully.

"Really? I was pretty nervous."

"If anything, you all looked fucking scary."

A voice from the side.

"Ello, Dave! You all right?"

I turn around. It's Beth, their drummer.

"Yeah, I was just waxing lyrical about your performance tonight."

"You enjoyed it?"

"Fuck yeah, last time I saw you was about a year ago. I was pretty gobsmacked tonight."

"Yeah well, we try," chuckles Beth.

"Seriously, I wouldn't have put money on you guys back then."

"I'll take that as a compliment."

"It really is!"

"Right, I'm off back in, see what shit Steakhouse is playing," cackles Beth as she leaves.

Stefania and Charlotte join her and I'm fully expecting Joanie to follow, but she remains in her seat, looking fragile and strangely troubled.

"You okay?"

"Yeah, I guess. . ."

"You seem upset."

She pats the seat next to her. Oh God, why did I ask? Now I'm going to have to concentrate and listen which is going to be tough, I'm very distractible this evening. I join her on the bench seat, strap myself in and do my utmost to give her my full attention.

"I just didn't enjoy it."

"Really? Why?"

"I don't feel it's my band."

"No way, you were great."

"I feel like a spare part."

"Well, I saw them a year ago and they sounded fucking awful. Don't underestimate the difference you've made."

She looks up at me like a child.

"Really? You mean that?"

"I'm deadly serious."

She smiles, bashfully. I think I've just become her dad.

"That's nice, thank you."

"Have you written any songs since joining?"

"No."

"Well try and write some. Make your mark."

"Yeah maybe. . ."

"Well at least have a go, see what you come up with. They might like it."

Joanie nods thoughtfully, looking vulnerable and troubled. I don't know why but I'm suddenly put in mind of Scarlett O'Hara. I lean forward and pick up my baccy.

"Don't overthink it, Joanie, just enjoy it. You were great."

I stand up to leave and she leans forward to kiss my cheeks.

"Thanks, that means a lot."

"'Ello? What's going on here, then?" interrupts a familiar voice from behind.

Oh fuck, it's Tigger. He turns to Joanie.

"You know how fucking old he is?"

Here we go again. . .

"Don't be a dick, Tigger."

He looks at me scornfully.

"Just a joke, dude."

"Yeah right."

He cocks back his head like a petulant child.

"Eeeeer."

Joanie is looking on, somewhat confused. I turn to her.

"Sorry about my friend here."

She smiles.

"It's okay," though her face says otherwise.

"Catch you later."

Joanie smiles and nods. Tigger looks on as I head towards the bar entrance. He catches up.

"What the fuck's the matter with you?"

I can't believe he's asking *me* that. I turn to face him.

"Why d'you always do that?"

"Do what?"

"D'you have a problem with me?"

"No, dude, it's you that got shitty."

"I can't ever talk with anyone without you hurling abuse."

"Come on, dude, it's just banter."

"No, it wasn't. Banter's supposed to be funny."

"Fackin' hell, lighten up!"

"It's just fucking boring."

"Well, stop chatting up young girls like an ageing groupie."

"You really are such a child."

"She's the child, dude."

Fucking hell, I can't be bothered with this bullshit, he's sucking the fun out of my evening. He's become my anti-woo.

"See you later, Tigger."

I walk into the bar area, still angry over his suggestion. Yes, Joanie is young and beautiful, but the last thing I'm trying to do is get off with her, or *anyone* for that matter. This is not what this place is about, it is and should remain a safe space for anyone but Tigger seems incapable of seeing past the lipstick, tits and bums,

"Yo, Dave!"

I spin round, a little startled. It's La.

"You all right?"

I shake it off.

"Yeah. Fine."

La looks at me curiously, unconvinced.

"Fancy a smoke?"

Even though I've just had one I nod and La leads the way, but we're intercepted by this guy practically bowling us over and he looks fucking insane, eyes bulging, talking incessantly.

"Do you know where Madonnatron are?" he asks in a raspy, stuttery voice, his eyes darting all over the place.

"Er, no I'm not really sure," replies La, eyeing him warily. "Nice T-shirt, by the way."

"Yeah. . ." he says, looking down. "I got it off Al Brown."

"I know Al," says La, brightening.

Al Brown is the man behind the Fluffer Pit Party gigs (the subject of his T-shirt), all set in the round like an old Shakespearean play.

He smiles, then refocuses on his mission.

"Have you seen Madonnatron?"

"I saw some of them earlier at the bar," offers La, "but I'm not sure where they are now."

Well, I know at least three of them have just gone inside and Joanie's at the back of the beer garden but feel I ought to hold this intel back from this crazy dude standing before us. Seems I *have* become her dad.

"Do you know 'em?" I ask.

"Yeah. I'm gonna put out their next record."

La and me both stare at him, surprised.

"Really?" I quiz.

"Yeah, definitely."

"Are they aware of this?" enquires La.

"Yeah, well not yet, that's why I wanna see 'em. They're fackin' mega!"

I shoot La a glance. She responds with a subtle *"what the fuck?"* face.

"What about Trashmouth?" I ask.

"Ah, don't worry about that"

"Really?" I say, puzzled.

"Yeah, Liam and Luke are mates o' mine."

His eyes start darting about again.

"If ya see 'em, tell 'em Jack's looking for 'em," and off he trots.

La and me stare at each other, exploding into laughter.

"Who the fuck was that?" I splutter.

"That. . . was Jack!"

Chapter Thirty

Trouble at Mill

I'll ruminate conspiracies, illuminating histories
I'm telling you to hear these totally compelling theories
But you know I'd never go right into dialecticism
With somebody with illuminati fluoride in their system
"Have a Baby" – Jeffrey Lewis

I follow La into the bar, still troubled by thoughts of Tigger. How have we come to this? It began going awry soon after he moved out of his marital home and moved in with Sadie. Almost overnight he stopped calling me for gigs, or anything for that matter, which also meant that I was now out of the loop. I'd become so reliant on him, perhaps too reliant. It needed a rethink. How can I do this without my mate, my gig buddy? I'm going to look like a right sad tosser turning up on my own, but after a few ignored texts pride kicks in and with it, an information void. I'm off the socials, just not ready to surrender my personality and core values to Facebook. Fuck that. It's hard enough wrestling Google out your life and even then, you never really can. They say they have to peek a bit for technical reasons, but the real reason is, they're a bunch of cunts who'd murder their own grandmother to achieve world domination. All the corporates are at it. You can't *buy* anything, *go* anywhere or *do* anything without being sent a fucking survey *"to help improve the customer experience"*. What a load of old shite, just more data harvesting. They even expect us to write reviews for them, like unpaid lackeys in their marketing team. Well, they can all fuck right off. Since when did buying a product obligate me to provide free market research? Let's be clear on this, whatever item or service I pay for, I just *expect* it to work, so if you don't hear from me that's a good thing, it means I'm reasonably happy. We all know the real reason is to help the bots fine-tune the profile they already have on us.

In the end I went old-school, checked out the Windmill's website, fully expecting the usual crappy online brochure, certainly not an ever-changing content affair. I was surprised and relieved to discover it was all laid out, the next three to four weeks of gigs, complete with bios, some of which were hilarious. So, one night I chose a set of bands I fancied and gave it a shot. I recall being wracked with fear as I approached the Windmill, rocking up there on my tod. Was I going to spend the whole night alone, like a misfit, a weirdo? You know, *that guy*.

Tonight, is no different. I had no specific plans to meet anyone, apart from a loose arrangement with La and Finn, having secured me entry to the Academy.

The Windmill is now stifling with body heat, like a rush hour tube in the heat of the summer, only way more fun. I need a drink. I probably don't, but I do. We work our way through the confusing mix, when La spots Finn and Zsa Zsa waiting to be served, so we bowl over. On the way I bump into Nathan Saoudi, his curly locks poking out from under a red beret.

"Hey, Nathan, how're ya doing?"

"Hey, man."

He puts his fist to his heart and I respond in kind.

"I need to fookin' lose this."

He holds up a black dustbin liner containing something pretty bulky.

"What is it?"

"My keyboard."

I don't recall him onstage tonight but perhaps I wasn't paying proper attention.

"Did you play with Moonlandingz tonight?"

"Nah. But I was there like."

"So, what d'ya think?"

"To what?"

"The gig."

"Oh, I was gonna watch them from the side, but I had a bit too much Ket."

I cough out a laugh.

"I 'eard 'em, but all I saw was the backstage ceiling," continues Nathan.

"Are you queuing for a drink?"

He looks around, assimilating his surroundings.

"Nah, I gotta get rid of this first."

"Piotr'll look after it."

He momentarily considers this option but dismisses it without explanation.

"Nah, it's all right, I'll find somewhere."

"Good to see you, man."

I move in, unintentionally beating Alex Sebley to the sweet spot that has opened at the bar.

"Oh, sorry mate."

"No worries, man, you were first anyway."

"You're a proper gent, Alex."

I really don't need a drink, I'm already beyond my natural peak. Still, I've caught Piotr's attention now.

"Pint a stout, please."

"You've already got one coming," says Piotr.

"Oh, really?"

I look down the bar and spot La waving at me then pointing to the part-poured stout settling on the bar.

"Thank you," I mouth.

I turn to Alex.

"It's pretty special what's happening here, don't you think?"

"What?" Alex queries.

"This place, these people, all these great bands."

"Yeah, it's quite something."

"This is history happening right here under our nose."

"That's true, man."

"Someone needs to document it."

"Yeah, but who?"

"Dunno."

"Do you write?"

"A bit."

"Well. . ." Alex moves in closer "I don't really talk about it much, but I have a publishing house."

"Really?"

"Yeah, if you write it, maybe I could help."

I'd heard he had some connection to publishing. that his grandma had been tight with Brendan Behan, something about her helping him get published whilst imprisoned for IRA terrorism.

"Tell me about your publishing house."

"Well, it's not-for-profit."

Okay, so now in my drunken head I've already made the leap from the idea to the publishing, next it'll be book sign-ings and film rights. Still, I find the whole idea interesting. Piotr arrives with my stout.

I turn back to Alex.

"So, what causes does it support?"

Alex looks puzzled.

"Your publishing house. Who benefits?" I clarify.

"Well, it's more like specific projects."

"What kind of projects?"

"Just projects."

"Yeah, but give me an example."

"Well, various things."

"Like what."

"Stuff I'm working on."

I chuckle.

"Why're you laughing?"

"I was thinking maybe something, I dunno, a little broader?"

A project? That could mean anything.

Alex looks a little put out and orders his drink.

I turn to my left to find Clams Baker in his white Stetson, leaning on the bar engrossed in conversation with someone. I turn around further still and there is Finn, freshly glammed up, now in a leopard-skin top with glitter all over his face. There are times the Windmill takes on a Lynchian quality.

Suddenly, I hear a voice I know too well, unmistakable in its northern charm.

"How can you not remember me fookin' name?"

It's Sadie. And she's berating Clams. What's her beef? I stare ahead to avoid any unwanted attention. Clams attempts to defuse the situation, though he's pretty wankered himself at this point.

"Well, I've only met you a few times," he replies in his American drawl.

"Yeah and every fookin' time I've had to tell you me name!"

Blimey, she's well cross with him.

"I'm a person too y'know!" she continues.

"Course you are. I was just saying. . ."

"You already think yer a fookin' rock star. It's all gone to yer head and yer not even fookin' famous!"

"Ah come on, there's no need to get like that."

"Egomaniacs the fookin' lot a ya!"

"I'm sorry, I don't know what else to say."

"You've said enough."

Clams turns away from her to face me. We've met before but I wouldn't say we really know each other.

"Hey man, how're you doing?" he asks me.

"I'm good. You?"

Sadie butts in.

"I bet you know this cunt's name!"

Really? Is this where we're at now?

Clams thinks for a second and then laughs.

"Actually, I don't." He puts an arm around me. "Sorry, man."

I turn to him.

"That's all right, Chuck, not at all offended."

Clams laughs, which seems to rile Sadie further, her face creasing into a scowl.

"Well, all you need to know is, he's a twat!"

This is insane, though I guess twat is a move up from cunt. Why is she being so aggressive?

"Sorry, Sadie, what *is* your problem?"

"Admit it, you're a twat – aren't you, Dave?"

How do I deal with this?

"Well, I guess that depends on your perspective," I offer, trying to keep things light, although her volume is increasing and we're beginning to draw a crowd. La and Zsa Zsa appear beside me.

"Well, from mine, you're a twat!" she continues, undeterred.

"You're a proper little charmer, aren't you?"

"Don't engage with her, Dave, she's clearly arseholed," says La quietly in my ear.

"Well, it's a bit hard to ignore when it's this in your face." I mutter back.

"I really wouldn't bother, let's go for a fag."

Sadie swings round to La, eyes ablaze.

"You can keep your fookin' nose out, it's got fook all to do with ya!"

"Excuse me?" La replies, bemused.

Clams shakes his head and makes a hasty exit to the smoking area. Zsa Zsa is looking troubled as the urge to intervene bubbles up in his brain and works its way through to his mouth.

"Come on, Sadie, leave it out!" he protests, like we're in an episode of *EastEnders*.

"It's all right, Zsa Zsa, we're just having a nice conversation." She turns to me with an icy stare, "Aren't we, Dave?"

I go to speak but La tugs my arm.

"Dave. Stop engaging, it's pointless."

This provokes Sadie further.

"Who d'you fookin' think you are? Did ya know he's fookin' married with kids?"

La looks at Sadie, puzzled.

"Yeah, sure I do."

"So why you fookin' him, then?"

There is a stunned silence. La and I turn to face each other in utter bafflement then burst out laughing. Probably not the right response, but at least it confuses Sadie into temporary silence. Zsa Zsa clocks Tigger passing by and intercepts, grabbing his arm, talking sternly into his ear. He looks like a mischievous schoolboy regretting the drama he's set-in motion, then breaks away and tentatively approaches Sadie, his face full of dread as he reaches over to her shoulder. She spins around as though she's ready to take him out, but freezes upon seeing it's him and throws her arms around his neck, exhaling with relief. Tigger talks into her ear, trying to reason with her I assume. Sadie pulls away abruptly.

"I'm not making a fookin' scene!"

Her eyes flicker around the group, before fixing on me.

"*You* know what you've fookin' done. *You* have to live with the truth."

What is she on about?

"You think I don't know what you been telling Sally?" she continues.

Ah, so that's what she thinks.

"Are you fucking serious?"

"You fookin' know! You're a snake!"

I shake my head. "This is paranoid bullshit, you don't even know me, let alone what I say and to whom."

"Oh, I know ya. I knows all about your type."

So, I'm a type now?

"And you've got a fookin' cheek," continues Sadie, "you haven't a clue about me. Call yer sen Tigger's mate? You've med no effort at all!"

With that, she storms off, Tigger limping after her, way more sober than he was just a few minutes ago.

There is a pregnant pause as we collectively wait for them to exit the building. As the door closes, the tension instantly dissipates and we all burst out laughing in relief. I turn to them all.

"Sorry you guys got dragged into all that."

Zsa Zsa is visibly shaken, but La just brushes it off.

"I guess she's not a happy drunk?" she observes.

"But why? What was it all for?" questions Zsa Zsa.

La turns to him.

"Fuck it, she's clearly wankered. Let's all have tequilas, for science and therapy."

"Good shout, La," adds Finn.

Zsa Zsa leans into me all close and intimate. He does that, especially when in gossip mode.

"Fackin' 'ell, Dave, what's she fink you've done?"

"Honestly, mate, I haven't a fucking scooby."

In truth, none of this has surprised me. The rancid poison coagulating under a skin of pretence has finally burst through, her rabid insecurity exploding into the cold light of day (if you consider the small hours at the Windmill to be such a thing).

I *knew* she had issues with me, my very presence feeding her paranoia; an open conduit to Tigger's pre-Sadie life, a single link in a chain leading straight back to his ex. Truth is, she knows nothing of me, hasn't really wanted to, much preferring a blank canvas to work with, paint me into any kind of cunt that fits the bill. Every vicious row, every insult thrown, every missile launched, I'm under suspicion, an invisible hand, leaking intel, loading the gun for every bullet fired in.

None of this is true. But what can you do? I shouldn't even *have* to defend myself, Tigger should have a bit more fucking faith than feed into this bullshit. We were mates and I supported him through it all, even put him up for a while, yet despite all this and more, I'm the one at the end of his girlfriend's pointy finger, in the dock, falsely accused.

"Right, you lot, paws out."

La is grinning, holding a salt cellar and a glass of sliced lime. The tequilas have arrived.

Chapter Thirty-One

Golden Syrup, Daddy Bear, Dragon Spit and Discerning Disco

Swinging on my pole in the back of a room
Pushing forty and you're facing parole
You got six months clean
But you gotta pay rent
And everybody's saying you're too old
"Standing on the Corner" – Warmduscher

We are all in The Shed now, laughing, drinking, bantering, Windmill normality resumed, the atmosphere far less cloying. I'm way too drunk to even attempt any kind of analysis, tequila shots have forced me to reside within the eternal now. Far less effort than meditation and arguably way more fun, if we ignore the aftermath. I drift off into a spectacular drunken haze and through the Windmill fog, I see Beth from Madonnatron. Which reminds me. . .

I clamber over the centre of the coffee table, something I only ever attempt when pissed, considerably increasing the odds of knocking over a punter's drink, but thankfully not this time.

"Yo, Beth!"

She looks up, her face widening into a smile.

"All right, Dave?!"

I move in closer, I don't wanna shout.

"There's this guy looking for you – well, all you Trons."

"Who's that, then?"

"Dunno, but he's pretty fucking mental."

"What's he look like?"

"Quite tall, well built, messy hair, big eyes."

"You don't know his name?"

Come to think of it, I think this time I do.

"Er. . . Jack?"

"Jack Medley?"

"I didn't get his surname. He was wearing a Fluffer T-shirt."

Beth laughs, heartily.

"Yup, that's him!"

"Is he all right?"

"Aw, Dave, Jack's a fucking megadude!"

"Thank fuck for that. I was a little worried for your welfare." I laugh.

"Nah, don't worry about him. He's lovely."

I give her a hug. "All good, then."

I clamber back to the group who are deep in conversation about who knows what, but I don't mind, I'm soaking up the atmosphere, beginning to feel at peace again. I fucking love this place.

"What're you lot gabbering on about?"

Zsa Zsa turns to me.

"Important stuff, man."

"Yeah, Dave. Matters," adds La.

"Way beyond your understanding," deadpans Zsa Zsa.

"Quite possibly, state I'm in."

"Tell me about it, I've got a show to do tomorrow. Talking could be a challenge," muses La.

"Yes, you *do* have work tomorrow," adds Finn, with ironic authority.

"Well, at least we'll have less of her babbling and hear some more tunes, eh?" I laugh.

La's mouth drops to the floor, simultaneously amused and offended. Have I just crossed a line? It's not uncommon for me.

"Ouch!" says Madame HiFi, giggling.

Finn and Zsa Zsa begin sniggering.

"I'm so glad we got you on the guest list, Dave," La returns.

Angus peers over, drawn in by the joviality, wondering what he might have missed. I meet his gaze, causing him to launch into me.

"So, when you gonna come to one of our fucking gigs, you cunt?"

He's like a drag queen with Tourette's and a well-practised "hills have eyes" vacant stare. When he does this, you have no choice but to front him out.

"So, if you're here, does that mean there might be some decent fucking music on now?"

"It's still my playlist, ya cunt, so fuck off," he proclaims.

"Ya can't DJ from The Shed, Angus."

He stares at me, then smiles like Batman's Joker.

"It's magic, Dave."

"No, Angus, it's a playlist. A fucked up one at that,"

"And therein lies the problem," adds La, almost loud enough for Angus to hear. He cocks his head, eyeing us all suspiciously, before turning back to his group.

I turn to the others, conspiratorially.

"Hey, guys, what d'ya reckon?"

"What?" queries Zsa Zsa.

"His laptop's unguarded."

They look up and smile a wicked grin.

"Yeah. . . go play somit fackin' decent," suggests Zsa Zsa.

I'm not sure, is that one step too far? A breach of Windmill protocol?

"Should I?"

"Go for it, Dave!" encourages Zsa Zsa, but then he always loves a bit of mischief.

"I believe in you," adds La, almost sincerely.

I lift myself from my seat and check on Angus, who is already eyeing me with suspicion.

"You, my friend, can fuck right off!" he booms, like the giant at the top of the beanstalk.

"Calm yourself, Angus, I'm just getting in some beers," which was also true.

"Oh yeah! It's your round, Dave," says La, handing me her empty glass.

Angus scowls, supposedly threatening, but because it's him it just makes me smile. I salute him, exit The Shed and re-enter the Windmill to the alien-sounding, throbbing electro beats of "Nag, Nag, Nag", Cabaret Voltaire's classic electro-punk stomper for the more discerning indie disco. Fuck the drinks, I head straight to the dance area to bounce in my own bubble of drunken nostalgia. A sweaty arm appears around my neck and someone is pogoing with me in unison. Yet again it's Angus, clearly loving it and the mere fact a track like this has transcended its generation, that someone so young could even know of this obscure experimental slice of post-punk industrial electronica, truly excites me. The song comes to end in a flourish of electronic white noise, Angus and me catch our breath, laughing helplessly, but before we have the chance to compose ourselves, the opening riff of Gun Club's "Sex Beat" echo round the room. I can't quite believe it, nor can Angus, but for different reasons. He is not supposed to have two good songs sandwiched together without a thick slice of cheesy pop as filling. Angus surveys the room suspiciously. Then, much like Goldilocks's daddy bear, he booms:

"WHO'S BEEN FUCKING WITH *MY* PLAYLIST?"

Angus clocks Honkies bass player, Tara, hovering near the mixing desk, trying not to laugh, but her guilt is obvious. He walks right up to her and looms over her tiny frame as he glares sternly for just a bit longer than is comfortable.

"I'm gonna let you off, because it's you," he says, causing Tara to giggle some more. Then he points at me accusingly. "Just don't let this cocklord anywhere near it."

He theatrically storms back through the bar, so I move over to Tara who is still giggling her head off. We both start jumping up and down to the hammer drill rhythm of "Sex Beat".

"Good work. You de-cheesed the playlist," I say.

"It's still his playlist, just did a bit of rearranging. It'll be Tuesday before we're back to his dodgy stuff," she smirks.

Then a familiar bass line kicks in and we simultaneously bounce into action, Tara whooping with delight. It's Joy Division. No, I'm wrong, it's "Thank You God for Making Me an Angel" by Country Teasers, which brazenly apes the bass riff from Joy Division's "Digital" and even includes the "Day in, Day out" refrain as a knowing nod. Despite the dark song it steals from, in the Teasers' hands it's a joyous, irreverent, ironic celebration of toxic masculinity. Within no time we're surrounded by various Windmill diehards, not ready to let the party end. Everyone's dancing, making shapes, even Zsa Zsa. Madonnatron's Charlotte, Beth, Stefania and Joanie are all here grooving away, for tonight it's their party and they're owning it.

Whilst dancing, I gaze at this crazy colourful spectacle and feel strangely moved. Yeah I'm drunk, which is why what I'm feeling is probably real. People use being drunk as an excuse for bad behaviour, when all it does is lift the veil on the more civilised version of ourselves, the one created for the world. All I know is my eyes are watery, there's a lump in my throat and I'm choked on emotion. What the fuck?

"You awright Dave?"

It's Zsa Zsa, misty-eyed, also drunk. It's been a long night. I hug him and speak into his ear.

"You know what, bruv? I fucking love it here."

He looks at me and his face melts into a golden syrupy grin.

"Yeah, it's special ain't it."

"And I love these people."

We both look around at the colourful human mass and return our gaze, all gooey with love. Somehow, we just light each other up, no idea why, no analysis required. If we were both so inclined, I'm sure we'd be a couple, or at least a filthy one-night stand.

"I love you, man," says Zsa Zsa. "You're a special person, Dave."

"So are you, bruv," I reply.

We are basking in mutual affection when a voice cuts in.

"Oh, look at you two, at it again."

It's La, smiling affectionately.

"I fink she's trying to get between us, Dave."

I turn to La.

"We were just saying how special all this is."

"All what?"

"All this?" I say, my hand gesturing around the room.

"The Windmill?"

"Yes, no, well yes, but this whole thing. It's pretty unique, don't you think?"

La internalises, as though she's never properly considered this before, perhaps too close to see the part she plays, yet continually championing it all on her weekly show, giving the whole movement a voice. Not from dry nerdy research, but complete immersion, providing background and context to all the magic brewing, yet seemingly oblivious to how integral she is. She looks up at us both and slowly nods.

"Yeah, you're right, it is special."

I'm suddenly distracted. What is that whooshing sound? I know that noise, that throbbing bass. I *really* know this. I wish I weren't so pissed. The beat emerges and my brain fuses, paralysing me to the spot.

"You all right, Dave?" asks La.

When the screeching guitar comes in it all makes sense, it's Girl Band's reimagining of Blawan's underground techno track "Why They Hide Their Bodies Under My Garage". Another gem from Angus's bizarre and extensive collection.

"Sorry, guys, I gotta dance."

I bounce into the dance floor, which has since become very pleasingly moshy.

Girl Band are from Dublin, not south London, but it matters not, they're musically linked, label mates with Goat Girl; toured with them too. Sonically, they're like nothing that's been before, a sort of techno Nirvana with lyrics by Rain Man, using instruments in ways never usually seen, making sounds never usually heard. My mate Simon Rumley introduced me, along with metal punk hip-hop band Ho99or. He persuaded me to come to *Visions Festival* back in 2015 where they both performed.

Girl Band blew my head off, one of the most intensely powerful performances I've ever seen and off the back of this experience, I persuaded my bro to make the unforgiving trek from Cornwall and join me at London's *Field Day Festival* in 2016, as Girl Band were on the bill. It also helped that Sleaford Mods, Goat Girl, Fat White Family, Steve Mason, PJ Harvey, Goat and heaps of other delights were also playing. The line-up was only marred by the inclusion of James Blake who has somehow carved a career out of millennial whining set to interminably dull beats and a wankometer turned up to 11. It amazes me what utter drivel people go for nowadays. Fat Whites, Sleaford Mods and Girl Band were our highlights. I recorded the latter belting out their single "Paul" for upload to YouTube (now owned by Google and the main leak in my data barrel).

After eight gloriously intense minutes, the song comes to a crashing close. My heart is thumping out of my chest and as I stagger back to the gang I'm ready to collapse. Zsa Zsa's now chatting with Alex Sebley and Madame HiFi's with La, having all since migrated to the bar.

"Was that fun, Dave?" asks Madame HiFi.

"Yeah, but I'm very thirsty now."

La suddenly animates.

"Yes! That's why I came to find you!"

"Fuck yeah, It's my round. Sorry La, got distracted."

"You're forgiven."

Ever since the 100 Club, just three nights ago, we've been buying rounds like it's an extension of the same night out. In that brief time, it has become apparent that La can drink me under the table and still look cool as fuck. I'm starting to think her very long legs might also be hollow.

"I need a smoke. Can I nick a bit of your baccy?" asks La.

"Sure"

"And a skin? And a lighter!"

"Have you lost yours?"

She frowns at me.

"What do you think, Dave?"

In the short time I've known La, she is constantly losing her tobacco and her phone, but it always reappears, as nothing is ever permanently lost at the Windmill - apart from a multitude of collective brain cells.

"Here," I hand over my smoking paraphernalia. "I'll be out in a bit."

La heads outside as I move towards the bar to order another quite unnecessary round of alcohol.

"What're ya having?" I shout across the bar just before La exits. She freezes a second, pondering the question, then shrugs.

"Whatever you're having." She smiles and exits.

Piotr appears with a glint in his eyes.

"Yes, sir?"

"Ah, just the man. Two pints of tap water, please.

"Is that all you want?"

"And two of your finest Bloody Marys, Mr Piotr."

I need to rehydrate and a Bloody Mary is my go-to drink when feeling peckish, like gazpacho soup with benefits. Piotr rolls his eyes and smiles.

"As you wish, sir."

You wouldn't get service like this in a normal pub.

"And a drink for your good self."

"Thank you." Piotr nods as he reaches for the vodka and tomato juice.

"Nice 'n' spicy, please."

Piotr smiles, devilishly.

"But not crazy spicy."

I stupidly said "nice and spicy" to Toby once and he served me dragon spit.

Chapter Thirty-Two

Gonzo Journos, FAC51 and the Neoliberal Hangover

Trapped in the mind
Of something else you've become
It's just the way it's been
When you've gone missing in the action
"Firewall" – Sleaford Mods

Whilst waiting for a more complicated drinks round than the lovely Piotr is used to preparing, I think about how the Windmill has forged a connection through time, back to the analogue days of my youth. . .

***

In the post-punk infused early eighties all we had for musical intel was John Peel and the written word. The *NME* was for the most part our main source of knowledge and back then it was a force to be reckoned with. We would devour it religiously every week, forever impatient for Thursday to arrive and if you knew a friendly newsagent you could get an early copy late Wednesday evening. It mattered then, it truly did, to be one day ahead of your mates, filled to the brim with news, single releases, album reviews, tours; it gave you a momentary edge. There was no instant access to info back then, the idea of a World Wide Web was the stuff of fantastical sci-fi. Nowadays you could be debating quantum physics in a field and settle an argument with a few taps on your phone screen. Okay, bad example, quantum physics arguments are never settled, but you get the point.

Weekly rags like the *NME* were crucial in these times, you would not always agree, more often their editorials would leave you seething, which was part of its draw. I cannot imagine such fervour and excitable anticipation for *any* rag nowadays.

To illustrate how far humanity has sunk the most popular news website in the entire world is the *Mail Online* and the *NME* has been reduced to another data-raping online zine with negligible impact on today's youth. Back then it was special, full of attitude, politics, hate and debate, with opinions strong, forceful, often unreasonable, with the power to lift a band to glory or kill them off mid-flight.

Not content to be mere reporters, these scribes blurred the lines between fan, philosopher and detestable critic, practically gonzo in their involvement, throwing petrol or piss on whatever embers of a scene bubbled to the surface.

They gave us a sense of geography, hardly bothering with London, as nothing meaningful was happening. The capital not only escaped Thatcher's wrath, but was the main beneficiary of her philosophy and in any artistic sense ceased to matter. It was having a "loads-a-money" party whilst the rest of the country became downtrodden and depressed. The results each culture spewed up said it all. Sheffield gave us Cabaret Voltaire, London produced Visage. Even in the late eighties, Manchester birthed the Happy Mondays, London shat out the embarrassingly awful Flowered Up. I could go on, but you get the point.

During the Thatcher-ravaged early eighties, the northern dignity of labour was replaced with soul-crushing dole queues and the next emergent generation found themselves blinking into the void, born into a world of no jobs, no money, no future, no hope. Things *needed* to be happening in these cities and from these post-industrial wastelands, all the anger, frustration, boredom and depression channelled itself into a smorgasbord of creative experimentation. Musical subcultures exploded all over Britain, giving us 57 varieties of post-punk and the *NME* documented it all, made the connections, gave it a political narrative, because back then the *NME* was unashamedly socialist.

Sheffield was the nearest place to me where anything resembling a scene was occurring, accessible within an hour by train and with so much to offer. The Steel City, where post-punk met Krautrock met experimentation – an industrial electronic primordial soup giving birth to all manner of musical organisms: Cabaret Voltaire, Clock DVA, The Comsat Angels and, my favourite of all, Artery, who combined fairground inspired music with witty, observational lyrics and intense live performances. Jarvis, also a fan, cited them as a huge source of inspiration to him, planting the seed that would give life to Pulp. Indeed, they launched themselves onto the scene that same year in 1978. The formula much the same: Jarvis Cocker drolly delivering his sexually repressed melodramatic monologues, accompanied by electronic arthouse disco. Over the years they became more polished, Jarvis's stage presence grew stronger, his lyrics even sharper, though it took seventeen years before they finally hijacked the nation's psyche with kitchen sink tales of rejection, revenge and sexual longing, capping it off with "Common People", their timeless anthem for the dispossessed. Even at the poppy end, Sheffield music was dominated by electronica, with the likes of Heaven 17, Human League, even ABC.

Simultaneously in Manchester, way before the Roses/Mondays/Oasis thing, or even The Smiths, existed an incredibly avant-garde post-punk scene centred mainly around Anthony H. Wilson's insane business folly *Factory Records*. And, of course, there was The Fall, but then there always will be, won't there? So long as your granny can find her bongos.

Manchester was technically within reach, if you didn't mind the four-hour mail collecting train, followed by a tragically long walk home. Aye, we had it rough. We were at this time obsessed with all things *Factory*, so often made this gruesome journey to visit the newly opened *Haçienda*. At the beginning, they were hosting some truly legendary gigs: The Gun Club, The Virgin Prunes, Bauhaus performing with Nico (which I'm 99% sure happened there, though the internet is silent on the matter). This was the *Haçienda* before Happy Mondays turned it into the 24-hour party people rave club it's mainly remembered for and which ultimately destroyed it.

I still have my *Haçienda* membership, a Peter Saville design, another utterly unviable idea bankrolled with the help of New Order and the late great spliff inspired Anthony H. Wilson. It was a plastic credit card continuing the silver/yellow industrial colour scheme utilised throughout the club with my name embossed across the front. A keepsake of a bygone era and an ominous symbol as to why *Factory Records* remained forever doomed, exemplifying one of the many reasons we should doff our cap to Wilson, for it was never about the money. And how can you not love the mad narcissistic cunt for that?

A trip down the M62 to Liverpool, another city, another flavour, leaning in a more psychedelic direction, where *Zoo Records* gave birth to Echo and the Bunnymen, Wah! Heat, Teardrop Explodes and a whole post-punk psyche scene.

Head down to the Midlands for another flavour still, where punk and ska were put through a blender, giving birth to the cultural phenomenon known as *2 Tone* and no band quite captured the mood of the nation more perfectly than Coventry's own Specials, nailing down the sense of hopelessness enveloping late Thatcher's Britain, whilst challenging the archaic attitudes towards race and culture. It was a simple message and the angry vulnerability of Terry Hall's delivery imbued their lyrics with a unique potency. Selector also came from Coventry, fronted by Pauline Black and Birmingham gave us The Beat, both releasing debuts through *2 Tone Records*, embodying the label's ethos from the make-up of the bands to their heart-on-the-sleeve political stance.

Wherever Thatcher enforced her anti-union, dole queue swelling ideology, a scene would coalesce and spew forth some ground-breaking music we've all since come to know and love. It can appear romantic, even magical, through the lens of nostalgia but at the time it was bleak and depressing and there really was fuck all else to do.

And here we are, 35 years later where it's happening again, something is brewing, but this time it's in the recession-proof capital and when you boil it all down, there's only one part of London where something like this *could* happen: the gentrification-resistant south, where a baseball hat with the slogan *"Make Peckham Shit Again"* has become a popular anti-fashion accessory.

Nevertheless, what is happening here is markedly different than the fate of the early eighties northerners whose brutal treatment was at the beginning of this neoliberal drunken night out. Now, with a financial hangover from hell, we are all staggering home trying to make sense of it all and the capital is also shelling out for the collapse of this economic Ponzi scheme through wage freezes and government cutbacks. Londoners, especially south Londoners, aren't taking it well. This colourful artistic community has sprung up from this austerity-driven shitstorm, priming itself before exploding into the wider culture. I could be wrong, but it feels like a new chapter of musical history is unfolding right here and the Windmill is currently its ground zero.

***

I'm snapped out of my misty-eyed nostalgia by Piotr coughing loudly with intent, holding two damn fine-looking Bloody Marys.

Chapter Thirty-Three

Low-Grade Weapons, High-Grade Tears and a Dog called Elvis

You ever get a feeling that nobody's listening
For a very good reason?
Pockets out of place, push comes to shove
You shrug it off, wrong season
"Vagina Dentata" – Fat White Family

I note with disappointment Angus has since regained control of his playlist. I've already had to suffer Dollar and now he's just playing Bon Jovi. He can be such a cunt. Most troubling of all is the amount of people dancing to it, including bloody Finn.

I cannot see Zsa Zsa and Madame HiFi, they must have joined La in The Shed, so I utilise what remains of my balance to weave through the crowd as I precariously carry four drinks. Nathan crosses my path again, still clutching his bin-bagged keyboard. Tim is there too, goading him.

"Bet you're carrying a low-grade weapon there."

Nathan looks puzzled. Though, to be fair, that's pretty much his resting face.

"What?"

Tim points to his bag.

"Yer keyboard."

"What about it?"

"Let me guess. A Casio CTK or a Yamaha YPT?

Nathan smiles.

"Or some other shite.", continues Tim.

"Some other shite." replies Nathan.

Tim cackles as he walks off and I continue towards the exit into the beer garden, nearly knocking over a bar stool onto a beautiful black Staffordshire Bull Terrier called Elvis.

He belongs to a grisly looking local called Gary who has the look of a south London Ian McShane and is not someone you wanna mess with. He's chatting with Stan, another local, who thankfully steadies the stool preventing a calamity and the very real potential of dog yelping/angry drunk man disaster.

"Aw bloody hell, thanks, Stan, you're a hero!"

He guffaws, says something incoherent which makes him laugh and winks at me. He's a good lad Stan, so long as you don't get him telling jokes, he grew up in a very different era.

When I enter The Shed, it's still pretty rammed. I cannot see Zsa Zsa or Madame HiFi, but I do see La in the far corner chatting with Lincoln and Edie.

She clocks me approaching somewhat unsteadily and quickly leans across the massive table that dominates The Shed to relieve me of drinks.

"You're a total star bar, Dave!"

"Ain't I just," I chuckle.

"I wasn't expecting supper though," says La as she inspects the Bloody Marys.

She takes a glug.

"Wow. Spicy," she continues.

"Too spicy?"

La savours it a while, then smiles.

"Just right. In fact, I didn't realise how much I needed this drink until now." She raises her glass in salute. "Cheers, Daaave!"

I smile and turn to Edie and Lincoln.

"All right, guys?"

Edie smiles, nodding and Lincoln holds up a bottle of Buckfast, his go-to beverage.

"We're fine and dandy, mama!" he exclaims.

"Anyone seen Zsa Zsa and Madame HiFi?"

"I think I saw them slink off," says Edie.

"Typical!"

Not one for goodbyes, Zsa Zsa always ghosts. Something I cannot do, as my deep-rooted sense of etiquette – or perhaps the need to have my existence constantly reaffirmed – forces me to say goodbye to everyone I know still present. It can make the act of leaving an exhausting ritual.

"Have you seen Finn?" queries La.

"Last time I saw him he was shaking his booty to 'Livin' on a Prayer'."

La cracks up at this, but then her laughter quickly dissipates. She nudges me and speaks quietly under her breath.

"Yer mate's back."

What's she on about? I turn around to face the entrance of The Shed where Tigger is now standing. Blimey, where did he come from? He is staring straight at me looking troubled, then slowly walks over.

"I'm gonna go check on Finn, see you in a bit," says La, standing up.

"Sure, see you later."

She nods to Tigger as she passes. He half-smiles back and then stares at me.

"Let's go for a chat?"

Does he wanna fight me now? Is this what we've come to?

I look at him quizzically.

"Hadn't you gone home?"

"Yeah, but I came back."

He nods towards the smoking area, around the side of the building.

"We got stuff to talk about," he continues.

I look around, no one's really noticed any of this as they're thankfully too engrossed in their own chat.

"Yeah, but now? Seriously?"

I *do* want to do this, just not now. This is daytime stuff, sober stuff. He looks thoughtful, earnest.

"Please, dude?"

What can I do? I can't just say no. In fact, I am struggling to say any words at all. Fuck knows how I'm going to hold down a heavy conversation.

Reluctantly, I follow Tigger into the beer garden where we find an empty table towards the rear and sit down facing each other.

Despite his previous state, Tigger looks almost sober. Has he spent the last two hours gorging on coffee and pure oxygen? He has an unusual calmness about him, an unnerving confidence. I clumsily breach the powerful silence.

"What the fuck was Sadie on about?"

Tigger shakes his head.

"It's not about her, dude. It's about us."

This is true, of course, but what kind of answer is that? He's deflecting, protecting her.

"You're not answering the question. Why did she tear into me? Where's all this shit coming from?"

He looks down and laughs. He's seriously winding me up.

"*You*, mate. You brought *all* this on."

Is he fucking serious?

"*Me*?"

"Yes, dude."

He has this air of calmness about him that just makes me want to hit him.

"That was such crap she was spouting. You do know that?"

He nods his head and looks down at his shoes.

"She was upset, she's only trying to protect me."

"From what? *Me*? Your mate?"

"She doesn't trust you."

Well, that's hardly a revelation. But where does he stand in all this? Has his mind been so warped already?

"And you?"

Tigger looks at me, smiles, before snorting out a tiny laugh. I just stare at him expressionless, waiting for a response I can actually understand.

He leans across the table and hugs me tightly.

"'Course I fucking do, ya cunt. You're still my bro."

An annoying lump has now taken refuge in my throat. Shit, not now. I pull away, hold his arms firmly and look directly into his eyes.

"What the hell's her beef, then?"

Tigger's shoulders slump as he lets out a slow breathy sigh and leans back.

"You never accepted her, dude. She can feel that."

"What're you on about? I've never been hostile to her."

"And you've never been friendly either."

I think about this. Is this true?

Perhaps it is. I wish I weren't so pissed right now, so fogged up with drunken emotion. I've always been friendly to Sadie. Okay, I haven't exactly opened my heart to her or really wanted her to do the same, much preferring to keep her at a safe emotional distance.

"Sure, you've been friendly, but not, ya know, *friendly.*"

Should I have tried harder? Got to know her instead of the avatar I've turned her into? It's not that easy though, the situation's way more complex. He may have left Sally, but she remains very much in my life, still my wife's best mate, always coming over, his kids too, so having any kind of intimacy with Sadie feels weird. Wrong even.

"You're always polite, dude, I'll give you that," continues Tigger, "but be honest with me, you don't like her, do you?"

I open my mouth to speak to deny this assertion, but then it hits me. I *don't* like her. Not one bit. Right from the off, she pressed all the wrong buttons and rang all the wrong bells.

Was it me? Did I kick off this hostile dynamic? Was my superficial veneer unable to adequately mask the utter contempt I have for this woman? Maybe politeness was not enough to prevent this psychological arms race escalating out of control. Of course, I logically accept it all, life goes on, things change, Tigger's happy despite the chaos in his wake. He makes his own choices, it's his life to live, love, fuck up, whatever. I supported him whenever I could, helped him get his head straight, gave shelter when in need, listened to him babble on and on and on about his traumatic divorce, how Sadie is now his everything, how she completes him, how amazing their sex life is – in unsolicited graphically gruesome detail. I was there through all of this, always positive, always standing by.

Yet despite all this reasonableness, this rationality, despite the conscious awareness of how to be human, something else, something inhuman was dwelling within and had taken residence within my core; festering, possessive, uncompromising dark matter, because deep down I resented her, for detonating the explosion that destroyed our family bond, our friendships, for taking away the fun times and for finding her way into Tigger's heart.

My face is wet. I must be drunk. Am I crying? Oh, for fuck's sake.

Tigger just sits there all calm, concerned even. I look up at him.

"You're right. I don't. I'm sorry."

Tigger embraces me and I sob into his shoulder.

"I just miss my mate," I blubber pathetically.

Tigger still holds me close, rubbing my shoulder.

"I haven't gone anywhere, you're still my bro, you always will be."

"Yeah, but it's different now."

I realise how pitifully needy I'm sounding, but at this point in the proceedings I'm significantly emotionally regressed.

"You're right, I did leave you hanging and for that I'm truly sorry, dude, I really am. I've just had shitloads going on, my head's been up my arse with the divorce, the kids, the house and on top of that, well, you know, I have this thing going with Sadie. And it's special, dude, I fucking love her."

"I know."

He's right, he's been living in a whirlwind and on top of everything else, he's loved up to the eyeballs.

Suddenly, I hear La's voice from the other end of the garden.

"Dave, we're gonna get a nightcap before heading off. Would you like to join us?"

I clear my throat with a cough.

"Sure, see you in a minute."

La nods before disappearing round the corner.

I turn to Tigger, who has that knowing smirk on his face again, eyebrows raised.

"Oh, for fuck's sake. Seriously?"

He bursts out laughing, opening his arms in embrace.

"Come here, ya cunt."

Chapter Thirty-Four

Fairy Godmothers, Black Sambucas, Tropical Rain and Lost Phones

I think about the heat
As it lowers itself on me
Past the closing hour
When the light in my phone
Starts to lose power
"B.H.S." – Sleaford Mods

Tigger's left again and I'm in the gents washing my manky face. Thankfully, I am spared the horror of seeing what state I'm now in as there's little in the way of functional mirrors, every spare inch covered with promo stickers and graffiti. I dab my face dry with loo roll and exit the loo. I'm not sure where me and Tigger go from here, but at least it was honest. Was it a breakthrough? I don't fucking know.

. .

La's with Finn at the bar and she clocks me approaching.

"Got ya drink here, Dave."

She hands me a glass containing some kind of brown-coloured cocktail. I give it a sniff. Hmm. . . ginger and rum, I think.

"What *is* it?"

"Dark 'n' Stormy."

"Like you, Dave," adds Finn, smirking.

We salute.

"To good times!" says La.

I take a sip. It's pretty tasty if not a little sweet, but a much-needed sugar kick at this juncture.

"Not bad. . ."

"Dave. They're fabulous," corrects La.

Finn slinks off to the loo.

"So how did *that* go?" she asks, nodding towards the garden.

"All right, I think. It's certainly been an unusual night."

"Another classic night at the Windmill."

"Yeah, apart from all the weird shit, it's been a *fantastic* night. Thanks so much for letting me tag along."

"It's been a pleasure, Dave. Truly."

"And so great to meet you both – I mean properly."

"And you."

She gives me a massive hug.

"What a time to be alive!" she proclaims.

She's right, it really is quite a time to be alive. It's also time for me to consider heading home. It's late, really late, any opportunity to catch a train long since passed, only Uber or the dreaded night buses. Now, whatever they say about Uber, it has revolutionised my social life and I can no longer do night buses on my own, especially this late - the closer to dawn you get the weirder the passengers become, including me. I look at my phone, battery's low but just enough.

"It's pretty late, I think I'm gonna head off."

Then from nowhere Kathleen appears, the Windmill's co-proprietor, who looks and sounds like a pantomime fairy godmother and for a select few, she can make late-night liquor wishes come true. Upon seeing me she floats over.

"How are you my lovely man?"

I kiss her cheeks. She really is so sweet, her entire face a big open smile.

"I'm past my peak, Kathleen, but just about hanging on. How about you?"

"Oh, I'm good. All the better for seeing you."

She can be such a flirt.

Finn reappears, still looking enviably fresh and grabs the remainder of his drink. I finish mine off and put the empty glass on the bar.

"Have a nightcap why don't you?" insists Kathleen.

I really don't need one but I'm already past the point of fucked, so what's it really matter? I look to La and Finn who both simultaneously shrug "*why not?*"

"Thank you, that'd be lovely," I reply.

"What would you like?"

I can no longer think, so point to La and Finn.

"Whatever they're having."

Black Sambuca as it turns out, pretty tasty at this time of the morning and dangerously moreish. Not that you need to ask as our hosts lovingly and liberally oblige. No money exchanged, no laws broken, just more brain cells and the rest of the weekend.

We are all chatting, but I'm struggling to hang onto to any kind of narrative. Is there one? I don't know. You might be feeling the same way, but I can't worry about you right now, I just need to get home. I pull out my phone to organise my escape.

"Hey, La, I'm booking an Uber, do want a lift home."

"Dave, I'm not on your route."

"You're *absolutely* on my route."

"I live in the sticks. I'm not on *anyone's* route."

"You're on mine and it's really no trouble."

"It's okay. I'm getting a cab with Finn."

This is puzzling.

"But he's going north, not west, isn't he?"

"I'll be fine, Dave," asserts La, shutting down the debate.

Of course, I understand her trepidation, La doesn't know me *that* well or even for that long and men can be *horrible*. I don't press the issue, even though part of me resents being considered a potential pest. I check my phone only to discover the Uber driver's fucking cancelled on me. Bastard. Why does this keep happening? I always tip and always chat, maybe I chat too much? Finn's also looking at his phone waiting on his own gig-economy transportation.

"Two minutes away," he informs La.

She grabs her bag and jacket from by the bar. They say their goodbyes and exit the Windmill.

Well, that ended strangely. . .

I do get it, you only have to look at the stats. After the age of 16, one in five women experience some form of sexual violence. With these odds how can women *not* be a tad wary? This is not helped by a more recent predilection of sad, pathetic guys who use crowded gigs as opportunities to grope women, stealing cheap kicks in the creepiest of ways.

I rebook my Uber and after what feels like an eternity, my hybrid carriage arrives and I say goodbye to Seamus, Kathleen, Tim, Toby, Nasos and Piotr, before heading for the door.

Outside, it's pissing tropical rain. I make a run for it, open the cab door, chat with the driver, then my phone rings. It's Finn. What could he want?

"Do you mind if I quickly take this?" I say to the driver as I take the call. "Finn?"

"It's me, La. Are you still at the Windmill?"

"I've just got into my cab."

"Fuck fuck fuck!"

I cover the phone and speak to the driver.

"Sorry, can you give me a minute before we drive?"

He nods politely. I return to the call.

"What's wrong?"

"I think I left my phone."

"Where?"

"Oh God, I don't know. I'm so fucked without it."

"I'll go see if they've got it."

"But what about your cab?"

"I'll let it go."

I apologise to the driver who speeds away, annoyed, no doubt causing my rating to plummet further.

"Stay on the phone, La," I continue as I head back inside.

Piotr's clearing up behind the bar.

"Has anyone handed in a phone?" I ask.

Without missing a beat, Piotr reaches behind him and holds up an iPhone.

"This one?"

I've been with her nearly all night and have no fucking idea. I describe the phone to La.

"Yes! Brilliant! I'm heading back now."

"Okay, I'll leave it with Tim."

"Thanks, Dave, you're super ace."

I book a fresh Uber, hand La's phone to Tim and chat with him whilst keeping one eye on my cartoon cab wending its way through the cartoon roads. When I'm certain it's arrived, I head for the door, give it a rattle but find it's locked, plus, someone is banging loudly from the other side. Tim's already following, keys in hand. As he unlocks the door, it immediately flies open and La bowls straight into me, utterly drenched, looking wretched. No one heard her banging through the hefty double doors and the noisy rain. I feel so bad for her but cannot hang around or I'll miss another cab. I say goodbye again, deciding not to go through the awkwardness of offering her a lift this time. I make a short dash through the pelting rain but just as I'm stepping into the Prius, Tim hollers after me:

"Hey, Dave!"

I look back but see very little through the tropical rain.

"What's up?" I shout.

"You're heading La's way. Can she share your cab?"

"Of course she can." I laugh.

So, with Tim's seal of approval, my trust quota improved, La steps into my Uber and we finally depart, drunk, tired, broken and decidedly wet, especially La.

As we head up Brixton Hill towards Streatham, we both stare out of the windows in easy silence attempting to assimilate the last seven hours. Such a long night. A long, dark, drunken night of the soul.

"Want some gum?" says La, breaking the silence.

"Yeah. Sure."

"It's yer favourite," she says smiling.

"Where d'you get that?"

"On my way back from the Academy."

I pop it in my mouth and my head explodes. It never fails to surprise me.

"Woo!"

"That was quite the night," says La. "Do you always have this level of drama in your life?"

"Seemingly." I sigh.

"And to think, the Windmill used to be such a quiet place."

"I seriously doubt that."

I have a strange feeling in my chest. Is it my heart? No, it's my phone vibrating in my inside jacket pocket. It's Zsa Zsa. I thought he'd be tucked up in bed by now.

"Hey, Zsa Zsa, where d'ya go?"

I hear coughing and muffling, then his raspy voice.

"Come over to ours, Dave, we got a few back for night-caps."

"Aw thanks, but I gotta get to my bed, I'm already a wreck."

"Stay at ours, we got a spare bed!"

"Ah I dunno, I'm in a cab with La."

"Cool, bring 'er along. I luv La. We all luv La don't we!"

This is followed by a motley chorus backing up Zsa Zsa's sentiment.

"The more the merrier, Dave," adds Zsa Zsa.

Before I know it and against ALL good sense, I'm updating my Uber destination with Zsa Zsa's address.

Upon arrival, I stumble out. La giggles as I steady myself against her window and lean in.

"Sure, you don't wanna come?"

"I do, but I really can't. I'm supposed to be on air in a few hours. I haven't done *any* prep and I'm wrecked."

Couldn't really argue with that logic. I currently have no such concerns, my wife and kids are away in Germany visiting my in-laws, so our place is empty (apart from our cat) and my diary has what my bro refers to as "a window of irresponsibility", not a big enough window to join Lincoln at a random festival, but enough time to re-acclimate to normal life. I am not good at going to bed anyway, I have serious FOMO issues which drives me to wring every drop out of every day, a symptom of my condition I'm told and if nothing else, a useful scapegoat for bad behaviour.

"I admire your resolve, La. I'm way too weak."

"You love it, Dave!" she laughs.

Just before the car pulls away, I lean in.

"Hey? If you're going to any gigs and would like a bit of company just give me a shout."

She smiles.

"I might take you up on that, Dave."

I make my way unsteadily to the front door of Zsa Zsa and Madame HiFi's gaff.

Chapter Thirty-Five

Treason, Treachery and the Gangster Poirot

I can be an idiot sometimes
I can say things I don't mean
And sometime when things come out my mouth
I instantly regret my speaking
"I Can Be an Idiot Sometimes" – Pink Eye Club

30TH JULY 2017, ZSA ZSA & MADAME HIFI'S PLACE

30TH JULY 2017, ZSA ZSA & MADAME HIFI'S PLACE

I follow Zsa Zsa through his hallway towards the source of the pumping loud music where everyone is gathered, the kitchen of course. Fats and Chris OC from Meatraffle are here, so is the very lovely Odette and her sweet big-hearted partner Gavin, who runs the Deli Lama; a lovely café in Streatham that magically transformed itself for Fat White

Family's after-party following their Brixton Academy show. There is also this coke-fuelled nutter spouting so much music biz hyperbole, he doesn't seem like a real person, more like a character from the pages of a John Niven novel. He's only in transmit mode, all receptors or any semblance of empathy having long since left town. Soon enough, he grabs a CD cover to get to work and as it turns out he's pretty good at sharing. Within no time we're all enjoying a late second wind, the kitchen alive with chat. Everyone's talking, no one's listening, no one really cares, tomorrow all will be forgotten.

The evening rolls on, Madame HiFi offering up all manner of nibbles though no one can relate to food anymore. Zsa Zsa keeps the rum flowing whilst simultaneously commandeering the music, never letting a song reach the halfway point, ever impatient to spin as many tunes as possible, mainly dub and reggae, then the odd track of his own, stuff he's working on, demanding a reaction in his cheeky, charming way.

I'm trying not to notice that dawn is upon us, bringing with it a sense of unavoidable guilt and one by one, people begin peeling away. The chatty guy went a while back after a text came in, a better offer, a better party. Chris and Fats are now leaving, so just me and my hosts remain. The conversation has somehow moved on to Tigger.

"He fackin' loves a wind-up," states Zsa Zsa.

"Yeah. . ."

I hold back, not really wanting to go into any of our shit, most especially at this hour.

"We gotta fink of a way of getting him back. Play him at his own game."

"Whenever he winds me up, I just bring up his voting record," I splurt out, without thinking.

Madame HiFi instantly glares at me, eyes widening. Zsa Zsa stops in his tracks, then shakes his head, confused.

"What d'ya mean by that?" he interrogates.

Shit shit fuck! He doesn't know does he. Did I know he didn't know? I'm not sure about anything anymore.

"I didn't mean nothing," I say, trying to gently dismiss it, move the conversation on. "Quite a night, eh?"

Zsa Zsa ignores me as he paces up and down, occasionally flashing me an intense look, before spinning on his heel like a gangster Poirot, piercing into my brain with his beady eyes.

"Did he vote fackin' Tory?"

I feel cornered, caught in his search light as he studies every line on my face like some south London Stasi officer. I don't answer, just shrug my shoulders, defeated, unable to maintain any pretence.

"I fackin' knew it! I knew he was a closet fackin' Tory!"

Madame HiFi bursts into fits of giggles.

"What a cunt!" Zsa Zsa spouts.

Oh Jesus, what have I fucking done?

Madame HiFi is now whooping with laughter whilst Zsa Zsa paces around his kitchen, like a boxer readying for a fight. I think I've told you that he was once a boxer. The best part is the reason he stopped: a punch on the nose would kick off a sneezing fit. Now, I don't watch the sport, but I'm pretty sure sneezing in the ring would be a significant handicap. All of this might be bollocks of course, as it all came from Zsa Zsa and he gets a kick out of spewing out spurious facts, see who takes the bait.

"Wait 'til I fackin' see him!"

Oh, shitting hell.

"Zsa Zsa. Both of you. You can't say nothing!" I plead.

"Good luck with that," Madame HiFi chuckles, nodding in Zsa Zsa's direction, who's still pacing the kitchen as if he's looking for something to smash.

"Please, mate, our friendship's already on a knife-edge. We had a bit of a breakthrough tonight. This could completely scupper it."

Zsa Zsa stops pacing, looks at me and nods. Slightly noncommittal, but he's knows there's bad blood between us and I think I've driven the point home firmly enough.

We have a final smoke, a cup of tea and some more of Zsa Zsa's musical choices; Paranoid London with Clams Baker on vocals and Mark Stewart's solo stuff recorded with Adrian Sherwood. The morning sun is now beaming onto the kitchen table and the conversation's grinding away. They both insist I stay and I'm in no position to argue, so escort me to their Marxist guest room where I promptly pass out, fully clothed.

Chapter Thirty-Six

Crispy Fish Fingers, Hungry Cats, Terrible Texts

You can't be splashing, you got no fins
You're getting salty, you ain't a fish
You're getting shirty
Your cheeky cuffy
Getting dragged 'round by your sleeves
"OBCT" – Sleaford Mods

I am gently awoken by the smell of cooking and the sound of music – the sound of Rush to be precise, not exactly Sunday morning hangover music. Madame HiFi likes Rush and Zsa Zsa's obsessed with them. Not me, our paths diverge on this one, but since it's Zsa Zsa and Madame HiFi's gaff, I cannot veto their musical choices, something

I am constantly accused of, particularly by my kids, on account of me banning Capital Radio, which is surely evidence of good parenting, like not buying them KFC or letting them date Tories.

Even though it physically hurts to do so, I lift myself out of bed and head for the bathroom, using my finger as a toothbrush, momentarily feeling like a student (even though I was only ever a pupil). I head downstairs towards the noise and aroma. My thoughts are foggy, fragmented flashbacks of the night before rattle through my head offering up nothing but confusion. Quite apart from the terrible music, something is bugging me. . .

"D'ya like fish fingers?" asks Zsa Zsa.

Wasn't quite ready for that question.

"Er. . . yeah, more than I like fucking Rush," he laughs, which quickly turns into a coughing fit. He's also ropey.

"We need a shop, it's all we've got," adds Madame HiFi.

Zsa Zsa's coughing subsides and he pokes around in the grill where he's cooking an entire packet of fish fingers.

"Sleep well?" asks Madame HiFi.

"I think I actually died and reanimated about ten minutes ago. Must've been the tasty aroma."

"He insists on grilling them but always smokes the place out."

"The *only* way. Crispier," asserts Zsa Zsa.

"I have to hide the bloody smoke alarms."

"Very considerate, that might have finished me off."

"Tea?" asks Madame HiFi.

"Aw, yes please."

I sit down at the kitchen table and retrieve my phone. It's dead.

"What time is it?"

"Just gone twelve," replies Madame HiFi. "Give me that, I'll charge it for you."

I hand it over.

"Hmm, so four hours sleep. Gonna hate myself by Tuesday."

"That's why Chris OC calls it 'Suicide Tuesday'," adds Madame HiFi.

"Looking forward to that," I shrug.

"'Ere ya go, this'll sort ya out," interrupts Zsa Zsa, placing a large plate of fish fingers on the table.

He then rifles through his fridge for appropriate condiments, returning only with some fancy mustard, Dijon with a hint of honey - pretty middle-class for a revolutionary.

"Want some? We ain't got nuffin' else."

I look at him and the mustard he proffers.

"Why not?"

I bite into the crispy breadcrumb coating to the moist, flaky, white fish. It tastes like heaven.

"Wow!"

Even the mustard strangely works. I must still be pissed.

"Nice ain't they?"

Okay, so we're not the 5,000 and Zsa Zsa isn't Jesus, but he looks well-pleased with himself. Perhaps it's the circumstances of their arrival or the fact that I'm craving carbs, in need of sustenance, but these really are the best fish fingers I've ever tasted. Seriously, I'm having a fish finger epiphany.

"They're fuckin' amazing."

From this moment on all my fish fingers will be grilled, so if you get nothing else from reading this, you can take Zsa Zsa's fish finger cooking tip away and for that and that alone, your life will be improved (unless you're a vegan). Or, you could just read the cooking instructions on the back of the packet.

After breakfast and my third cup of tea, I decide to leave my lovely hosts to their Sunday, bid farewell and head for the nearest station.

30TH JULY 2017, HOME

I step through the door I had left 20 hours earlier and feel utterly wrecked. I put on some mellow music and crash out on the couch.

I'm awoken some hours later by my needy cat padding my stomach, a little too forcefully, claws fully out. She's probably hungry. She's definitely hungry. I sit up and check my phone. It's already 8 p.m. and I feel a wave of guilt over my neglect of the non-human I live with. As I drag myself to my feet and shuffle to the kitchen, I'm thinking about my chat last night with Tigger. It feels like we both shouldered some responsibility. Did we burst the boil and squeeze out the poison? Maybe we can now be mates again? Get back to our old escapades, those "anything can happen" nights out. I hope so.

I'm physically wasted, but hungry, so make myself some pasta. As it's simmering away on the hob, I have a flashback to my chat with Alex Sebley the previous evening. . .

A glass of wine would be good. A nice healing glass of red. Just the one. I settle in front of my laptop with my wine and pasta to begin writing. I'm not entirely sure what or how or where it will even go, but I resolve not to overthink it, just vomit it all up like a good old-fashioned exorcism. I begin slowly at first, tapping away on my keyboard, filling the blank screen with words and before I know it, I've lost all sense of time.

My phone vibrates on the work surface as a message comes in. Maybe it's Tigger. Perhaps a sign that last night did mean something. I grab my glass and walk over to the counter, pour myself another then lean back on the counter as my cat rubs forcefully against my legs, making certain I'm aware of her presence. Shit, I still haven't fed her! I take a gulp of wine, grab my phone and check who's been texting. It's from La:

Dave, thank you so much
for getting my drunken
self home last night.
You're a total star bar!

Well, that's nice. The cat is still working my leg. I reach for her food and finally fill the bowl. My phone vibrates again. Another text. This one's from Tigger. As I read, my legs involuntarily buckle and I lose my footing, sending the cat's food bowl scuttling across the kitchen floor along with the cat in a furry ball of frightened panic. I grasp the counter and inelegantly pull myself to my feet. I read the text again:

Thanks for the stab in the
back re your little chat
with Zsa Zsa last night. . .
proper mate you are.

"What the fuck?" I say out loud to no one but the cat.

I flashback to my chat with Zsa Zsa and Madame HiFi in the wee hours and then it hits me. Oh fucking hell! I had somehow blocked it out like an inconvenient memory. Fucking Zsa Zsa! Couldn't keep his big mouth shut, couldn't wait to wind him up. Was it such a big ask to expect him *not* to confront Tigger about the fact he'd voted Tory? Let me think? Zsa Zsa – a self-proclaimed Marxist, only holidays in communist countries, especially Cuba, Meatraffle's debut album artwork's a portrait of Lenin painted by Zsa Zsa himself. He's not just left, he's left of left – fascist left. Furthermore, he and Tigger frequent the same local and Zsa Zsa is a mischievous fucker to boot. This was perfect intel for him, so expecting him to keep a whopper like this to himself was a pretty tough call and clearly, he had totally failed. Nonetheless and politics aside, he's still a cunt for doing it.

I need to deal with this head-on. I try calling him. Pick up. Pick up, you fucker. It goes to voicemail.

Jesus, am going to have to try and explain myself via text? I hate heavy talk via text. It's impossible when tensions are high, all intonation added by the reader, nuancing the words with unintended meaning. Oh fuck, here we go:

Tigger, I am genuinely sorry
for politically embarrassing you
– it was not intentional at all,
we were just very drunk and
shit. If it's any consolation,
Zsa Zsa has mates that STILL
vote Tory. At least (thanks to
Sadie – cos I couldn't convince
you), you have seen the fucking
light! Now stop sulking ya cunt
and have a listen to this:

I send him a clip of I, Ludicrous's brilliant single, "It's All Free". An attempt at normalisation.

He replies:

You don't get it, I'm not
politically embarrassed,
I'm spitting fire. I've been
let down by someone I trusted,

who I thought was a brother.

No drama, just empty.

Oh man, this is all way out of hand. I try calling him, re-peatedly, but every time I do it just rings to his voicemail. Not switched off, just not picking up. I text again:

Ffs take my call dude,

let's have a proper chat

After a long pause, he replies:

Here's a song for you. . .

He sends a link to "Broken Heart" by Spiritualized. I mean seriously, is he taking the fucking piss? Perhaps it's all a wind-up. Levity, that's it. Must be. I mean we were close, but not exactly lovers. This is all a stupid joke. Delib-erately over the top, I bet he was cackling to himself when he sent it. I text back:

Now you're overdramatising

things a tad dude, doncha think?

I assume he'll just roll along with the banter.

Fuck you.

I try calling again. No answer. I send another text:

What's wrong with talking?

No response. Nothing. He's deadly serious.

I stare at all the texts in stunned silence. I cannot believe it. How can I have been such an idiot? What was I thinking? Was I even thinking? Had this pent-up resentment some-how bubbled to the surface in an outwardly innocent slip-up, a drink-fuelled faux pas, some passive-aggressive shit-stirring? Had I subconsciously put the worm on the hook hoping Zsa Zsa would bite? Me and my big stupid drunken mouth!

All along, I had convinced myself, no doubt convinced you, that I was the innocent target of Tigger's weakness of character, his mistrust of me, his utter fickleness and of course Sadie's malevolent influence. Not me and my inability to accept change, to go with the flow, demanding more from Tigger than he could possibly give and in the process pushing him further away, yet all the while casting myself as the blameless victim. I should know this about myself, it's a pattern in my life, I can blame my ADHD but that's just a fucking cop-out, an easy moniker to hide behind, excuse myself and make me less culpable.

I should know all this, my ability to bury the hurt, outsmart my true feelings and intellectualise them away. Then, as if from nowhere, when my fractious brain is pickled with alcohol or whatever, they rise to the surface, take control of my mouth and wreak havoc. Whatever the reason, whatever the motivation, my mouth ran away with me and hung a friend out to dry to someone he loved and respected.

After all this and all that has happened, I've just hammered home the final nail in the coffin of our friendship. It is finally over.

What a total fucking cunt I am!

Photos: Batch Three

Dan Carey (Producer, Speedy Wunderground Founder), Streatham, 2019
Photograph by Holly Whitaker

Squid: Ollie Judge, Labelmates Festival, Moth Club, Hackney, 2019
Photograph by Anna Yorke

Black Midi: Morgan Simpson, Electrowerkz, Islington, 2018
Photograph by Anna Yorke

Black Midi: Geordie Greep & Cameron Picton, Electrowerkz, Islington, 2018
Photograph by Anna Yorke

PVA: Josh Baxter & Ella Harris, SXSW fundraiser, Windmill Stage, 2020
Photograph by Anna Yorke

Pink Eye Club's Haydn Davies, Windmill Stage, 2020
Photograph by Lou Smith

Background: Clams Baker, Jack Medley & Stage Invader. Foreground:
head-locking security goon, End Of The Road Festival, Dorset, 2019
Photograph by Lou Smith

Warmduscher's Ben Romans-Hopcraft, Test Pressings Festival, Hackney,
2019
Photograph Anna Yorke

Warmduscher, Village Underground, Shoreditch, 2019
Photograph Anna Yorke

Jack Medley (on glitter cannon), La Staunton & members of Horsey, 93 Feet
East, Shoreditch, 2018
Photograph by Lou Smith

Beth Soan & Dave Ashby leading Jack Medley's Procession, Brixton Hill,
2019
Photograph by Lou Smith

Jack Medley's Megarave Procession, Brixton Hill, 2019
Photograph by Lou Smith

Gavin Mysterion, La Staunton & Chris OC, Windmill Beer Garden, 'Jack Medley's Megarave', 2019
Photograph by Lou Smith

Misty Miller & Gaby Lydon, Windmill Beer Garden, 'Jack Medley's Megarave', 2019
Photograph by Lou Smith

Trixie Malixie (Scud FM/Superstation Twatville), Windmill Stage, 2019
Photograph by Lou Smith

Cat Yong (MeU), Windmill Stage, 2019
Photograph by Lou Smith

Tiña: Josh Loftin & Calum Armstrong, Windmill Stage, 2020
Photograph by George Cannell

Madonnatron performing as Jack Medley's Secure Women, Windmill Stage, 'Jack Medley's Megarave', 2019
Photograph by Lou Smith

Phobophobes (L to R): Chris OC, Jack Fussey, Bede Trillo and Jamie Taylor,
Windmill Stage, 'Jack Medley's Megarave', 2019
Photograph by Lou Smith

P

SLEAZE: Dave Ashby & Jerome Alexandre, 'Jack Medley's Megarave',
Windmill Stage, 2019
Photograph by Lou Smith

Meatraffle: Tingle and Zsa Zsa Sapien, Windmill Stage, 'Jack Medley's Megarave', 2019

Photograph by Lou Smith

Fat White Family: Lias Saoudi, Windmill Stage, Meatraffle SXSW Fundraiser, 2020

Photograph by Anna Yorke

Fat White Family: Saul Adamczewski (seconds before wacking lairy member
of Hard Fi with fretboard), Windmill Stage, 'Jack Medley's Megarave', 2019
Photograph by Lou Smith

Baxter Dury, Shepherds Bush Empire, Hammersmith, 2018
Photograph by Anna Yorke

Reprezent FM presenter Glory, with Prince Harry, Meghan Markle & Finn
Whitehead, Reprezent FM studio, Pop Brixton, 2018
Photograph by Dominic Lipinski (Getty Images)

Team Lose-it (and Helpers): Cheryl Rad, Beth Soan, La Staunton & Fin
Doran, Hammersmith Apollo, 2019
Photograph by Dave Thomson

Jamming in the Shed, with: Hank Dog, Jessica Winter, Lias Saoudi, Nathan Saoudi & Saul Adamczewski' s hand/guitar, Windmill Shed, 'Jack Medley's Megarave', 2019
Photograph by Lou Smith

Mural painted by Charlotte Aggett (Madonnatron) to commemorate south London legend Jack Medley, Windmill Shed, 2019
Photograph by Lou Smith

PART TWO

LATER...

Chapter Thirty-Seven

King Midas, Prophetic Moths and the Legendary Swordsman

The dawn is on fire
Bacteria divides
A black colossus gallops
Across the three shires
"Black Hanz" – The Moonlandingz

5TH JUNE 2020, KITCHEN TABLE, HOME
Before this virus forced its doors to close for what feels like an eternity, the Windmill was the gift that kept on giving, all manner of emerging new talent began their musical

journey from this tiny stage in this breeze-block carbuncle of a venue.

We had a very worrying time last year when the usually jovial Seamus became critically ill, shrinking before our eyes in what seemed like a matter of weeks before disappearing from view completely. Hospitalised. The lovely Kathleen often seen returning to the Windmill late at night, tears just beneath the surface of her thousand-yard stare. Then, after ten tense weeks involving two major surgeries, Seamus came through and everyone exhaled. He and Kathleen are so utterly integral to this place, rare beasts in pub-land, as few would put up with all the madness, mayhem and melodrama – all vital ingredients in the creative energy of this place. Within six months, Seamus was back to his bonny old self and Kathleen has been walking on air ever since. Order in the universe restored. What a time to be alive. . .

Then along comes Covid-19, fucking up everything in its path.

If we were still inhabiting that *other* world, the *old normal*, I would at this very moment be getting drunk with my mates in Brockwell Park, just south of Brixton, at what was to be the very first *Wide Awake Festival*. The bill was going to be amazing, some of the finest emerging new music this city has to offer. Keith Miller who runs Bad Vibrations, the event's promoter, had included a Windmill Stage in acknowledgement of where much of this festival's line-up had begun life.

On top of this, the annual music and media festival, South by Southwest (SXSW) was so blown away by Windmill acts in previous years, the organisers invited Tim Perry over to Texas to curate a Windmill-themed venue. So, this March Tim was all ready to treat Texas to Meatraffle, PVA,

Black Country/New Road, Sorry, Drinking Boys and Girls Choir (a Korean band he's rather fond of), not to mention his pet favourites HMLTD. For everyone involved this was a really big deal, but sadly other forces were now at play and no one really knew quite how far this virus had travelled, causing this significant event to be cancelled only days before it was due to commence. Now, along with heaps of other festivals across the world, its future hangs in the financial balance.

The Windmill's stature has increased over these past three years as it finds itself on the receiving end of considerable attention from a variety of quarters. Unsurprisingly, next-big-thing-goal-hanger Steve Lamacq now claims the place to be his own. In fact, he took over the venue for a celebration he held last year with IDLES headlining. It was a private affair, I certainly wasn't invited and don't suppose I'll be at the next. He also ended his "Homecoming Tour" at the Windmill as part of "*Independent \Venue Week*" (*IVW*). He even interviewed Tim in The Shed.

IVW is a wonderful enterprise, founded by Sybil Bell with support from the Arts Council, though it would be entirely understandable if you'd mistakenly thought it was Lamacq's innovation. No, his is the snappily titled "*Wear Your Old Band T-Shirt To Work Day*", or *WYOBTSTWD* for short.

Now, along with other pubs, bars and venues across the UK, the Windmill's ongoing viability is at the mercy of this virus, surviving only on crowdfunding and the goodwill of a loyal clientele involved in all manner of fundraising projects, unable to contemplate coming back to a world without it. For when Rishi Sunak was throwing *our* money around in frightened panic, the Windmill fell through the cracks in the funding criteria, simply because of its trading style.

Despite all this recent attention, the Windmill has resisted any attempts at gentrification, except for the addition of a gold tinsel stage backdrop and *Ladies* and *Gents* signage above the toilets, both of which are reassuringly counterbalanced by the interior of the gents which remains the same as it ever was: grim.

After fifteen years pulling pints, head barman and all-round good guy Piotr decided to hang up his beer towel and return to Poland, assured of a better quality of life than this country now has to offer, Third World poverty blossoming on every urban austerity-deprived corner. This was a worrying turn of events, as humanity-hating Toby took over as head barman. Yet, something strange happened, something quite unexpected: Toby became nice. I've since had an opportunity to get to know him better when he joined a group of us for a gig at the Social in Soho. Turns out, without the demands of punters on his back, he's a lovely fellow with a wicked sense of humour. Why hadn't I seen this before?

Tim Perry is still the same cantankerous yet loveable train driver, still putting on an endless stream of new acts, still surprising us with special one-offs and unadvertised word-of-mouth gigs, hosting bands that have long since outgrown the venue. Even Kae Tempest turned up in 2018 for a rare, intimate performance. I stupidly asked Tim how he'd managed to pull it off. He stared at me, poker-faced.

"It was our shared love of HMLTD," he cackles as he strides away.

The real reason, I later discover, was because the person behind tonight's billing, including post-punk Dublin upstarts Fontaines D.C. was Speedy Wunderground maestro,

Dan Carey. You can hear Kae Tempest perform an exclusive song "My New Love" on a compilation called *Live at the Windmill*, recorded that night and released during Lockdown through *Bandcamp*. If you haven't bought it already you should; one of the many collaborative initiatives to help raise a fighting fund to meet the demands of an unforgiving landlord.

Whilst Fat White Family drew focus on all this, it was Tim Perry's extensive musical knowledge and keen ear for emerging talent that gave it all a sense of cohesion. Now, Dan Carey has managed to whip the whole thing up into a frenzy. He was always a big champion of the place, harbouring a long-held fantasy that he'd one day recreate this charming fleapit of a venue at *Glastonbury Festival*, whose 50th anniversary has also been cancelled along with the rest of our future.

Up until lockdown, the Windmill has arguably been Dan's main recruiting ground, having produced Black Midi, Squid, Black Country, New Road, Tiña, Goat Girl, Lazarus Kane, PVA, Sinéad O'Brien, Fontaines D.C. and two albums for Warmduscher, many of whom honed their craft here.

Dan has a keen eye for left-field talent and his Speedy Wunderground label has gained a certain character; a unique flavour, an attitude, like Fast or Factory or Creation, yet much like the whole south London thing, there's no dominant genre.

It's not a signature Dan brings, but an approach, part of which is to pile a band into a dark laser-filled smoky bubble of urgency, with a non-negotiable curfew and an agreement to include a Swarmatron somewhere in the mix. All of which spawns a freshness and spontaneity often lost in the formulaic approach of modern production methods.

Warmduscher's recent album *Tainted Lunch* took just four days to nail down, *Whale City* only three.

Earlier this year, at the 2020 Music Producers Guild Awards, Dan walked home with "Producer of the Year" award – the top accolade. He wasn't expecting it, didn't really think anyone was taking that much notice; this mad professor of music furrowing into the night, tossing musical gems over his shoulder, rarely coming up for air.

He told me last year he'd missed Girl Band when they toured their album *The Talkies* (a band he absolutely loves), as he lost himself inside a guitar loop for a new Goat Girl track he'd been working on. He fully intended on making the gig, but all of sudden it was 2am, so he napped a few hours in the studio, woke up and continued with the track. Dan is no industry whore, he just follows his nose, trusts his instincts and musicians love recording with him. Real success in life is when the world clocks on to something you're already passionately doing and now every Speedy Wunderground release is met with a whirlwind of buzz, for Dan Carey's at the top of his game, south London's very own King Midas.

It's not just Speedy Wunderground's domain, however, there's countless other acts who've made their name at the Windmill over recent years. Like, for example, Nuha Ruby Ru, a fascinating artist with a powerful voice and a mesmerizing, sometimes terrifying stage presence. Or Sleepeaters, a more straight-up rock and roll outfit, heavily influenced by The Gun Club and The Scientists. Or Deep Tan, a trio of three uniquely interesting women, with their own brand of cold-wave electronica. Or Lynks Afrikka, who've unexpectedly found a receptive audience at the Windmill for their sharp-tongued, straight-baiting disco-pop. Or Sweat and their thinking person's funky electropop, formed by brothers Dante and Gamaliel Traynor. Not a new act, but their involvement in this collective is significant, indeed their musicianship can be heard throughout much of Fat White Family's more sonically adventurous third album, *Serfs Up*.

We also have the likes of Peeping Drexels, Great Dad, Pet Grotesque, Lazarus Kane, Superstation Twatville, Sonic Eyes and Children of the Pope, all of whom are uniquely fabulous and worthy of further investigation, the latter of which include two Brazilians (João and Fells), who literally upped sticks to move here after falling in love with it all from afar, courtesy of Lou Smith's YouTube channel.

Pink Eye Club have also been playing tons of gigs, a solo vehicle for Haydn Davies, a man who three years ago had so little confidence, he could not stand without stooping, or look you in the eye when talking. Despite this, he summoned up sufficient fortitude to launch his own one-man-show, in which he delivers droll observations on the challenges of modern life, all set to disco samples and club beats. It's been so heartening to see Haydn thrive at the Windmill, no longer stooping or socially awkward, he's now hosting his own nights and Pink Eye Club have become a line-up staple. It is also rumoured that Blang Records have been eyeing him up.

Legendary beat poet and raconteur Mr Patrick Lyons has surrounded himself with a talented bunch of musicians, calling his band MeU and if you can imagine the bastard love child of Howling Wolfe and Allen Ginsberg backed by The Aristocats, you'll be roughly in the right terrain. Plus, there is a cat in MeU, not a feline creature, but Cat Yong, their visually striking, flamboyant bass player. We met at

Test Pressings Festival last year in Warmduscher's mosh pit and have remained friends ever since. MeU's line-up also includes Harry on sax, another character I continually bump into at various gigs across London. In MeU, Patrick Lyon's has single-mindedly pursued his true passion, not allowing his age or his health to slow him down, his band providing the perfect accompaniment for his beatnik prose. If you like Sun City Girls, then check out MeU, who prior to all these lockdowns were performing regularly to a very receptive audience, for its simply impossible not to love this man.

Another great act to have emerged from the Windmill's primordial soap is Tiña and their forthcoming album *Positive Mental Health Music* is going to be Speedy Wunderground's first full-length album release (if we ignore their single compilations). As a live experience there is beautifully vulnerability about them with subtle shades of Daniel Johnston, Nirvana and The Lemonheads in the mix. Josh Loftin, their pink Stetson wearing singer, has a voice capable of switching from Sylvester falsetto to full-on Cobain roar in an instant. He has also, somehow, made the colour pink their brand.

Phobophobes are still working on their second album, whilst guitarist Jack Fussey plays guitar in an another interesting band called Muck Spreader, currently making waves on 6 music with their broody spoken word prose. A sound that is becoming a genre in itself with the likes of I Like Trains, TV Priest, The Lounge Society, Sinéad O'Brien, The Yard Act, The Cool Greenhouse (one of a handful of bands that can pull off a Fall cover) and the Ukrainian folk-tinged, existential melodrama of Black Country, New Road.

PVA's warm-up party for the already cancelled SXSW was the last gig I dare attend before the fear of the Covid-19 was too overwhelming to take further risk in the name of entertainment. Much like A Certain Ratio or LCD Soundsystem, PVA make organic dance music with a post-punk twist and as a live spectacle they are something to behold, guaranteed to get your granny on her feet. Lauren Laverne has been frequently spinning their remarkable Dan Carey produced debut "Divine Intervention" on her 6 Music morning show and it's abundantly clear that PVA are destined for greatness. I hope so, because I have a wager with Josh Baxter, co-founder of the band, they'll be headlining *Glastonbury*'s dance tent and if I win, he has to sort me a triple A pass. I'm not sure if Josh quite realised there was no upside for him in this bet.

Black Midi have been wowing everyone with intense live shows having played their first gig at the Windmill to a largely empty room. I've seen them a number of times and whilst their jazz inflected math rock is not up my musical alley, Tim Perry is utterly enthralled, having championed their cause from day one.

Meatraffle decided against releasing (or even writing) a second album, leaping straight to their third, entitled *Bastard Music* "on account of the music's indeterminable origins," so claims Zsa Zsa.

In bright yellow letters on the back of his parka are the words "I Got Remixed by Andrew Weatherall", which is true, as the legendary swordsman cooked up a dub version of "Meatraffle on the Moon", which turned out to be one of his final collaborations. An honour for sure, of which Zsa Zsa has not been shy at letting the world know.

Though who can blame him? In the true sense of the word Weatherall was a legend. His unexpected death earlier this year has almost been forgotten amongst all the legends

Covid-19 has since taken, but the impact this man had on the coalface of popular music cannot be overstated: injecting dub, samples and beats into Primal Scream's New York Dolls/Stooges influenced rock and roll. It was the moment rock fused with dance, inaugurating a cultural revolution. Ecstasy-fuelled acid house was already in full swing, but it was Weatherall who invited all the pasty-faced indie-rock kids to the party. He went on to work with everyone, from My Bloody Valentine, to St Etienne, to Fuck Buttons and finally Meatraffle, possessing a deft touch when it came to reshaping the work of others. Weatherall was never in it for the glory, consciously avoiding all that "superstar DJ" swagger, which I assume was because he preferred herbs over powder. Either way, his passing was a great loss to music and humanity.

Tim Siddall, another Windmill performer, known to all as Flame Proof Moth and accurately described as *"Mark E. Smith meets Jake Thackray,"* released an uncannily prophetic single in October last year entitled "Yes, Ban Planes"; a demand to the world that we ban air travel, shopping and find something else to do with our time.

Within six months his wishes became our new reality. . .

Chapter Thirty-Eight

Right-Wing Socialists, Public School Buffoonery, Serfdom and Servitude

The truth is an unnamed source
The truth is not available for comment at this time
The truth is an infinite playlist
The truth is not what you expected
The truth has over one hundred million views
The truth is unverified and unverifiable
"The Truth" – I Like Trains

5TH JUNE 2020, KITCHEN TABLE, HOME

This virus has properly spooked us, made worse by the fact that we've no fucking clue where the outbreaks are happening until they've already done their worst. Back in February, at the beginning of all this, the virus *was* being tracked.

Then, on the 12th of March, with a total absence of logic, justification, or science, Johnson brought all 'track and tracing' to an end, switching off the only light we had, leaving us all in the dark with an invisible, mystifying, yet brutal enemy. That a Prime Minister of a country would do this to their own citizens is profoundly disturbing.

Seems like our more paranoid fears were justified, Johnson *did* want us all to catch the virus, all part of his scientifically flawed *Herd Immunity* approach. And despite a rhetorical retreat from this loathsome position, his entire methodology is solely focused on slowing down the speed at which deaths occur, not actually preventing them from happening.

Most of us did not wait for the government to tell us when to isolate from society, as it already seemed too late. So, we hunkered down in our homes, venturing out for essentials only, avoiding humanity, hating humanity; moronic shoppers, aggressive joggers, righteous cyclists, drunken teenagers - *all* of them lacking spatial awareness. Then, the tedious ordeal of our return, carefully removing our outerwear, washing the Coronas away in the shower and cleaning our essential shopping with overpriced alcohol wipes purchased on Amazon. We turn on the TV to see much of the world in varying versions of lockdown, Saturday afternoon city centres throughout the globe, eerily deserted. The *new normal*.

Then, eleven days ago in Minneapolis, a toxic white American cop called Derek Chauvin changed all this, when he forcefully pushed George Floyd's face into the tarmac, with a knee across his neck. A move made all the more disturbing by the callous ease this disproportionate method was employed and all the more sickening by the smug satisfaction on Chauvin's face.

George Floyd, a black man suspected of using a counterfeit $20 bill at his local shop, breathlessly and politely pleads with Chauvin to stop, claiming he can't breathe, calling out for his late mother before finally gasping, "Tell my kids I love them. I'm dead."

And within minutes, he was. Murdered in broad daylight as Chauvin's colleagues casually watched on like it was just another day at the office. And it was for a US police officer, as they kill over 200 black people a year, many entirely innocent, like Tamir Rice, a 12-year-old boy with a toy gun, or Walter Scott, a 50-year-old man, shot in the back whilst running away over a faulty tail light.

Across all races they manage to notch up around 1,000 deaths a year, but when you interrogate these numbers further you discover the victims are not only disproportionately black, but twice as likely to be killed by a cop than a white suspect.

Amnesty International have for many years accused Israel's military of severe human rights abuses towards Palestinians, yet across the US, police departments have received hands-on training from them.

On top of this, they all have access to military-grade weaponry, the result of a controversial Defence Department enterprise known as the *1033 Program*, initiated by Clinton, restricted by Obama then liberated by Trump, who decided *no* weaponry should be out of bounds to the US police force. As a result, over $7 billion of excess military equipment has been sent to 8,000 local US law enforcement agencies – sniper rifles, automatics, grenade launchers, armoured vehicles – all provided freely. The US government had to do *something* with it following their retreat from Afghanistan and Iraq, the result of which is a military-trained testosterone-fuelled police force, armed to the hilt like Robocop.

Whilst many other killings have been filmed, in the case of George Floyd, the brutality was recorded by many horrified onlookers and the footage went instantly viral. Another positive example of how social media can benefit humanity, by democratising the news and enabling the dreadful visual truth to drive the narrative. Because you can be sure as eggs is eggs, if the footage had not been uploaded in real time, George Floyd's death certificate would read *very* differently and Officer Chauvin would still be on the streets of Minneapolis spreading his hate.

Protests instantly sprang up across America and the Black Lives Matter movement quickly went international, with over 2,000 protests in over 60 countries as the entire global community mobilised into action. The moment when the fear of Covid-19, our invisible enemy, was pushed aside by righteous anger at the visible enemy, the unrelenting pandemic of institutionalised racism.

George Floyd's death did not change the conversation, it just reminded the world of the one it had avoided finishing, because having a black US President did not bring an end to this struggle. As symbolically powerful Obama's inauguration was, systemic racism continued unabated under his watch and being black in America still means you're destined to be poorer, with minimal career opportunities and significantly more likely to be killed at the hands of *so-called* law enforcement.

After four days of protests – four days after George Floyd was choked to death – Officer Chauvin was arrested for manslaughter and later charged with murder. This is hopefully not the end of the story but the beginning of a brand-new chapter, the dismantling of a system that has processed 432 indigenous deaths in custody since 1991 and only produced two convictions. Yet, this time the momentum feels unstoppable and Governments are finding it hard to ignore the international outrage, all too aware that this could be a flashpoint, a spark that ignites a wider rebellion.

***

But what of the British experience? Nowadays we do not consider Ole Blighty to be racist, certainly not on a par with America. Yet the numbers speak for themselves. Black people make up 3.5% of the UK population yet represent 8% of deaths in custody and 20% of police taser use. Imagine if these cops were *all* brandishing guns? The depressing truth is black suspects are twice as likely to experience violence and brutality at the hands of the UK police.

The problem is not *just* the police however, racism is still so ingrained into our cultural perspective shaped by phony notions of patriotism, as evidenced by the ridiculous national outrage when someone spray-painted "*Churchill was a racist*" on his statue during the BLM protests. The part he played in defeating Nazism made us conveniently forget the racist bile he spewed forth throughout his entire life.

Even as recently as 2002 you lot voted him "Greatest Briton Ever", a man who wished to use the slogan "*Keep*

England White" for the Tories 1955 election campaign. So, it really should come as no surprise that we end up with his biggest fan as Prime Minister.

Johnson dresses up his own racism in public school wit and childish polemics, yet in his rear-view mirror are the carcasses of many a loathsome position and whilst you may have heard many of these already, we cannot be reminded enough:

He stole a page from Enoch Powell's "Rivers of Blood" speech referring to children within the Commonwealth as "piccaninnies", the people from the Congo having "watermelon smiles" and suggested the people of Papua New Guinea were all cannibals, for a laugh it seems, nothing more.

He spoke out *against* Britain's efforts to prevent the practice of female genital mutilation in Uganda. No one even knows why he took this position.

He accused Barack Obama of harbouring *ancestral dislike* for Britain, due to his Kenyan roots, simply because Obama suggested that Brexit might not be such a cracking idea.

Within an article on Britain's ex-colonies in Africa, published in *The Spectator* whilst he was editor, he wrote, "The problem is not that we were once in charge, but that we are not in charge anymore."

He stoked the fires of right-wing populism by suggesting women who wear niqabs look like letter boxes or bank robbers, within an article defending their right to wear them.

It took nine days before Johnson offered up a response to George Floyd's chilling death. And when Trump tweeted "when the looting starts, the shooting starts" during the BLM protests, Johnson said nothing, even after receiving a letter signed by 40 cross-party MPs imploring him to condemn Trump's glorification of violence.

Don't be fooled by that "blustering Boris" bollocks, the veneer of public-school buffoonery, it's all a sinister calculation appealing to both sides of the debate, whilst fanning the flames of Islamophobia, racism and hatred, tapping into that populist right-wing sentiment. You think he actually gives a toss where his votes come from?

And so, we hand him the keys to Number 10, because just like the people of America, we look up to these idiots, these so-called *men of the people* and sadly this country still has an unspoken deference to the elite.

***

I'm still reeling over the trouncing Corbyn suffered in last December's election which not only ruined Christmas, but sucked any semblance of joy into a black hole of despair, as I finally abandoned any vestige of hope that a more decent society might be possible.

Following this devastating result, Labour appear to have misread the tealeaves as to what had caused their support base to swell so massively, why exactly, so many young people had become politically engaged, ultimately concluding to be voteable they really need to become a bit more Tory again.

Their solution? Sir Keir Starmer; another soft-left leader guaranteed not to upset the Ruling Classes applecart. Indeed, you could not get much more Establishment than the former 'Head of the Crown Prosecution Service and Director of Public Prosecutions'. So yes, when the time comes, Starmer *will* be allowed into No. 10 and nothing will really change.

On reflection, I don't really know *what* I was thinking, caught up in the fervour like everyone else, boxed in by my own algorithmic echo chamber thinking swathes of other folk felt the same way and there was no way this cock-sucking Etonian Churchill-wannabe could ever win this election. *Of course*, people would see through all the blag, bluster and bullshit and remember all the numerous times Johnson had been an out-and-out cunt. So, the bitterest pill of all to swallow was the realisation we'd all been *played*.

It seems so long ago now, a world away from our current state of existence, but earlier this year I'd arranged to meet some friends to see Adult Entertainment's debut London show at The Social in Soho. Not an easy band to duck-duckgo, you try searching a band with *that* name playing London's red-light district.

Adult Entertainment is Adrian Flanagan' latest project, the madcap genius behind Eccentronic Research Council and Moonlandingz. Within Adult Entertainment Adrian performs as a duo with artist/poet/singer Charlotte Cannon, a live wire make no mistake, oozing so much fevered sexuality, even Prince Andrew would work up a sweat in her presence, though at 24 she's way beyond his usual proclivities.

21ST FEBRUARY 2020, THE SOCIAL, LONDON

Adrian is a lovely chap, yet he does have that old-fashioned perspective many northerners have of London's populace, stemming from the misapprehension that London is actually full of *Londoners*, like we're all a tribe, completely missing the multi-layered international magic of what this city is really about. Most of my mates live in London, but very few are *from* London (or the UK for that matter). The truth is no one gives a shit. Still, during his in-between song banter in which he makes jokes about Corrie being better than EastEnders, he barks at the audience:

"Don't tell me you all voted Brexit?"

Everyone looks on bemused, confused even. I'm standing near the stage, already a few pints deep and a strong urge bubbles up in me to correct him on the matter:

"No, mate, that was all the northerners!" I holler.

The place goes quiet, Adrian gives me a stern-faced glare, then Charlotte whoops with laughter, exclaiming, "He's right!", punching a welcome hole in the mounting tension.

It was true, though. It *was* the northerners who enabled Brexit *and* a fucking Tory landslide. It wasn't their fault, they were very cleverly groomed and just to be clear, it wasn't *all* northerners but *enough* northerners to carry Johnson to victory.

These traditional Labour strongholds, generation upon generation of Labour party voters, socialism embedded in their DNA, who'd chew off their own arm than *ever* vote fucking Tory, makes the truth of what happened so much harder to take, but with the clarity hindsight provides we can unravel the game theory at play:

It began long ago, accelerated by the refugee crisis our geopolitical wars gave rise to. The one Cameron referred to as "*swarms of migrants at the border*". For some time, they'd been shipping refugees to these already under-resourced, criminally neglected northern towns and villages, services at breaking point, a further pummelling by Tory austerity in all its various forms of bleakness, fighting even harder for a GP appointment or a place for their kid at the local school.

Who do they blame?

Not the government, that's way too abstract. No, they blame those Syrians, those Iraqis, those Romanians, those foreigners, those *Others*. We all remember the posters, an army of "migrants" marching upon us tailing back to infinity, with the simple slogan "Breaking Point". The image was a lie, it was a Slovenian border crossing, but it worked a treat and the link to immigration policy was made front and centre. To these northern socialists the simple slogan *"Take Back Control"* meant *"Send 'Em All Back"*. The term *Brexit* was filled to the brim with the same connotation, causing all those who voted Leave for socialist reasons to go into hiding for fear of being misjudged a racist.

So, when Boris enters the election with no real policy platform, just haughtily charging around the country squawking *"Get Brexit Done"*, it translated to *"Get These Foreigners Out"*. The oldest divide and rule trick in the book, for when people feel desperate, all they need is something (or someone) tangible to blame. They make the solution simple, a trick they stole from the Nazis, along with their simple messaging techniques, for it matters not they're peddling lies, with enough repetition they *become* the truth.

Whether through nurture or opportunity, the Cummings/Johnson alliance used this methodology to powerful effect, successfully breaking the Herculean knot that for generations had bound these voters to Labour. And for those who couldn't stomach crossing the floor all the way to the Tories, Farage offered up a Brexit candidate, his new and very personal rebranding, having already lost UKIP to Tommy Robinson and the ultra-right. Was it really just an off the cuff decision to only put-up Brexit candidates in non-Tory held seats? Or part of an overarching Establishment plan to stop Corbyn at all costs? Answers on a disinfected postcard please.

The other question is, why would the Establishment want Brexit? Of course this all depends upon which Establishment we're referring to here, because you can be sure of one thing, Brexit was not favoured by the neoliberal Establishment, a philosophy that still has the EU spellbound, despite the poverty it's creating and the planet it's destroying. No, we have to wind the clock back *way* further, all the way back to the old British Establishment, the ruling classes, represented by the likes of Rees-Mogg, Johnson, Cummings and of course Cameron, the tosser who set this whole shitshow in motion. He who pretended to be a Remainer yet a self-confessed Brexiteer right up to the moment he became PM – a fact the media neglected to report and one he's denied ever since.

So back to the question, *why would* the Ruling Class Establishment want Brexit?

The answer is depressingly simple. . .

Tax.

The ruling class are still mind-bogglingly wealthy and believe that tax is just for us, the proletariat, a mentality that goes back to the days of the old aristocracy, the bloodline of which is still alive, kicking and fully in charge today.

The EU had been compiling a blacklist of tax havens, an important yet grossly under-reported development during the years leading up to the EU referendum. Our government spent years indignantly arguing how it did not "*believe it fair to refer to its overseas territories as tax havens*", defending the spider's web of British "territories" spanning the globe, such as Panama and the Cayman Islands, where corporation tax is set to zero.

This is why companies such as Starbucks establish their head offices here, legally basing themselves in the UK, thus, granting themselves unfettered access to what is nothing more than a humongous tax avoidance scheme, all achieved by the use of a technique known as "offshoring".

Put simply, by ensuring their intellectual rights are held in a British territory, all it takes is a nifty bit of accounting, some overpriced licensing fees and they can push any profits into one of these tax havens, thus *legally* avoiding *any* tax.

Currently the conglomerates that make up the FTSE 100 have over 1,600 subsidiaries based in British Territories so they can sell their shit to us tax fee, upon which our government adds on a thick slice of VAT, ensuring *we* effectively pay their taxes for them.

Britain is the world's number one tax haven for globalised corporates or any revoltingly rich individuals and currently there is around £15 trillion sitting in offshore accounts around the globe, all funnelled through the UK into one of these British territories. Why this is not common knowledge only demonstrates how powerful the media is at controlling the narrative.

So, whilst HMRC spend much of their resource intimidating individuals and small business owners, using anti-money laundering rules to destroy the lives of plumbers for doing the odd cash job, or haranguing holidaymakers for sneaking too many fags through customs, they allow these aristocrats and corporate fuckpigs to get away with trillions. These laws apply to us all, but you've gotta be filthy rich to afford the structures required to employ them.

Well, the EU wanted to put a stop to this, create a more level playing field and ensure no members are rigging the game, the UK being the worst offender by a long yard (or metre). This did not go down well with the ruling class who employ the same techniques, exploiting offshore family trusts to ensure most of their wealth is not only owned outside the UK for tax purposes, but has (technically) been gifted down the family tree to ensure the next generation of useless chinless wankers avoid losing any of it to inheritance tax. To illustrate this point, our own fucking Queen has over £10 million of her personal wealth within offshore tax havens. "One does not like paying money into one's own *Revenue and Customs.*" The irony would be laughable if it weren't so sickening.

Nevertheless, when her Maj pops up on television during lockdown to offer up some scripted platitudes, over 27 million of you shit-larks tune in and the media fawn over her every word like they actually fucking matter, having seemingly forgotten her favourite son was a fully paid-up member of Epstein's paedophile Ponzi scheme, no doubt paid for by our taxes.

So back in 2013, like a good royal soldier, Cameron sent forth a missive to the European Council's President insisting these British territories should not be dragged into the EU's crackdown on tax avoidance, otherwise, they might have to do the unthinkable and share their wealth with wretched poor people. For many years previously, the UK had significantly slowed down progress, but now the game was up. The EU's legislative tanker was stopping for no one, especially not Cameron. In fact, they scoffed at his insolence, ignored his protestations and continued with their tax avoidance crackdown.

Within two years, Cameron announces an In/Out EU referendum. Funny that?

This is the true meaning of "Take Back Control" and so-called *sovereignty*, not the dog whistle racism used to win the Brexit vote and the 2019 election, but to maintain our very British territories – our tax havens. Like I said, we've all been played.

***

Before Extinction Rebellion and Black Lives Matter hit the streets, this country had lost the art of civil unrest and even when we do hit the streets, even when it feels like change is almost a certainty, all that really ends up changing is the news cycle. Okay, we're good at signing petitions as they fall into our inbox, just a few keystrokes and our names are on another meaningless list, ignored by its intended recipients, forgotten the following day. Us Brits are masters at the art of moaning, yet not only accept the Establishment shitting on us every day, we keep voting the fuckers back in so they can shit on us some more.

Whilst the French have their own problems with embedded racism, we could certainly learn a thing or two from them about resistance. They understand the power of people *en masse*, the authoritative strength of collectively giving the middle finger and bringing their entire fucking country to a halt. I guess having a successful revolution embedded in their gene memory infuses them with a certain swagger. Not here, though. After ten years of punishing austerity, in full knowledge that Johnson is not just an opportunistic chancer, but a lying, racist, incompetent bully, we reward his cuntfuckery with a landslide majority. Much like the French, we too have gene memory, just one of serfdom and servitude.

Within months of him becoming PM, Johnson not only succeeds in racking up way more Covid-19 deaths than any other country in Europe, but also ends up in hospital, allegedly fighting for his own life, just two weeks after brainlessly boasting about shaking hands with infected patients. People who are not usually religious prayed for him, though not all for the same outcome.

Then, between March and April this year, when the entire country was in lockdown, whilst the deaths were peaking, Johnson's government moved 25,000 patients out of hospitals into care homes throughout England, with the stated aim of freeing up more hospital beds. We later discover not one of these patients had been tested for Covid-19 before being admitted and we all know what happened next.

After failing to gaslight the entire Care sector into shouldering responsibility, Johnson then had the gall to proclaim that back in March he did not appreciate the virus could be spread asymptomatically. An utterly blatant huge fuck of a lie, because we all knew this to be true, it was all over the media, all on record, discussed at length within Sage meetings as far back as January. I guess it's better for the nation to judge Johnson's government as incompetent clowns than sadistic murderers and if nothing else the state benefit bill will be lower, the obvious silver lining for a morally bankrupt government.

But seriously people, you voted him in! What were you thinking? Or maybe you weren't thinking, maybe none of us were, just lab rats unwittingly compliant in a game of three-dimensional chess, engineered by sociopathic dark master and Brexit architect Dominic Cummings, a Goebbels for the digital age. A man whose ruling-class father-in-law, Sir Humphry Tyrrell Wakefield, a close friend of Prince Philip, owns a horse named Barack because it's half white and half black.

Chapter Thirty-Nine

Marxist Anthems, Glaswegian Gents, Fat Whites Soft Play

Now, you know these rules, they don't apply to me
I'm just a motherfucking bastard, as you can see
But gentlemen and ladies, I think you'll agree
You must stop fucking each other's lives up
"Hitlers and Churchills" – Country Teasers

5ᵀᴴ JUNE 2020, KITCHEN TABLE, HOME

You may recall the band No Friendz? Well, as bands often do, they imploded in vitriol. Angus went all Ziggy, sacking their guitarist Adam Brennan with Dan GB following traumatised by the psychodrama that unfolded.

Zsa Zsa swiftly came to the rescue, inviting Adam to add guitar licks to his solo performances. This coupling soon became a trio when Madame HiFi joined, adding percussion and further vocals, all of which kicked off the idea for his latest project, Scud FM. So, Zsa Zsa quickly set about recruiting further members: Gavin (of Deli Lama fame) providing percussion, keyboards and vocal support, Dan GB on drums, who'd left No Friendz after a disastrous Cabbage tour support slot that almost landed them at the wrong end of the *Me-Too* movement. Nothing came of it, but Cabbage were still smarting having only recently shaken off similar accusations. Finally, Trixie Mixie on bass (whose own band Superstation Twatville already has me smitten after hearing their debut "Vaping Monkey"). As a live experience, Scud FM are a mighty force and quite possibly the finest purveyors of Marxist pop anthems since, well, *ever*. To illustrate the point, the chorus of "Oliver Twist", their joyous and life affirming mosh pit shout-a-long, ends with the line "*But you can fuck off if you are a Tory.*"

Lias Saoudi had also been eyeing up Adam Brennan's guitar virtuosity and after a bit of road-testing, invited him into the Fat Whites as an official family member. Adam couldn't quite believe it and was totally bricking himself about telling Zsa Zsa, in fact, he asked me to do it. I declined, of course, but spent the remainder of the evening winding him up, impersonating Zsa Zsa's reaction:

"I fort you were a comrade, a bruvver. Didn't fink you'd go for the money and fame."

"Fuck off, Dave!" he would hiss.

Joining south London's premier league almost turned Adam into a cunt. I remember walking into The Shed where

I found him basking in the adoration of two young female fans, newfound attention for his newfound status.

"Dave? Get me a drink," he demanded.

"Adam? Fuck off!" I replied.

After this exchange, the girls looked at me like I was the unreasonable party, such is the nature of fandom.

Thankfully, over time, Adam calmed down and is almost back to his old sweet self, with only a tiny hint of Kanye about him. In the end, Adam managed his internal conflict by joining Fat White Family, whilst continuing his membership of Scud FM (unless, of course, the Fat Whites are touring).

Angus, on the other hand, was left standing alone, his band name prophetic, for he did indeed find himself with *no friends*. I have seen or heard little of him since, which is a shame for he's a terrific performer with so much untapped potential. I am sure he'll be back, in fact, there are already murmurings, for Angus has more than just a hint of Kanye in the mix.

Fat White Family still roll up at the Windmill to smash through some of their old classics, mainly for fun, but sometimes other reasons. After a touring hiatus lasting nearly a year, they performed in August 2018 for an incredibly special fundraiser in aid of Dale Barclay, known mostly for fronting hell-raising Scottish outfit Amazing Snakeheads. I had planned to see them play at the 2015 NME showcase in London where they were scheduled to perform alongside Palma Violets, Slaves and Fat White Family, but news came in the band had sadly split up the day before the gig.

The Glasgow music scene not only echoed but also cross- pollinated with south London, in fact Meatraffle have quite a following up there too. Dale was known for lending support to others along the way, like fellow Glaswegians Sweaty Palms. He also played guitar for the Fat Whites, replacing Saul during one of his stints in rehab.

Then, an unwelcome bolt came out the blue. Dale developed grade 4 Glioblastoma, a rare form of brain cancer. The NHS removed 90% but he needed specialist treatment to remove the remainder which had since mutated. It was a high-risk operation, unavailable on the NHS due to budget constraints, for even if your raison d'être is saving lives, you must still behave like a business with all its checks and balances.

Still, Dale praised the NHS on his GoFundMe page for all their care and treatment, but went on to say, "*I need specialist care. I am officially a customer. This is the reality.*" His survival was questionable, his options limited, but he was still young and wanted to live. This was his last throw of the dice.

Lias Saoudi and Tim Perry hit upon the idea of a benefit gig to help Dale pay for the specialist treatment he'd invested his possible continued existence in. A special event, with Shame and Peeping Drexels also on the ticket and a rare chance to witness Fat White Family perform on the tiny Windmill stage, the place which played such a crucial role in their ascendance.

The grim reaper threw down the gauntlet, the odds were not good, but Dale picked it up, gave it all he'd got and went under the knife. Days went by with no updates on his GoFundMe page. Then everything we feared was confirmed when his steadfast partner Laura St Jude posted her last update: Dale had lost his battle. Complications following surgery. We lost another great frontman. I never got to meet him but those who did all say he was a true Glaswegian gent.

This was one of a handful of gigs the Fat Whites had played since their Saul-less 100 Club gig back in 2017. To be fair, many of the Fat Whites had been involved in all manner of other projects: Adam Harmer with Warmduscher, Lias with The Moonlandingz and Saul mainly with Insecure Men, though he'd been involved with them all at their genesis. Prior to enrolling Adam Brennan, the Fat Whites added another full-time member: Alex White, classically handsome, tidy facial hair, long flowing locks and an exceptionally talented multi-instrumentalist. If Saul, Lias and Nathan were the Three Musketeers, Alex would be their D'Artagnan. Okay, this band are always shedding members and absorbing new ones, having spat out over a dozen hopeful musicians, catching up fast with their hero and departed legend Mark E. Smith. Though, Alex brings with him new instruments, assuring him a certain degree of permanency, if such a thing exists in a band such as this. The saxophone's his secret weapon, for despite the considerable efforts made by eighties sax players to destroy any credibility it once had, Alex has taken the baton from his forefathers and somehow managed to make the instrument sexy again.

The Saoudi brothers and Saul each contributed four songs to their third and more wide-reaching album *Serfs Up!*, with Nathan penning the single "Feet," a surprisingly catchy number that gets under right your skin and makes you itch, but in a good way.

Adam Harmer also contributed an even funkier track, allegedly tossed aside by Saul during the recording process. As luck would have it, Adam also plays lead with Warmduscher, so they decided to record it instead. The song?

6 Music favourite and Warmduscher's biggest hit to date "Disco Peanuts". Which just goes to prove, a good song will always find a way.

The Fat Whites also played *End of the Road Festival* in 2018, though their set was late Friday afternoon on the main stage, which is still the morning for them and so a little more subdued compared to their usual rabid performances. This is what makes their antics all the more authentic, as there's no plan or choreography, the Fat Whites just go with how they feel, even if it means Lias keeping his cock inside his pants. I mean, if it became a thing, a routine, they'd lose everything they've come to mean to us all. When Lias removes everything but his stained, saggy Y-fronts (and sometimes they come off), his utter indifference to any humiliation is compelling as if tapping into an inner yearning, a primordial need, a psychological freedom we all secretly crave.

But not this time. Something happened about halfway through the set, considerably altering the dynamic. As the band launch into the family-friendly singalong "Is it Raining in Your Mouth?", above all the bobbing heads I spot a young boy about eight years old, seemingly crowd-surfing my way. I was confused, it looked properly insane, then I clocked it was a clever illusion created by his dad bravely (and perhaps irresponsibly) charging into the frenzied mosh pit chaos, whilst holding his child horizontally above the crowd.

Fortunately, people are inherently decent, even in a Fat Whites mosh pit and gave way to ensure the young lad safe passage. It was quite funny and pretty cute, well at least at first. The idea caught fire, however, and before the song had even finished the mosh pit was awash with kids dominating the skyline caused by hordes of dads attempting to emulate this display of fatherly manhood, making it feel more like a soft-play activity centre than a Fat Whites mosh pit.

So, no unveiling of Lias's cock onstage that day - he does have his limits.

Chapter Forty

Medley's Meddling, Clams Ranting and My Fluffing

Forty minutes, record a track and get it mastered
Spent the last three nights getting plastered
I feel sick, I feel lost
But you know what?
I like to. . . lose it
"Lose It" – Jack Medley's Secure Men

Despite our city-minded reluctance to camp in a noisy field in deepest Dorset, the bill for *End of the Road* in 2018 was too difficult to ignore. Apart from all the south London bands who'd collectively invaded this west country festival that year: Fat Family White, Warmduscher, Shame, Insecure Men, Black Midi – all different, all remarkable, it was also

peppered with living legends, like John Cale, Damien Ju-
rado, Yo La Tengo and Josh T. Pearson. We were also looking
forward to some wonky pop from Ezra Furman, a good ole
punky knees-up with IDLES, and the electro-pulsing tree-
themed visual spectacle that is Snapped Ankles.

I was there with La, Finn and Lou Smith, so technically
part of the Reprezent FM crew. We were press filth, media
scum, though the only equipment I had was my phone,
so technically superfluous to requirements, an interloper,
a ligger – but fuck it, I was there with my mates and I
was in for free. As an added bonus, my bro and his partner
trekked up from farthest Cornwall to be there too, somewhat peeved I couldn't get him on the Reprezent crew list.

According to Finn, we bottled lightning that year and
he's not wrong. These things can go tragically wrong when
a disparate group is thrown into the domestic intimacy
of camping together, witnessing more of a person than is
comfortable and from which some friendships never re-
cover. Not this time, though, no tantrums, hissy fits or politics, we just effortlessly clicked and developed a kind of
hive mind, albeit with intoxicated bees. All the revelry was
scheduled around professional duties, several band interviews had been lined up for La to undertake. Lou was to
film, Finn direct and quite by accident a role developed for
me, that of *Interview Fluffer*.

Just to be clear, this did not involve me having to maintain other men's erections between takes, but it did involve
my mouth. At the beginning of each interview, Finn and
Lou would fiddle with their hardware, as La paced around
summoning up questions from the ether. She's never prepared, but if she *were* organised it would be at the expense
of her lively tension, for the main reason La comes over so

natural as a presenter is because she *always* wings it. So, whilst everyone's pissing about it can start to feel uncomfortable as band members hover about, awkwardly waiting and I'm just hardwired to prevent social unease, so I fill the void with chat, banter, any old bollocks, it doesn't matter, so long as it relaxes the people I'm with, because if they're relaxed, so am I.

It soon became apparent my inane blatherings did appear to help band members loosen up, coaxing them into a chattier mode of being. My fluffing began with Shame, (a lovely bunch of spirited hedonists), followed by Snapped Ankles (my particular highlight, as Paddy and Micky are just funny as fuck). Also, Bristol punks IDLES (who after the interview covered my copy of *Joy as an Act of Resistance* in lewd graffiti), then finally, Ezra Furman (more on this strange encounter later).

Now, a quick word on IDLES, since they've been on the receiving end of quite a bit of flak from a variety of quarters, particularly their singer Joe Talbot, who is a lovely fellow but made the decision to take the self-righteous virtue-signalling baton from Chris Martin, on loan from Bono who'd stolen it from Sting. Now, whilst I cannot disagree with much that has been said about Talbot and his band, I've seen them play live a number of times, so here's my take. It is quite possible that *some* of their audience might just as easily have been EDL supporters had they happened upon a different, more right wing flavoured punk. So, it is surely a good thing that Talbot's stomping anthems have them chanting along to songs concerning the difficulties of toxic masculinity or why immigrants might actually make good mates. Okay, subtlety is not part of Talbot's schtick and he does have a tendency to crack open his woke-filled nuts with a wrecking ball, but as a live experience they are undeniably infectious, throwing everything they've got into every performance. They even made a *Jools Holland's Later. . . Special* unexpectedly special. So, for me, despite their crass messaging and the fact many of their songs turn into spelling lessons, there's something wonderfully joyous to witness their entire audience bouncing up and down chanting *"My best friend is an alien!"*

Still, as good as they are live, when it comes to punk attitude, they could not hope to reach the heights of one particular act the festival offered up that year. An utterly unique gig experience that felt historic, like the Pistols playing 100 Club, or Joy Division at Pips Disco: and a shared memory furthering the friendship bonds developing between us.

31ˢᵀ AUGUST 2018, END OF THE ROAD, DORSET

We are inside the Tipi Tent before the band, before the crowds and it's so bloody bright in here that I've had to put my shades back on. Have we screwed up our timings and somehow missed them? I check my phone but the screen's blank. No, it's not – I'm wearing sunglasses. I lift them onto my head. Only 1:20 a.m., 10 minutes early. So why are the main lights still on? It's more like a village hall after bingo night than a rock venue about to play host to Warmduscher, one of the most anarchic bunch of musical psychonauts on the circuit, a band which over the course of the past year have become one of my favourite live acts, even equalling the Fat Whites.

A kind of south London supergroup, constituent parts from Childhood, Paranoid London and Fat White Family members, originally created onstage with no rehearsal when

Saul Adamczewski helped Clams Baker fulfil a gig commitment after his previous band Black Daniel had fallen apart.
This irreverence and their collective ability to not give a flying fuck about anything has enabled them to hit upon a
sound that is uniquely their own. A very different live experience to the Fat Whites, which can be like a night in Bedlam. Warmduscher just hype it all up into a riotous party,
satisfying your intellect whilst making you wanna dance –
feel-good music with a knowing wink. Yet much like the
Fat Whites, Warmduscher also break the fourth wall, but
instead of piling into the audience, they invite the audience to pile onstage and become part of the show. From a
bunch of mates having a piss about, they have morphed
into a musical tour de force and *Whale City* is my album
of the year – a musical soup of crunching riffs, sleazy funk
and garage soul, over which Clams Baker recounts tales of
an anarchic mythical city at the decadent fag end of the
American dream. It just blows away the blues, kickstarts
the dopamine and makes you wanna party – it really is *that*
good.

Zsa Zsa Sapien played a small but important role in their
ascendance following a session with 6 Music's Marc Riley
earlier this year. The ex-Fall bassist asked for some band
tips and Zsa Zsa suggested getting Warmduscher in for a
session, which Riley did just a few weeks later, an experience that blew him away, not just the session but also the
surreal madness of this loveable bunch of lunatics. He was
also heartily chuffed when gifted an inappropriately sleazy
jingle by Dr Alan Goldfarb, the bands delightfully surreal,
unofficial publicist.

So here we all are, leaning on the metal bar in front of the
stage in the wee hours of Saturday morning waiting for the

action to begin. My bro has interpreted my text directions as to where we're positioned in this increasingly busy tent and has now joined the gang. Between the bar and the stage is a two-metre no man's land patrolled by steroid-pumped security goons. I turn to my fellow travellers, confused by this strange and unexpected environment.

"This is weird."

"What is?" asks Lou.

"All this." I point to security and the wide gap before the stage.

"Press pit?" says Lou.

"Goon pit more like," counters my bro.

I turn to the others. La appears to have zoned out, though it's hard to tell with her shades on.

"It's too fucking bright in here," I observe.

And as the words leave my mouth, the main lights dim.

"Looks like they heard you, Dave," sniggers Finn.

"Don't tell him that, he'll believe it," groans my bro.

"Was that me?" I say, only half-joking, such was my state of mind at this late festival hour.

"See what I mean?"

"All right, Dave, sort the stage lighting, too, will you?" demands La from behind her shades.

I look at her wryly and put on my best Jarvis.

"I'll see what I can do. . ."

But then, without fanfare, ceremony or any sense of occasion, members of Warmduscher appear onstage.

First to step up is the always affable mop-headed gangly stickman that is Quicksand (Adam Harmer when in the Fat Whites). He plugs in his guitar, plucks out a few notes and makes minor adjustments before banging out a few riffs. He looks over to the soundman and points to the ceiling.

He's soon joined by the handsome, dreamy Mr Salt Fingers Lovecraft, casually strolling on, fine-tuning his bass and garnering the soundman's attention, pointing to the heavens. He surely is one fine-looking man and if I were, I would for sure, no question – though fully accept that if he was, he probably wouldn't.

Next up, Lightnin' Jack saunters across the stage, takes his pew behind his kit and hammers out a few beats before looking to the soundman and also pointing skywards. Looks like they wanna be loud tonight. They begin strumming and crashing away, not really in sympathy but the odd recognisable riff to tease the crowd.

The Witherer (aka Little Whiskers) appears, bald head, full beard, black mac, incredibly cool, albeit in a slightly odd and unsettling way. He clutches his mysterious black box from which he can distort any instrument or vocal of any band member at a whim, like a god of weirdness.

Finally, Clams Baker III (to use his full title) marches onstage dressed in black, no Stetson, no Vegas costume, just a pair of shades, a baseball cap and a head full of attitude.

The crowd let out a huge welcome cheer but the band don't seem to notice us and chat amongst themselves, twanging their instruments like they're in a rehearsal space, not onstage with a lively excitable crowd waiting for the show to begin. What is happening here? Where's the grand entrance? Their keen sense of theatre? This is not what we've come to expect – apart from except perhaps at the Windmill where simple logistics make grand entrances tougher to execute.

I look around at the audience who are strangely mesmerised.

Snapping out my thoughts, I turn to La.

"What's happening?"

She looks at me smiling, dazed, her pink hair illuminated by the over lit stage.

"Dunno, Dave, I'm spangled."

So am I, we all are, certainly most of the fleshy pods of consciousness who at this late hour have peeled away from their cosy camps and travelled across the festival site before pouring into this oversized tent to bear witness to this insanely brilliant bunch of musical thrill seekers.

Then the beat kicks in and Warmduscher crash straight into "Uncle Sleepover", their sleazy ode to familial affection. The lights remain on, the sound's not great either but the band don't seem to give a toss and bang out a mighty racket all the same. Clams is in angry form, leaning into the mass of revellers, spitting rhymes like a semi-automatic. The whole tent lifts off as the moshing kicks off in earnest.

The song ends abruptly. Clams addresses the audience.

"Okay, rehearsal's over. Let's get on with the show."

The band launch into the powerful riff of "Big Wilma" and the whole tent goes wild. Various bodies pass overhead, but security intercept, successfully preventing any divers breaching their no man's land and reaching the stage.

When the song ends, Clams addresses the crowd again:

"Don't worry about them!" he shouts, pointing at the security goons. "Any of you guys wanna party? Come! Join us, you motherfuckers! You're ALL welcome!"

The stage manager is on the side-lines, gesticulating his unhappiness at this suggestion, putting his security team on notice. Why does it matter? I haven't a clue, but in that moment, sides are taken, lines are drawn and positions harden. The crowd, already in lairy form, need little encouragement, but we still get plenty from Clams hyping up the crowd like an evangelical cowboy preacher. Revellers keep trying, security continue intercepting, but the stagediving intensifies and some almost make it. Security are clearly spooked and, much like frightened dogs, they step up their aggression. The crowd respond in kind, for it's no longer about stagediving, it's a fight for freedom and liberty, a gig-based allegory for "sticking it to the man."

More security appear, the tension is palpable, this could all go very wrong and it feels so fucking great!

Then, right in front of me, this subhuman muscly goon decides to show off his manhood and security training by clasping some poor guy's neck between his legs, much like a typical white American cop's interaction with a black guy. He stands there smirking, mock whistling as he tightens his grip on this punter's neck. This poor bastard shelled out £195 to be here and is now being physically abused. If this does descend into a full-blown riot, it will not be because of the band, or the audience, but this moronic slab of meat. I take out my phone to film this fucker's abuse of power, but as I do, another goon blocks my lens with his hand. The whistling goon quickly releases the poor reveller, suddenly aware that his antics might not play well on social media.

I look around, furious, unable to get my head around all this. The crowd are really going for it now and when all the goons are momentarily preoccupied with several divers at once, I see it, a moment of opportunity; an unprotected spot right in front of us. A girl to our left is jeering at security, furious at their heavy-handed antics. I tap her shoulder.

"Wanna get up?"

I would go myself, but at my age and in my current state I might not coordinate the jump. She turns to me, smiles, then nods clearly excited by the prospect. I shout over to La.

"Hey La, give us a hand?"

Then in one elegant move, we launch the girl into the air and hope for the best. Thank Fuck. She lands centre stage, arms aloft in anarchic triumph and the entire Tipi roars with approval. The air is electric, the seal has been broken, the power has shifted and it's all so beautifully chaotic. Security are quickly overwhelmed by the sheer quantity of stage divers invading the stage. Clams is feeding on the tension, swinging the mic round his head like a lasso as he continues goading the audience, fuelling the adrenaline as the tipi transforms into a pressure cooker of hysteria.

I grab my phone and hit record; I need something to remind me this is actually happening.

Clams addresses the crowd:

"You wanna be my friend? You wanna be my fucking friend? Then come up! I said come on up!"

The stage manager is by now apoplectic, darting around the stage not even sure where or why. Then, it seems he can take no more as he marches purposefully over to the power supply and waits, readying himself for the right moment to pull the plug and bring an end to this madness. Warmduscher are onto him and don't give him a chance, crashing full tilt into the next song, leaving no space, no musical lull. The powerful, menacing riff of "I Got Friends" hits home and the audience go ape-shit as the band stretch this two-minute anthem into a ten-minute epic, with Clams ranting and hollering at the audience before very noisily and theatrically introducing each band member, aided by The Witherer and his magic box of twisted distortion.

The stage manager looks on at the sea of bodies crammed into the Tipi and then at the mayhem onstage. His face drops as he bottles it and retreats from the plug bank for fear of sparking a full-blown riot. By now, punters are darting around the stage like ninjas avoiding capture at the hands of security who've also invaded the stage. One woman takes the mic, screaming along to the throbbing riffs the band are pumping out, another reveller pings around like the metal ball in a pinball machine, skilfully avoiding capture, then twerking at the security beefcakes before bouncing away.

Saul Adamczewski has been watching from the sidelines, no longer in the band on account of having a fistfight with Clams some months earlier. Unable to contain his excitement over the madness unravelling before him, Saul throws himself at a member of security, enveloping them in a bear hug to prevent them ejecting any more punters, for anyone caught breaching this no man's land is thrown out the Tipi, never to return.

Fear not, though, help is at hand in the scurrilous form of Jack Medley, for as stage invaders are escorted out, Jack slips them all backstage passes. Well, he does until the excitement is too overwhelming and he can no longer resist invading the stage himself. The security goons are further confused when punters they've ejected come bouncing back. Clams is delighted to see Jack has made it, instantly handing him the mic whose face lights up like a child being offered candyfloss. Jack launches into his own insane version of the lyrics like a bloodhound with Tourette's as the entire tipi, already wild with excitement, whoops and cheers along. This is fucking priceless.

After their riot inducing version of "I Got Friends" they segue into "Standing on the Corner", before closing their set with a thunderous version of "Johnny's Blue Khaki". Then, as if escaping from a crime scene, they quickly vanish, leaving in their wake, euphoric revellers, baffled security and a stage manager with hypertension.

We all regroup, our minds well and truly blown. My bro is wide-eyed with confused excitement.

"Shitting fuck – that was insane!" he shouts.

"For that and that alone this festival was worth the ticket," I exclaim.

"Er, you got in for free, Dave," points out La.

"Yeah, ya fucking ligger!" pokes my bro.

"I got motherfucking friends!" I shout.

"And we've got ourselves a fluffer." La smirks.

My bro looks mystified.

"Are you shooting a porno?"

Something about his expression sets me off giggling, I'm still hyped from the gig. He rolls his eyes and pulls out his tobacco pouch.

"I need a fag, I'll see you outside, then you can tell me all about your fluffing moves."

We decide to do the same but as I turn to leave, I'm confronted by an unexpected apparition: Tigger.

Oh fuck, really? Sally had mentioned he might be coming, but until now our paths had not crossed. I'm certainly not ready for an encounter, he doesn't fit my current reality and there's fuck all to say anyway. I would sooner walk away, but that would be such a lame move and the last thing I want to do is embolden the cunt.

Fucking hell, let's do this. I make my way towards him and as I approach his face hardens with that overconfident smile, though not quite reaching his eyes. Instinctively, I offer my hand, rather formal I know, especially considering the environment, but like I said, I'm always polite and hugging would feel insincere. Tigger clasps it firmly, a proper bloke handshake.

"You all right?" I ask.

He fixes his eyes on mine, still smiling, then cocks his head.

"Yeah, I'm great."

"Good."

"So . . ."

"So. . ." I reply.

"So, you here with La, then?"

I nod. No need to justify myself to him.

"That's nice. . ."

Here we go again. . .

"Yeah, it is."

He nods his head slowly.

"You camping together?"

"Yeah. And?"

"Just asking. . ." he says with that annoying smile; raised eyebrow, knowing stare. God, I'm so fucking bored with this.

"Together, together?" he continues whilst delivering a cheesy wink.

"Seriously, Tigger, you need to fucking evolve."

Tigger cocks his head and locks onto my eyes again, an annoying trait he must believe adds gravitas to whatever shite's about to fall out his mouth.

"So, when you gonna apologise?"

I instinctively recoil.

"Are you serious? For what?"

Then, with childish superiority, he shakes his head as he slowly retreats before merging into the stragglers exiting the Tipi.

I'm frozen to the spot processing what has just happened. An arm wraps itself around my shoulders which thankfully belongs to La.

"You all right, Dave?"

"Yeah. . . I think so?"

I should really bring you up to date with the Tigger situation, though, there's really nothing much to tell. No resolution, no healing heart-to-heart, no cathartic coincidence, no mind-expanding epiphany. We both heard voices for a while, now the rest is history and since that night in July 2017, we've remained estranged. Initially, I kept bumping into him, mainly on account of Zsa Zsa's various reconciliation attempts, such was his guilt over our fallout. I guess he had no idea how divisive the issue would become and the responsibility weighed heavy on him. He would often invite me to some gig or other and when I turned up Tigger would also be there. On such occasions, Zsa Zsa would make clumsy attempts to kick off a conversation, like we're all just mates together, but it was always tense and would invariably disintegrate into a heated exchange as Zsa Zsa looked on helplessly.

"I feel like it's all my fault, Dave," Zsa Zsa would often confess, fishing for absolution.

"That's cos it fucking was, ya big-mouthed cunt."

I do not *really* blame Zsa Zsa. I've come to realise it was never about letting slip that Tigger had voted for Cameron back in 2010. He'd have found another reason, this was just an easy hook on which to justify my expulsion. When Tigger ceased communicating, it was hugely frustrating, never being able to express my version of events. I felt bruised, unheard and misunderstood. If only I could somehow right the wrong, correct the misjudgement, make everything good again. For a time, my head was muddled with theories, but it was clear we could no longer be friends, the things that we've learnt are no longer enough and the clock cannot be unwound. Over time one thing became clear to me: our friendship had become toxic and it was time to move on.

I found solace at the Windmill. I would frequently go there alone, but after a while that did not seem to matter. Once I stepped through the door there'd be Nasos, Tim, Seamus, Kathleen, Piotr, Toby, old locals like Stan, Gary, or fellow ageing music obsessives like Herman Noel, Ed King-pin or Simon Adamczewski and whoever else was about. And there was always *someone* about. I was completely at ease, everyone was just so open and friendly. It took me a while to trust that it would be okay. I guess, like we all do to varying degrees, I suffer from social anxiety. I push through it all the time. I've learnt to quickly break the "stranger danger" tension, someone has to because we're all feeling it, but really it is only theatre. Don't get me wrong, it's still me, just a version of me. We all do this. It's how we get through the day, through life. I'm as honest as I can be within this social construct, this personality, but to allow anyone beyond this point I need good cause to feel safe, yet to keep *everyone* at this distance is a tragically lonely place to be, I've learnt.

Once Tigger was out of the picture it became easier to develop friendships, being alongside his lust-fuelled madness had become an irritating social constraint, more so within the confines of the Windmill. On my own I had the freedom to really talk with people, find common ground and over time, piece by piece, trust would build.

This happened in a big way with La. Perhaps there was something we recognised in each other. She is equally wary, yet similarly adept at hiding behind a façade of witty charm and supreme confidence, scattering any social tension away at a stroke, all the while protecting her more vulnerable side from scrutiny. I didn't expect us to become mates, certainly not in the way we have and I do not claim to fully understand how or why it came to be, but the connection feels almost familial and we just seem to *get* each other. It began as gig buddies, but over time we've become closer and she's now more like a sister, albeit from another mister. Our relationship feels more emotionally real than I've found possible with guys and almost devoid of dick-swinging alpha battles, though, we occasionally have those, especially when fighting over what music to play.

La's striking, no question, simultaneously asexual and sexy, but never flirty, at least not with me. Any tension that arises infuses our friendship with a certain power, the intergender dynamic offering up new dimensions, a creative energy the very act of fucking might actually destroy. The truth is simple: she is a dear friend for whom I have heaps of uncomplicated love. When out together, we're a unit, a team, a teeny gang and even if we spend most of the night in the company of others, we have the comfort of knowing we're never alone, that we always have each other's back. We cannot imagine us being ex-friends, but we can envisage us being ex-lovers, so we've made a pact that we'll never fall out or shag each other.

"He asked me to apologise," I explain to La.

She screws up her face.

"Tigger? For what?"

"I have no idea."

"Fuck him. You don't need pricks like that in your life."

"I'm beyond it now."

She looks straight at me, unconvinced.

"But are you *really*, Dave?"

"You know what?"

"What?"

"I like that you give a shit."

The concern on La's face melts into a smile.

"Come on." She grabs my arm, nodding to the exit. "Let's find the others."

Chapter Forty-One

Festival Tent Saunas, Limp Mojos, Royal Rapists and Damn Fine Coffee

Prescribe me some time for dreaming
Prescribe me some time to waste
How I love the feeling
I just can't stand the aftertaste
"Bite the Apple" – Phobophobes

I wake up in a steamy tent, mouth so dry it is stuck together, yet I'm soaked, lying in a warm puddle on my non-
porous air bed. Have I pissed myself? Fucking hell, how

wankered was I? I mean, sure, it was a pretty messy night, the sun already out when we climbed into our tents, but this has got to be a first, my air bed transformed into a paddling pool of piss. On top of this, my bladder's achingly full and I desperately need a wee.

Now, this is confusing. How can my bladder be so full if I've already emptied it onto my air bed?

What time is it? 10:30 a.m. Shit. We're supposed to be interviewing Ezra Furman in half an hour and I'm in a sweaty tent sitting in a puddle of my own piss. I can hear a chorus of snoring and a welcome waft of coffee odour has somehow managed to infiltrate the moist air permeating my tent.

I drag myself off the air bed and smell the puddle. It's not piss. Is it rain? It hasn't rained, though. Has it? No, Jesus, it's sweat! I guess that's more bearable than lying in my own urine. Seems the intolerably hot sun transitioned my tent into a canvas pressure cooker and my body provided the only source of moisture. Judging by the amount and my sandpit mouth, I'm in dire need of some serious rehydration. I grab the jerrycan and take a large swig of what is very warm water, then wipe myself down with a damp towel before throwing on a T-shirt and shorts.

I poke my head outside. Lou's making coffee and he looks up at me, smiling.

"Mornin', Dave."

"Mornin', Lou. That's a damn fine smell happening there."

"Thought the aroma would do the trick." Lou chuckles.

"Are the others up?"

"No sign of life yet."

"What about the Ezra interview?"

"My thoughts too."

"Finn? La?" I croak pathetically in the general direction of their tents.

There's some movement emanating from Finn's tent, then out pops his wayward morning hair head.

"Oh God. . . fucking hell. . . morning."

"Sleep well?" asks Lou.

"No, my tents become a sauna."

Not just me, then. Tents aren't designed for the nocturnal existence of festival life, especially during a major planetary heatwave. Now *there's* a gap in the market for all you *Dragons' Den* wannabes.

"I'm off for a wee," I say, heading for the nearest loos. Then I turn back and holler, "Think you need to get La up!"

La loves Ezra Furman and would hate herself (and quite possibly all of us) if she missed the opportunity to interview him simply because we over-partied.

I return. Finn and Lou are drinking coffee.

"Where's La?"

"We can't wake her up." Finn laughs.

"So, we don't know if she's even alive. What if she's dissolved in her own sweat?"

"I think she's okay, I heard some movement," reassures Lou.

"She'll be well fucking annoyed if we *don't* wake her," I point out.

To be fair, La does have a sprinkling of the diva about her, which can make people somewhat wary, but I quite like that about her, maybe cos I'm a bit of one myself. I march over to her massive tent (La having the only one you can stand up in) and unzip the main entrance before stepping into the living space. I holler through the canvas wall to her bedroom.

"La? LA?!" I shout.

I hear her stir and groan.

"Ugh. . ."

"Ezra Furman. You still wanna do it?"

"Shit! What time is it?"

"Ten forty-five."

"Fuck! Really?"

"Yeah, really. . . Lou's made coffee," I offer.

"Excellent!"

I re-join the others and after some unzipping La emerges from her canvas palace in a white summer dress.

"Did I hear rumours of coffee?" she asks whilst rearranging her morning face into a smile before pulling on her socks.

"Coming up," replies the ever-reliable Lou.

He's a proper Boy Scout, has all the shit, definitely someone you'd want in your tank come the apocalypse. He leans over to La with a double expresso, which she gratefully knocks back before tying up her massive festival boots.

We're now all ready to go, so lift ourselves off the grass to begin our unsteady amble across the baking festival site, hollowed out, crusty, chronically dehydrated, only the sun on our face and the caffeine in our system to nourish our perished souls. Within no time we arrive at the backstage entrance. One of the many wonderful things about this festival is you can get anywhere super quick, it's just the perfect size. We arrive at our rendezvous and a friendly festival official escorts us backstage to where Ezra Furman is nervously waiting at a picnic table.

The others begin setting up, talking camera angles, backdrops, techy stuff, all the while La's pacing around thinking of questions to ask, so I just sit down across the table from

Ezra to chew the fat, relax him a bit as my new role de-
termines. But something's wrong. Where's my superpower?
My fluffing mojo? The magic ain't happening, the conversation's limp, flaccid, in retreat, all my fluffing efforts failing.
Something about me is freaking him out and Ezra stares at
me with panic in his eyes. Is it my demeanour? My morning
face? Perhaps I stink like a badger. I have no idea, but I cannot engage with him, not one bit. He flicks me suspicious
looks, paranoid eyes darting everywhere, in fact, he *can't*
look at me, he's actively avoiding eye contact, like I'm going
to hypnotise or abduct him or something even weirder.

Fucking hell, I'm not enjoying this, not one bit and Ezra
definitely isn't. Is he on some kind of spectrum? Perhaps
he's experiencing a heavy festival comedown? If either is
true, we have more in common than he realises. Yet right
now, we're each inhabiting very different universes.

After what feels like an eternity, the gang finally get their
shit together and we all head for Ezra's white canvass dressing room which contains only white furniture. Ezra turns
to me and somewhat awkwardly asks me to leave. Fuck it.
I grab one of the free bottles of backstage breakfast beer,
go back to the picnic table and wait. Interviews are boring
anyway. Then, from the adjoining tent, comes the angelic
harmonies of a live choir. Poor Ezra, sitting on a pure white
couch, in a pure white tent, with an angelic choir beautifully harmonising whilst being interviewed by punky angel La, also dressed in white. It must feel like he's in some
strange Lynchian heaven.

The breakfast beer has kicked in quick, probably should
have eaten first. I lie down on the grass to soak up some vi-
tamin D, but the sun is unrelenting, so I find myself some
shade. From what was a long cruel never-ending winter, we

leapfrogged spring and careened headfirst into the most intense heatwave in recorded history, most of the planet literally on fire. Yet, here in Ole Blighty, no one dares complain for fear of jinxing it. I mean, when do we ever get holiday weather like this? There is, of course, another reason we're all so stymied by this heat: the silent hidden guilt we carry, the collective realisation we've now passed the point of no return, that it's finally escaped our control and this little blue planet is already fucked. Sorry, kids, for destroying the future of the entire human race.

***

"You ready, Dave?"

I wake up startled. La, Finn and Lou are standing over me, smirking. This must be how it feels to be in a grave if you haven't died. Guess I must have drifted off.

"How'd it go?" I ask, pulling myself into a sitting position.

"Well, apart from the choir. . ." complains Lou, rolling his eyes.

"Oh, I think we should have a choir *every* time!" proclaims La, excitedly.

I take off my shades and rub my eyes.

"So, what's his problem with me, then?"

They all burst out laughing.

"Don't fucking laugh." I lift myself to my feet. "I'm having a mini crisis. I think I might have lost my fluffing mojo."

"Aw, Dave," says La, giving me a hug as Finn and Lou continue laughing. "It's not you, he's just incredibly shy."

"Plus, you do look at bit scary this morning," adds Lou, unhelpfully, but probably truthfully, because what you reliably get from Lou is dour honesty, not one for gilding the lily.

"Plus, he thought you were a cunt," chips in Finn, giggling his spiky head off.

"Fuck off," I reply.

"I think our fluffer needs fluffing," teases La.

"Well, you can't win 'em all," I sigh.

"I'm starving," says Finn, rubbing his tiny belly.

"Yes! Right, let's get breakfast," asserts La.

And so off we trot, La leading us out of the backstage area, which to be frank is tediously boring, there's no fun to be had with all the tense and precious artists and their entourage, the party's happening out here with all the hoi polloi, the fun seekers. As usual, La's striding ahead, way too fast for the rest of us, stopping occasionally to bask in the sun to quell her growing impatience for us three useless blokes.

"Jeez, you is too fast for a festival," I wheeze after her, out of breath.

"Come on, princess."

"Funny you should say that," I reply.

La turns back, eyeing me warily, unsure if I should be encouraged. I continue regardless.

"According to word-of-mouth, well, family mythology. . ."

"What's he on about now?" shouts Lou from behind.

"I expect we're about to find out," groans La, with a sigh.

Despite their lack of enthusiasm, I press on.

"Well, my great-great-great-great-grandma was a maid for one of the royals."

"Really?" asks Lou.

"So I'm told. Anyway, nothing unusual happened, nothing out of the ordinary. Well, not for them, especially back then."

La rolls her eyes, impatient to get this over with.

"What happened, Dave?"

"Er. . . well. . . my great-great-great-great-grandmother was. . .er. . . raped by her royal boss."

"Oh, Dave, really? For fuck's sake!"

"Go on, Dave, tell us more," sniggers Finn, using me to wind up La further. I oblige of course.

"Well, it resulted in a child, a bastard child to be precise. And that child was my great-great-great-great-grandma."

"That's horrible," protests La.

"Well, I'm here because of her."

"That's the horrible bit," quips Finn.

"Well, technically it means I have some royal blood in me," I say, theatrically.

"That actually wouldn't surprise me," say La, rolling her eyes.

"You might even have a claim to the throne," says Finn, egging me on.

"King Dave? Can't see it," dismisses Lou.

The thing is it might actually be true. I cannot imagine a story involving rape would have travelled through all these generations if it were fake, but who knows?

"I'm quite possibly the eighteenth pale descendent of some old queen or other," I quip.

"Dave, if you continue quoting Morrissey at this time of morning, I *will* hit you," threatens La.

"And I wouldn't stop you," adds Finn, chuckling.

I turn to him.

"Yeah, but if I *were* a royal, you'd only be brown-nosing me, just like you did Meg and Harry."

La and Lou crease up.

"You utter cunt, Dave!" gasps Finn.

Last year I was just randomly watching the news, when a report came on about a royal visit to a Brixton radio station. I was only half paying attention when all of a sudden, Finn's on the telly standing next to Meg and Harry. I couldn't fucking believe my eyes. Turns out the royal couple had paid a visit to Reprezent FM, slumming it in three shipping containers within Pop Brixton.

When we next spoke, I asked Finn what they were like.

"They were sooo sweet!" he gushed.

I'm sure they fucking were, living off the back of every single person they meet just because one of them entered the world through a specific vagina. I mean seriously, what are they even? A living remnant of a tyrannical dictatorship in which one inbred family lords it over the rest of us. We say we have democracy in this country, more like a power-sharing agreement. The House of Commons, representing us common folk, hence its name and the unelected House of Lords: the monarch's representatives. All UK legislation requires old queenies rubber stamp, which is why the idea of Charlie being on the throne is a frightening prospect (to them and possibly us), for fear he might one day use his power and veto a piece of legislation. What then for so-called democracy?

The ruling class are still thriving in Ole Blighty and if you need any convincing just look at the fucking Cabinet. Old queenie and her protégé remain perched at the top of this pyramid and for reasons of quaint tradition and tourism, this blue-blooded behemoth remains on the back burner, all their powers intact, just a tacit agreement they will never exercise them for fear us common folk might revolt.

Yet still it remains, on the back burner. . .

We continue walking, Lou still chuckling, La visibly exasperated, no doubt worsened by low blood sugar, having sacrificed breakfast for Ezra.

"How about here? Coffee looks good," suggests Lou.

"YES!" asserts La, leaving no room for doubt.

And so, it was agreed. We order our food, take it to a shaded picnic table and fill our wretched bodies with some much-needed fuel. It's a truly delicious brunch and whilst savouring every mouthful, I look around the colourful festival site and at the sun-dappled shade over my lovely festival companions as they study the programme, babbling away, discussing the day's possibilities, making plans for the evening ahead, plans we shall inevitably fail to follow. I do not really understand the feeling I am having right now, or why it's even happening, but I do recognise that these are the moments we live for. It's always the small things, never the big.

***

For the rest of the weekend, we hop around various gigs, sometimes together, sometimes apart, regularly regrouping at our camp to refresh, replenish and occasionally retire. Before we know it, it's 9pm, Sunday night.

We had made it a non-negotiable to see Velvet Underground legend John Cale who is due to play very soon. So off we all trot. Unfortunately, the John Cale tonight is not the one we know and love. Instead, we get a minimalistic, avant-garde, art house-wailing John Cale and we're surrounded by people who shushed at us if we spoke too loud, like it's Ronnie fucking Scott's, not a field at a music festival.

The inescapable truth is my head couldn't deal with John Cale's set despite my deep and utter respect for the

mad Welshman. I dropped any pretence I was enjoying it
and it turned out we all felt the same, but to be fair to John
Cale, we had our party heads on and this was no party. So,
we tiptoe our way out, weaving through the serious mu-
sos clearly getting something out of Cale's performance we
were far too shallow to understand.

We decide to check out the Tipi and caught some of
the Marmitey Ariel Pink, all talented and weird in his "look
at me I'm a freak" kind of way, but he came over like an
overindulged American brat. So, La drags us off to the
Silent Disco, something I was dreading, but quite unexpectedly turned out to be the best fun ever. After an hour or so,
Finn beckons us all to remove our headsets.

"We really ought to go to this party now."

He's referring to the festival after-party occurring backstage. He'd promised the promoter we'd attend, so attend
we must.

"Will it be any good?" I ask.

"The beers are free," replies Finn.

So off we trot. . .

Now, the idea of going to a backstage after-party might
sound uber-cool, glamorous even, but in my experience
they're usually the opposite of either. Invariably awkward,
stilted, often networky and surprisingly un-rock and roll.
The musicians are all right on the whole, finally relaxing
after the stress of performing, it's all the music biz folk
who surround them, here for business, not pleasure and
partying's just not their forte, especially nowadays, with
the industry populated by clean-living, politically inoffen-
sive, woke-to-rule millennials. The ones who look down
their nose at my generation, shaking their heads in con-
demnation at our immature behaviour. All of which stifles

any potential for a balls-out, crank-up-the-music, hammer-down-the-drinks, dance-your-tits-off party.

We arrive and it is exactly as expected, only worse. There's a disco tent they try coercing revellers into throughout the night, but zero thought has been given to it. The whole room is brightly lit with bare white bulbs and a crappy sound system pumping out unimaginatively dull music, not even so bad it's good, or comically cheesy. It's hard to imagine how the people who put this together coordinated an entire fucking festival. Still, there are people here we know and everyone's trolleyed off their tits at this hour, so we make do and mend. What's more, the ever-resplendent Jack Medley is here, causing mayhem as only Jack can. He also thinks the event is a dog's dinner and persuades us all to stuff our pockets with free booze and take the party back to our camp.

We met Jack earlier on our way to the backstage area to interview IDLES. He was lying in the grass with a bunch of young women. He asked La to get his copy of their new album signed for him.

"You've got a backstage pass, why not come with us?" she suggests.

"Yeah, well, I would but, er, well, like, er, words got round about me," replies Jack in his nasally rasp.

I love his self-awareness, that he fully accepts their verdict. I don't suppose his escapades during Warmduscher's set helped any.

We're all in a circle in La's tent palace, Jack is telling us about the album he's working on, *Secure as Fuck*. La's been playing his debut single "Lose It" on her show for some months now.

"I got a new one I can send you," rasps Jack.

"Excellent! Is it radio friendly?" enquires La.

"Yeah, yeah, yeah, it's fine."

"What, as in *no swearing*?" presses Finn.

"Yeah, yeah, none."

"Wicked, send it over," enthuses La.

"Yeah, I will, just got a few tweaks but I'll get it over, yeah. It's fuckin' all right it is."

"What's it about?" I ask.

"Well, it's about Saul. . ." Jack becomes momentarily distracted. "Oh yeah, there is one swear word."

"Okaaay. . ." says Finn, expectantly.

"Cunt. I say cunt. Just the once," he adds with childlike innocence. "That's all right innit?"

The merriment continues through until 10 a.m., by which time the sun is out, doing its worst. Jack wanders off in search of his tent, he was relying on a lift back to Brighton and needed to pack. The sun's unforgiving, way too hot to climb inside my tent-come-steam room; so I grab my bedding and camp down in the shadow cast by La's ginormous tent, sinking quickly into a deep slumber.

I am woken by security guards. It is now Monday lunchtime and our field is completely deserted. Everyone has packed up and left. Even Lou's ghosted. I'd somehow slept right through it; we all had. The showers at the edge of our field have been dismantled, but we've no time for cleanliness, we have to pack up our shit and re-join what we've come to accept as civilisation.

As we travel back to London, La's phone pings, a message from Jack Medley and his new song "Sauly", along with the collective realisation that this man is quite possibly a genius.

Chapter Forty-Two

Abnormal Normality, Reptilian Illuminati and Kafkaesque Feedback Loops

And I hear that the insects are all still dying
Even though I took out all my recycling
And apparently the ice caps are all still melting
Even though I turned off my central heating
"The End of the World" – The Cool Greenhouse

5TH JUNE 2020, KITCHEN TABLE, HOME
Much of the future we had previously expected has now disappeared, some optimistically postponed, more a fervent

hope than a confident plan. Now we live with the insecurity of not knowing how much of the universe we left behind will still exist when we do return. There'll be more than the devastating body count to assimilate, for the world we knew will have significantly altered in our absence – indeed, *by* our absence.

Throughout all of this, social media has been streaming with lockdown flavoured memes, a few of which provide some much-needed levity, punching a hole of relief through the wall of grimness and a never-ending news cycle that marries *Groundhog Day* with *Contagion*. All we get is wall-to-wall Covid-19: how far it has spread, how many have died, personal anecdotes, incompetent ministers, idiotic presidents.

Amongst all this noise and babble, it's easy to forget all the other shite that had previously been raining down on us, all of which *and more* is still with us, just ignored and forgotten in the face of viral hysteria and a criminally in-competent government, currently implementing counter-intuitive moves to reignite the economy and in doing so, providing this over excitable virus with a constant supply of fresh meat, never letting go of their *Herd Immunity* ap-proach, sociopathic eugenics in action.

We are living through strange, febrile times. Something is off, thickening the atmosphere of an already restless world and hanging in the air like a bad smell. Truth and reason so far out of reach there's nothing left to grab hold of, just a feeling in our bones that we're at the end of something and the beginning of something else, yet unable to envisage pre-cisely what.

Since that night in Brixton almost three years ago, long before we entered a universe of facemasks and frequent hand washing, the world was already going insane and went rocket-fuelled mental when Trump became president, his orange, bloated comic-book-villain face hovering over our daily lives, impossible to ignore.

The mere fact such an astonishingly moronic narcissist with the emotional volatility of a rabies-infected puppy, was elected leader of the free world, is so utterly bizarre, so surreal, so off-the-scale nuts, comedians have struggled to take it any further. It's simply un-satiriseable. Trump is the living embodiment of how fucking insane this planet has become.

The slow-reveal truth of how Cambridge Analytica focused all their efforts on the swing states in the US electoral college, manipulating the floating voters, dubbed "The Persuadables", is a diabolical distortion of democracy. Not messing with the ballot papers, but the psyche of the voters, merely the illusion of a fair vote. Goebbels would have been proud.

Meanwhile, on this side of the pond, we've been forced to endure a short succession of three uniquely incompetent Prime Ministers, who collectively played their part in making Brexit the most painfully tortuous journey possible.

Cameron for calling the vote, then quitting his job and ducking for cover the moment the result came in.

Theresa May stepped into the breach, took control then quickly lost it, following an electoral gamble that smashed a hole in her government's parliamentary majority, that could only be filled by a ragbaggle of ultra-right, Union-obsessed pro-lifers. Most definitely *not* strong or stable, her legacy a litany of failures: the mishandling of the Grenfell tragedy, her dreadful role in the Windrush controversy and an election manifesto that included a tax on dementia.

Like a wounded dog, her government limped along as she dragged the entire nation into a Kafkaesque constitutional feedback loop, repeatedly pushing forward a Brexit bill that Parliament kept shooting down, but much like one of Romero's zombies, simply refused to die.

Soon enough and in typical Tory fashion, a darkness enveloped Ms May, knives were being sharpened, the game was finally up and then *poof*, she was gone.

Celebrations had not even begun when events took an even darker turn. Something we fervently hoped *wouldn't* happen, that many believed *couldn't* happen, ended up happening. Boris Johnson became Prime Minister.

Within a matter of weeks in the job, he decided the only way out of this constitutional mess of clashing ideologies was to circumvent any need to consult Parliament at all, through a previously unknown medieval practice termed *proroguing*. In simple terms: *become a dictator*. He would have gotten away with it too were it not for the intervention of the Supreme Court who concluded Johnson's advice to old queenie *"was unlawful, void and of no effect"*.

We were about to celebrate again, but then Johnson called an election. A Brexit election, which he won by a landslide, for reasons previously stated. He then audaciously attaches an impossible timetable with extra conditions attached, expressly designed to infuriate an already exasperated EU, propelling the nation towards a no-deal Brexit or a deal that enables Britain's spider web of tax havens to continue, unhindered and unabashed with their state endorsed tax-evasion. A key service industry to the world they serve.

Not *our* world, of course, the world of the super-rich, the mega-powerful, the inherited bloodlines, the Bilderberg collective, the reptilian illuminati. Call them what you like, they exist all the same.

Still, it was good to see one of these lizards caught in the glare of the international spotlight, when creepy android Zuckerberg was grilled by Congress after Cambridge Analytica revelations went from tinfoil-hat conspiracy theory to front and centre mainstream news. He claimed to know nothing, didn't mind looking stupid and cared even less that we all *knew* the cunt was lying, for *any* admission of guilt would have sent Facebook's shares plummeting. What else matters to the corporate psychopath?

Just before our ability to roam the world was curtailed and our every movement controlled in some way, I visited the old Stasi headquarters in Leipzig, Germany, now a museum preserving a one of the darkest periods of European history, during which you could, quite literally, not trust your own grandmother. The Stasi went to extraordinary lengths to build files on every single citizen, their characters, their associations, their habits, their dirty little secrets. Yet fast forward only 30 odd years and you Facebookers are giving it all away freely, as you trivially sate your fragile egos and validate your existence. Indeed, the level of detail you wilfully surrender would have given the German Democratic Republic state a hard-on.

Zuckerberg famously said, "*I don't know why. They trust me. Dumb Fucks.*" In this commoditised, neoliberal system, if you believe something is *free*, it can only mean *you're* the product, so it really should come as no surprise that every dimension of who you are as a person is up for sale. Cambridge Analytica could not have enabled Brexit or helped Trump into the Whitehouse without Facebook's support. Seriously people, isn't this *enough* to make a stand? Only participation gives Zuckerberg power and in return he sells your digital avatar to the highest bidder so they can fuck with your heads. What more motivation do you need to delete your accounts?

Maybe you're thinking "no need to worry now, we got GDPR to protect us". What a scam that turned out to be, sold to us as regulation to *protect* our data, yet nothing more than a legal framework through which to *sell* our data. Surfing the internet has become the online equivalent of dodging guided missiles whilst crossing an ever-changing minefield surrounded by snipers.

Remember the days when you could open a web page and just *read it*? Not now, half the page you want is often faded out or disabled and there's a massive banner with a large flashing ACCEPT button. If you proceed, the page will open, but so will your online life to a whole host of bots and cookies for whatever nefarious purposes they're being paid for.

The alternative is to look for the small link called *preferences* or *settings*, or *more info* through which you're thrust into a rabbit hole detailing all the data harvesting organisations that want to get to know you better. You are then given the tedious task of switching each of them off, or even worse, they send you scuttling off to various third-party websites. Revisit the same site where and make you do it all over again. And seriously people, what the fuck is *legitimate interest*?

GDPR is a legislative Trojan horse stacked in favour of the corporates, not the people. They grind us down because life's too short for this perpetual tedium. We end up hitting "Accept" and in doing so release swarms of bots into our digital universe observing, following, recording, analysing, suggesting, manipulating and subverting every aspect of our online life. Bots now account for over half the internet traffic; remember that next time your Netflix boxset series glitches. The idea that GDPR is protective legislation is a joke. If they were truly serious about this, our starting position would be one of anonymity. Only *we* should own our data and decide how visible we want to be; how much of what we reveal and to whom. That should be a basic human right. Right?

Our democracy has failed us, our economic system has morphed into nothing more than a confidence trick adding no tangible value to our lives, just ravenous consumption, annihilating our climate and, ultimately, the future of our species. This is the hangover from Hayek's neoliberal financial orgy, humanity reduced to commoditised, algorithmicised consumers. The market ruling, the market deciding, chewing us up, spitting us out, caring for nothing but itself and certainly not the fucking planet.

Homo erectus appeared around a million years ago, Homo sapiens a mere 300,000 years, yet the dinosaurs roamed the planet for 170 million years before they were staring extinction in the face. For, whichever way you look at it, most of these new viruses are caused by human behaviour, even if their origin is technically zoonotic, because with the arrogance of demigods we have bitten the hand that feeds us; abusing the planet and every species we share it with, plundering it for food and minerals, unlocking carbon it took millennia to safely bury. Yet still, we continue with our ecocide in full scientific knowledge of all the damage we're doing, so cannot even blame ignorance. Covid-19 is a symptom of a much bigger disease and the day of reckoning is upon us.

I am not completely devoid of hope. They keep banging on about a *new normal*, a term now imbued with the notion that our liberty will be compromised – and it will, that much is clear. Yet this could also end up liberating us. Our response to this *could* birth a new way of thinking; a dismantling of current constructs; a reimaging of how society functions. This *could* be one of those moments in human history where we question the world we were born into and say, "*Hang on, isn't there a better way of doing this?*"

Chapter Forty-Three

Human Centipedes, Official Bears, Venn Diagrams and Spectrum Dwellers

I've been here before
And I am there still
Mid-aftermath
Heroic and colossal baby
When you look back
"When I Leave" – Fat White Family

6TH MAY 2019, MY BED, HOME

I regain consciousness to a vibrating sound on the wooden box beside my bed. I stare at the ceiling and my phone vibrates again, sounding more urgent than friendly.

If I attempt any movement my head pounds, so I'll just lie here a while, try and recombobulate, maybe dredge up some memories from the preceding eighteen hours, if only to counterbalance quite how broken I feel.

Last night, Warmduscher made an increasingly rare appearance at the Windmill. They were trying out new material for their upcoming album *Tainted Lunch*. It was rammed to the hilt, a pressure cooker of madness and mayhem. The Windmill is usually reliably great, in fact if I were a hippie I'd go there with dowsing rods searching for ley lines, because if you get the right night it can be extraordinary, everyone just powered along by a magical energy. This was one of those nights, still in full swing long after the bar had closed. Toby and Seamus called time on The Shed but no one wanted to just go home, so an impromptu after-party was hastily organised and we all scuttled down to the Deli Lama on Streatham Hill. This place has form, known for its legendary below-the-radar all-night parties.

My memory's fragmented but buried in the depths, beyond the damaged neurotransmitters and a cerebral cortex demanding healthier working conditions, something is troubling me. I'm receiving random flashbacks, but struggling with specifics, just the guilt over my alcohol-withered state in the Uber ride home, my night ending as the normal world began, people jogging, walking dogs, going to work. It was like peering into an alternative universe from a Prius-shaped space shuttle. I remember it being nearly 9am when I finally stumbled through my door. I vaguely remember crawling up the stairs. I don't remember cleaning my teeth, but recall my harrowed state as I stared at the ceiling hoping sleep would come soon, that I would survive this.

As I lie here now, head pounding, mouth like sandpaper, bladder uncomfortably full, I wonder if it really was worth it. Slowly, I lift myself up, bring my feet to the floor and grab my phone. Fuck. It's 2:30pm! Most of the day lost to a drunken coma. I'm no Catholic, or anything for that matter, yet still feel wracked with guilt, primed and ready for some self-flagellation.

I scroll through my notification alerts.

The last text is from La:

Oh god

I spoke to Beth

Jack's gone

What the fuck? Which Jack? We know loads of Jacks, the Windmill's teeming with them. Does she mean Jack Medley? Surely not. I wrack my brains trying to make sense of it, yet it did kinda makes sense. He was supposed to have played support to Warmduscher last night. In fact, I was wearing his trademark Venn diagram "Secure as Fuck" T-shirt containing his stock phrases "Suck it up", "Deal with it" and, of course, "Lose it". La took a picture of me wearing it and sent it to Jack to help cheer him up, so gutted was he at not being well enough to play. He didn't respond.

I quickly stand up, too quickly, causing the blood to drain from my head and everything goes dark. I fall back on the bed and close my eyes. In short waves, the memories begin washing back in. As the night continued La continued messaging Jack, but failed to elicit a response. And he *always* responded. A text maniac, spinning off random messages to whoever took his fancy at any time of day or night. Suddenly, I flash forward to the Deli Lama and a conversation I had with Beth Soan of Madonnatron. It must have been around 4 a.m. and we were both profoundly inebriated. Jack and her were super tight, always hanging out together, but last night she was concerned and emotional, weighed down by a deep sense of foreboding. Jack hadn't responded to any of her calls or texts since the previous evening and he'd been diagnosed with pneumonia only three days before, but promptly sent home.

No room at the NHS Inn.

A cold wave shudders through my body. I frantically text La back:

What? As in died?

She replies instantly:

Yes

For the remainder of the day, shocked disbelief ripples through south London, Brighton and beyond. Jack Medley was only 41 years old and really ought not to have died. Some would argue it was inevitable and perhaps it was, because he lived life large and to the max, burning his candle brightly and from both ends.

I spoke with La later that evening.

"I'm angry with him, Dave. He was a fucking tank; he had no right to die!"

She's right, he was a tank, a tall strong beast of a man with a mop of messy hair shaved around the back and over his ears, much like a Wildling from Game of Thrones, though not clothed in bits of animal skin, more likely donning a band T-shirt, loose jeans permanently hanging off his arse.

The socials flooded with posts, photos, videos, funny stories, moving eulogies - a digital celebration of all things Jack. People began to mobilise; calls were made, gatherings arranged, mostly informal remembrances-cum-sob sessions, but amongst it all, one thing was unanimously agreed upon: something had to happen. La and Beth took control, immediately approaching Tim Perry to sketch out plans for a commemoration in Jack's honour. They drew up a list of his favourite bands and called them all up, inviting them to play. Not one declined.

26TH MAY 2019 – WINDRUSH SQUARE, BRIXTON

It's 1:30 p.m. and already a colourful ensemble of characters have assembled, easily over 100, many carrying odd-shaped cases, because inside these cases are instruments, mainly brass, but also a large marching bass drum. There are two bears holding clipboards. Official bears handing out pink armbands as they chalk people off their lists. An important job, for this occasion has been put together for family and friends, which is why one of these bears is the ever-reliable Finn, or MC Husky as Jack Medley fondly dubbed him during our time with him at End of the Road.

There is also a Brighton collective in attendance, for it was Jack's adopted hometown. There's no specific theme or dress code for the occasion, except for vague instructions to dress up, so I decided upon 1970's American border town pimp, a costume I created for a televised Japanese New Year party held at 93 Feet East: a truly insane event featuring Warmduscher, Goat Girl and Jack in charge of a glitter cannon.

Today's commemoration came together in record time, just three weeks after Jack shuffled off this mortal coil to *"go collect his triple-A pass for his Megarave in the sky,"* as Warmduscher's Clams Baker dubbed it in a warm, funny, heartfelt post he made upon hearing the sad news. It was this post that inspired the title for today's one-day festival:

"Jack Medley's Secure as Fuck Megarave," taking place at the Windmill, just half a mile up the road.

You might be wondering why Jack's passing has inspired such an enormous turnout of friends and fellow musicians. How could one man, relatively unknown in any cultural sense, be the sole cause of this incredible tribute? What person could give cause for this growing mass dressed in all manner of crazy garb to congregate here, before forming a New Orleans-style procession led by a thumping marching band and dancing bears? To really understand this, you would've had to experience Jack first-hand. If you didn't have this pleasure, I'll do my best to do the man justice.

Jack Medley was a force of nature, a one-man riot, a living breathing art project. a crazy mad ball of unmarshalled energy and a loveable, spectrum-dwelling, fiercely intelligent stream of consciousness. When you met Jack, you *really* met him, of that you were left in no doubt, for it wasn't a meeting you'd ever forget. He lived by a set of rules entirely of his own making and quite often not in accord with those of the world around him. He was intense, abstract, random and hilarious. Jack challenged all accepted norms, societal customs and rules of engagement. He was not just in your face, he would pummel his way through your cerebral cortex and crash-land into the epicentre of your pleasure receptors, suspending logic and any semblance of rational thought. He was high-minded, bighearted and generous to a fault. A vinyl aficionado who would give away his last record to make a friend happy. He was never selfish in his fun-seeking antics, Jack wanted everyone to get on board his happy train and did his level best to make that happen. A night when Jack was in the house was always an event, his hyperactive energy making the world a brighter, wilder place to be.

He was a massive supporter of many a south London band, most notably Madonnatron, Fat White Family and Warmduscher, an honorary mega-fan, his name permanently etched at the top of their respective guest lists. Charlie from Madonnatron set about capturing his essence within a wonderful mural, complete with all of Jack's aforementioned catchphrases, so now Jack's portrait adorns the wall of the Windmill's Shed. Clams from Warmduscher set up a GoFundMe page to raise £2,000 to help realise Jack's dream and give his *Secure as Fuck* album a vinyl release, a target met within just 11 hours. No one had envisaged this brilliant and hilarious album would end up being his swansong, his last goodbye.

It's hard to describe Jack's music on paper because there are no benchmarks. He doesn't really sing, more like a raspy rap and his often-bizarre lyrics are a stream of consciousness meshing his real life with his imagination. All of which are set to a twisted lo-fi techno-disco backdrop and grungy guitar riffs, provided by fellow Secure Man, Dom Keen, a producer and musician who's previously worked with Dark Horses, Holy Magick and Death in Vegas. "Lose It", the song that kicked it all off and routinely played on La's show, is a deranged hyperactive celebration of basically *losing it*, as in, having that ill-advised final shot or drinking way too much White Ace. Basically, losing the plot and being totally fine with it.

If you have not already guessed, Jack had named his project primarily to wind up Saul Adamczewski, whose critically acclaimed side project went under the moniker Insecure Men - he even copied the typeset. Throughout the last year, Jack managed to nail down enough songs for an entire album.

Many rumours circulated about Jack, most of which he no doubt began himself, some so utterly preposterous, so unverifiable, you would quite understandably take them with a pinch of salt, yet they would often turn out to be true.

Like for example, that he used to own a whole heap of Bitcoin, which led to him living it up like a rap star for three years, during which he literally partied his digital stash away.

Jack once told some of his mates he had to pop out briefly "to see a man about a dog," which they quite understandably took to mean drugs were being acquired, but he came back with an actual dog. A fully grown Rottweiler. They were meant to be clubbing that night, so Jack's solution was to smuggle this canine beast into the various bars and nightclubs they attended. He was never asked to dog-sit again.

In October 2018, before treating us to his Secure Men Windmill debut, Jack was leaving The Shed for he was due onstage. I followed him into the bar and he turned to me, twinkle in his eye.

"I've had to sack eighteen band members already."

"Really? Why d'you go and do that?" I asked, humouring him.

"Ah!" he snorts. "They were all so demanding, it was doing my 'ead in!"

So armed with a sampler, a backing track and various gizmos, Jack hits the stage, with additional rhythmic and moral support provided by Beth Soan, who like me, in fact, like everyone watching, howled with laughter throughout most of the set. Not at him, but with him, for Jack was a natural performer, with comical anecdotes and in-your-face banter punctuating each song. Despite Jack's constant brain battering, he was sharp as they come and spellbinding to watch.

I saw Jack Medley's Secure Men several times since, each performance shambolically unique. He supported Warmduscher at the Dome in London, with additional guitar licks provided by Fat White Family's newest member, Adam Brennan.

Only last February Jack brought his live spectacle to The Five Bells in New Cross, joined onstage by Misty Miller, a hugely talented performer with an effortlessly beautiful voice. Together they treated us to a very touching rendition of "Anyone Else But You" (The Moldy Peaches classic). This was the last time I saw Jack.

La is live streaming the whole procession as we slowly work our way up Brixton Hill. Beth is leading the way alongside SLEAZE frontman Dave Ashby, both sporting hi-vis, followed by dancing bears and a solid thumping brass band, appropriately sound-tracking our journey with poignant renditions of "Ghost Town", "St James' Infirmary" and of course "The Bear Necessities". Some are singing along, others respectfully silent, many crying, but everyone feels the positivity of the occasion, a warm glow running through and connecting every member of this colourful human centipede.

Jack's family are here too, obviously moved, not quite able to comprehend this other life of their son in all its barmy kaleidoscopic glory. Warmduscher's Lightnin' Jack Everett bashes out the marching rhythm on the bass drum, proudly held by Jack Medley's dad as he stoically fights back the tears. Passers-by reach for their phones to film us, cars slow down, honking in tribute to this unknown soldier. During "Ghost Town", the people at the head of this centipede spontaneously burst into The Specials refrain "Ay, ya ya ya ya ya ya ya", which ripples down the procession like a choral Mexican wave.

Jack's favourite people, his favourite bands, all heading to his favourite venue. It really couldn't get much better. And let's be clear about this, we're not talking about a bunch of lo-fi no-marks, but some of the hottest acts on the circuit right now: Warmduscher, Fat White Family, Meatraffle, Insecure Men, Phobophobes, SLEAZE, along with Jack's old band Filthy Pedro, Pit Ponies, Misty Miller, Scrappy Hood (from Milk Kan) and Madonnatron (performing as Jack Medley's Secure Women) – all held together by MC, poet and raconteur Mr Patrick Lyons.

As we turn into Blenheim Gardens, Tim Perry is hovering by the Windmill's entrance and upon spotting us, he grabs his phone to capture this loud crazy colourful procession snaking its way towards him.

The entire venue, including the beer garden (and especially The Shed) has an atmosphere never felt before. No tensions, no dramas, everyone's egos left at the door or back at Windrush Square, for today is not just a heap of bands performing to an audience of fans, it's a communal gathering in honour of someone who has touched us all. A celebratory wake and, as it turns out, a loved-up, life-affirming, fuck-off Megarave.

From Warmduscher's incendiary opening to the Fat Whites cathartic finale, this is undoubtedly the event of the year. But the focus today is not the bands, for as good as they all are (and they are life-changingly good), we're here to honour our dear departed friend, so to them, it's about doffing their caps to a fellow traveller, a kindred spirit and the energy permeating the Windmill enriches every performance to epic proportions.

The revelry continues in The Shed with intermittent jam sessions right through until closing. And whether through a collective sense of loss, or in a more metaphysical sense, one thing was universally acknowledged; we could all feel his presence, it was tangible. Jack Medley was in the house. Good job too, for he'd have been well fucking annoyed if he'd missed this banger.

5TH JUNE 2020, KITCHEN TABLE, HOME

Jack's *Secure as Fuck* album was finally released on the 18th of October 2019 in glorious splattered pink vinyl, pressed and printed on a not-for-profit basis by Blang Records, run by Joe Murphy, Paul Finlay and Jules Dakin. They had history with Jack, including a legendary night on the town when Jack decided to go naked for the evening, just for a laugh, successfully gate-crashing various venues before, inevitably, being thrown out by confused, discomfited bouncers.

Beth and La propelled Jack's album release forward, carrying everyone along with them. They roped me into accosting Sleaford Mods fans with Jack Medley's Secure Men flyers as they poured out the exits of Hammersmith Apollo last year. Prudence and Fin from Rocket PR, often seen at the Windmill, provided pro bono support to help promote *Secure as Fuck* and within no time at all Iggy Pop was playing selected tracks on his 6 Music show, totally smitten by Jack's whole schtick. He even provided the backstory as to how the album came to be, namechecking La and Beth along the way no less. Dr Pop is massively into Sleaford Mods and Warmduscher, so Jack's album is right up his street. He also didn't seem to mind Jack and Dom aping a Stooges riff. Even Lamacq's been playing "Lose It" on his show, having observed Jack's mural on The Shed wall during IVW, momentarily redeeming himself in my eyes until, that is, he referred to him as "Jack Smedley," proving once again he is still very much a cunt.

I see a lot of Beth nowadays and she has the power to send me into melts of laughter with a well-timed glance. It was Jack's sudden death that brought her into the foreground of my life and now we have a special bond for which I doff my cap to our dear departed friend. We once, perhaps ill-advisedly, went to see Bill Callahan perform in London, but the church-like atmosphere produced a form of hysteria between us and we could not even look at each other, let alone speak. The more we tried to contain it the worse we became. By the end of Bill's performance, our faces were wet with tears and the seats around us empty. We are both quite ashamed of this now.

During lockdown Beth and La organised a tribute album in honour of Jack, entitled *Songs in the Key of K*, all proceeds going to the Windmill's Covid-19 survival fund. It features exclusive tracks from SLEAZE, Madonnatron, Misty Miller, Saul Adamczewski, Clams Baker and many more, further evidence of the lengths this community will go to, using whatever skills, resource, or energy they can muster, mobilising together for the greater good. In fact, one of my lockdown highlights was the live launch of the album on social media in May this year, via the Windmill's platform. If a band failed to provide a video of their own, La and Beth stepped into the breach with hilarious results, all segued together with surreal visuals and some guest appearances from the late Jack Medley himself, reminding us all why we miss the mad fucker. For despite the trials and tribulations, the psychosis and turmoil, wherever each one of our boats happened to be sailing, Jack's passing was a humbling moment that brought the entire collective back together for comfort and support, very much like an extended family. Which is precisely what it is: an insanely dysfunctional, creatively prolific, glorious, loveable family.

Chapter Forty-Four

Shit Sandwiches, Awkward Elephants, Glassy Dudes and WOO!

I'm a turgid fucked-up little goat
Pissing on your fucking hill
And you can't shit me out
'Cos you can't catch me, 'cos you're so fat
So, fuck ya!
I'm Miami
"Miami" – Baxter Dury

I have tried hard not to label what has been happening in south London as a 'scene' even though every other bug-ger is, including 6 Music and all the music journos. But how can it be considered in this way when it has no definable identity or sound? It is certainly not like anything I've experienced since arriving in London over three decades ago.

I guess more than anything else, it's a community, because everyone looks out for one another and because it's *not* a scene in the usual sense of the word, it's hard to envisage it ever coming to a natural end. Even throughout this pandemic it has continued to remind us of its relevance, particularly the Windmill, banging the drum loud, releasing a tremendous live album, hosting virtual gig nights, social media band takeovers and all manner of activities surrounding this unique venue to raise awareness and vital funds.

This organic evolving micro community pays no mind to what's in or out, or *trending* within the wider, homogenised, narcissistic culture, perniciously creeping into every corner of our lives. This collective exists within the fringes, beyond the mainstream's critical eye, at least until a band is ready to take the plunge. Still, all this recent attention is a bit of a worry, the current buzz from the *next-big-thing* culture, hardwired to be fickle, fresh meat to feed their short attention spans, who swallow without tasting before moving on to the next.

Yet, this shape-shifting musical community refuses to be nailed down or turned into a strapline and *this* is what makes it exceptional.

***

"So, what's your book about?" is the question that has dogged me these past three years. My bro was the first, when, during a long phone conversation, during which I debriefed him on my text break-up with Tigger, I also told him I'd started a book. . .

30TH JULY 2017, KITCHEN TABLE, HOME

"So, what are you reading?" asks my bro. "No. I'm *writing* one."

"Oh. . . right. So, how much have you written?"

"Six pages."

My bro chuckles down the phone.

"For fuck's sake, I only started a couple of hours ago." He's still chuckling.

"Why are you laughing? Are you stoned?"

"No. Well. A bit."

I laugh.

"Well, we've been here before," he continues, referring to the various unfinished symphonies littering my various hard drives.

"Er. . . well yeah, I guess."

"So, you gonna actually publish this one?"

"That's the plan."

5TH JUNE 2020, KITCHEN TABLE, HOME

My plan was not to be constrained by a plan, but in retrospect, a plan might have been useful, because for much of this time I've been wrestling with the curiously impenetrable world of publishing. I am of course breaking a cardinal rule by carping about this, but fuck it, if you've come this far, you're probably past caring.

Many published writers are already journalists, with heaps of contacts, an established media profile and a portfolio of published work they can point to, all of which means they have more than a toe in the door, because in the world of publishing the marketing campaign matters way more than the book. I wasted half a year with a pretty serious agent representing many of my personal heroes.

I cannot deny being flattered by such esteemed attention, it was an exciting development. At least at first. I was asked to provide a full proposal, which if you've ever seen one, is almost a book in its own right. After a painfully slow six months, things came to an abrupt and disappointing end. The short version is, they flirted a little, teased me a while, even showed a bit of leg, but ultimately concluded there was a conflict of interest. It was one of those happy sandwich missives, initially pouring honey over my hopeful ego:

"...passionate and witty... an engaging and natural voice. .. captures the energy... this definitely feels like we're getting the inside track..."

And then comes the filling; the turd nestled between the complimentary slices.

"Unfortunately, I've just done a deal for a book about the Fat White Family by Lias Souadi [sic] and Adelle Stripe," concluding it would represent a conflict of interest for him.

What the fuck? Lias not only knew about my book but I'd also emailed him extracts and not unsolicited. Our paths have crossed many a time since, but not a word has been said. Nothing. It began to feel like he was actively avoiding me, though it's hard to tell with him as he's aloof by nature. Still, I wasn't going to press him for a response, the ball was in that motherfucker's court. He knew I was talking to Adelle Stripe's literary agent who'd just published "Sweating Tears with Fat White Family" for *Rough Trade Publishing*. Now this agent is representing *him*. Why couldn't he have just levelled with me, instead of skulking away every time we met? I mean seriously, what a total cunt!

Maybe my expectations were unrealistic, but the way it came to be felt so right, a result of La and Beth having a boozy session with Blang Records, following a Jack Medley's Secure Men album release meeting, during which they apparently discussed my book. One of them just happened to be best mates with this guy. Neither La nor Beth have any recollection of any such conversation, but whatever they said did the trick. Several emails later and I end up meeting him, then things got proper exciting.

I guess we've all been there, those moments in life when it feels like something could really be happening. You're defying gravity, walking on air, because you might finally make that quantum leap into a more exciting, self-actualised existence.

Then, it comes, the unwelcome tap on the shoulder, the cold water in the face and a beautifully worded rejection that has the power to turn your entire world grey in an instant. I fell back to Earth with a painful thud, along with the castle my imagination had built, now just useless rubble littering my landscape. It wasn't just the rejection, but Lias Saoudi being part of the reason – ironic in a way Alanis Morrissette could never hope to understand.

After a few days, my darkness is replaced by a kind of *fuck you* fury and as the Butter Man says, anger is an energy. I resolve to cut out the need to deal with the tedious machinates of the publishing world, waiting for someone's approval, for the light to go green so I can be let into their dusty old club. I'll do it the punk way. Plus, I want to get mine out before those two fuckers!

Funnily enough, I attended Adelle Stripe's book launch at The Social in Soho last year. During the Q&A session she was asked about her favourite music. She offered up Snow Patrol; said they were the best band of the noughties. Seriously, how fucking worried should I be?

So, fuck literary agents, fuck publishers, fuck Lias. Fuck them all!

2ND MARCH 2020, BANK, CITY OF LONDON

Five days since my rejection letter and I'm finally venturing out. Not really in the mood, but my bro and his family have travelled to London especially. We all have tickets to see Jarvis Cocker play a one-off gig at The Steel Yard in the City.

When we arrive, my bro and his family join the queue to the venue. We agree to regroup inside as I've arranged to meet some friends at a nearby bar. The nearest one I can find is called The Banker, so I head towards it whilst retrieving my phone to call my mates. It's the wrong bar, they meant by the station, not the venue but since I'm nearer our ultimate destination, we agree to meet here, at The Banker.

I enter the modern corporate interior, charm and authenticity replaced with homogenised sameness, not helped by the fact it's full of loud cocky bankers.

As I'm waiting for my stout to be poured, I survey the pub for anyone I might know. Then, to my surprise, leaning against one of those stand-up tables, I see Lias, alone, nursing a pint of stout. What the fuck? Why is he here of all places? He's the last person in the world I want to see right now.

I stare at my phone before he clocks me, scrolling through my texts, not registering a thing, just weighing up the fucking weirdness of the situation. What strange twists of fate this universe offers up. I mean Lias, the man who brought me to all of this, who opened up my eyes and ears again and part of the inspiration for writing this fucking book, is standing just a few feet away and all I want to do right now is kick him in the bollocks.

He's seen me now, I can feel him staring. How long can I stand here ignoring him? It's beginning to feel weird.

Fuck it, I casually look around, feigning surprise when our eyes connect. Quite bizarrely, he seems pleased to see me. Maybe just relieved to not be standing on his own surrounded by Jodrells. He chats away at me, funny, erudite, disarmingly charming, but the elephant has not left the room and I will never forgive myself if I let this opportunity slip. Time to grasp the nettle.

"Congratulations on the publishing deal."

Lias looks at me, puzzled.

"How do you know about that?"

"Matthew told me. It's brilliant news."

His confusion over my positivity is apparent

"Oh, thanks, man."

"Seriously, well done, I know it's not easy."

I'm not going to pretend this is easy either, but it cracked the topic open.

"Yeah, I haven't started writing yet. I was supposed to have done some today but kept fuckin' procrastinating."

Fuck me, he's got a publishing deal and there's not even a book!

"So, when's it coming out?" I probe, cheekily. "Early next year, well that's the plan."

"Next year?"

Lias nods. Of course, he means next year. Fuck it, I'm definitely self-publishing now.

I go on to explain that whilst his band feature in my book, it is not specifically *about* them. The more we talk, the more apparent it is how different our respective books will be and most certainly not in conflict.

We continue chatting, way more re laxed now the elephant has left the room. Quite what has been resolved remains unclear, but my resentment appears to have subsided, my anger quelled, so, if only on a psychological level this unexpected meeting has served its purpose, but more importantly, it has established an understanding - we are *not* in competition.

That said, I'm getting mine out first.

Lias checks his phone.

"Baxter's gonna be joining us shortly."

"Baxter Dury?"

"Yup."

"Cool." I nod, blasé as I could muster.

Fuck me, the Lord of Ladbroke Grove, the king of swagger, the man who wowed us all with his surprise sweary hit "Miami" and the glorious album that followed, is joining us for pints! Woo!

Moments later, in he strides, the urban goose, the sausage man, working his way through the city boy slickers until he reaches our table. Lias introduces us and we chat a while.

Baxter's been touring, so I ask if he'd had a good time.

"Yeah, but it's not like we're getting on it all the time, partying every night. My band are practically Quakers," he winks.

Baxter has a relaxed, convivial manner and a certain old-school gangster charm about him. As he orders himself a pint he asks what we're having. My glass is already half full, causing my sense of etiquette to overrule my fandom and I decline the invitation.

That's right, I've just said *no* to Baxter Dury buying me a pint. If only my glass had been half empty.

We stand around the table, each nursing a pint of stout, similarly attired in tweed coats and peaked caps as we discuss the impending doom of the Coronavirus. At this point only an abstract fear, pictures on TV from Wuhan and now Italy. It was heading right for us, we should be bricking it, but already too jaded after SARS and MERS failed to ignite anywhere much beyond their countries of origin. Baxter is worried, his new album is scheduled to come out next month.

"We're supposed to start our European tour next week. Fuck knows what's gonna happen. They've already started locking down over there."

"Yeah, we had to cancel all our dates," adds Lias.

"Your tour of China?" I interject. "Probably a lucky escape!"

"Yeah, but there's about forty grand we'll never get back."

"Fucking hell, really?"

"Yeah, it's a bit of a pisser."

"But on the other hand, it might just have kept you alive," I counter, trying to give the loss of £40k a more positive spin.

Lias isn't persuaded.

"Our London show is supposed to be happening right at the time they say it's gonna peak over here," adds Baxter.

Which is what we're jabbering on about as my mates arrive, somewhat surprised at the sight of us three huddled together round a table. I go to the bar with them and get in a round, extending the invite to Lias and Baxter, then neck them back quickly as Jarvis is due onstage very soon.

We hoof down to The Steel Yard. The place is heaving and there's a buzz in the air. The Witherer from Warmduscher's on the decks and I bump into Bobby Gillespie in the toilets – all clear signifiers that tonight is an event.

The design of the venue means everyone is funnelled through a narrow entrance to the main auditorium and its bottlenecked with punters, making it almost impossible to navigate the Cunt Wall. It's a mighty thick one and certainly a challenge but after a few failed attempts it is finally breeched. Not without hostility. Still, it was worth the frissons of hate, for the closer to the stage the more chilled people become, plus I manage to locate my bro.

Jarvis is in sparkling form, delivering surreal witty monologues throughout and treating us to his soon-to-be-released new single "House Music", an instant classic reminding me of why this man is still so relevant. No one writes intelligent pop quite like this, its lyrics an uncanny premonition of a world that awaits.

After the gig, it is the usual north of the river bollocks; lights on, bar closed and before we've got our heads around the gig ending, or get a chance to even chat, bouncers are coercing us out.

As we head for the exit, I bump into Lias again, still hanging with Baxter. We wish each other luck with our respective writing projects, say our goodbyes and head off into the night.

***

Turns out the agents 'conflict of interest' with the Fat White Family book was just misdirection, as whilst occupied with my own book proposal to him (the 'homework' I'd been tasked with), he'd been cooking up his own plans, roping in a music journo he represented, quickly releasing their own miniature version of what they thought this book was about.

Whilst I like to entertain the image of these two hunkered down in Soho House, casually scheming over a few brandy's as the agent strokes a Persian cat nestled in his lap, I'm remarkably okay about it all. Moreover, I find it oddly flattering for my ideas to be considered worthy of such plagiaristic behaviour and this discovery ultimately strengthened my resolve to stop pissing about and finally get my shit together.

Plus, *anything* that brings attention to the Windmill at this very crucial time can only be a good thing.

30TH JULY 2017, KITCHEN TABLE, HOME

"So, what you gonna call this book?"

I didn't have a name, hadn't even thought about it until the question was put to me.

"WOO!" The word just flew out of my mouth, but it kinda made sense.

My bro is quiet as he mulls it over.

"As in W. U. Like Wu-Tang Clan?"

"No. W. O. O."

"Ah. . . okay. . . *woo.*"

"And an exclamation mark," I add, with a slight chuckle.

"An exclamation mark?"

"Not *woo.* WOO!"

WOO! is that little dopamine hit we sometimes get that knocks us out the groove of our conditioning, enabling us to let go and fall into the present. It can be any number of things and is different things to different people, but it's not about *things,* it's about those moments that help get us through the day, through our lives and imbue it with meaning. That irrational excitement, those accidental connections, those little hits of love that cut through the banality of everydayness, catching us off guard, causing the ice to thaw around our hearts and our senses to momentarily heighten.

We knew this when we were kids, open to anything, alive to everything, excited by the small things when life had texture, colour, even magic. But life is hard, busy, stressful; rattling through the days as we chalk up the years, powered by fear, arrested by anxiety, numbed by repetition and if it all gets too much there's always drugs and alcohol. These moments of pure joy become a rare treat needing ever greater stimuli to find our way back or we just forget they even existed. Disconnected beings craving connection, desperate to control the outcome yet isolated by the effort. Passions once held dear pushed aside by necessity and the struggle to survive, then forgotten like a Polaroid left in the sun, image erased along with the sentiment. Much like the proverbial boiled frog, we just don't feel it happening to us.

As for me, my beating heart was like an old boiler with a dodgy thermo-coupling and a pilot light hungry for gas. Then, when least expecting it, something came at me from left-field and suddenly it was back. It had never really left, the flame had grown dim, expectations diminished but the gasman cometh, replaced the dodgy part, a roar of gas is propelled full force at the pilot and WOO! My head giddy, my stomach tingling, my face beaming, disorientated, off balance, I can feel again, I'm still alive.

It was like falling in love. I *had* fallen in love.

You may recall the moment for me, a Fat White Family gig at the Electric Ballroom, which feels like a lifetime ago now, but was just six years.

"Okay. . . I get it. WOO!" proclaims my bro.

"You think it's okay, then?"

"Might need a subtitle?"

"You reckon?"

"Probably. . ."

There is a pregnant silence we both shatter with laughter.

I have other reasons for calling this book WOO! It was a popular sign-off on all the socials from the bands and characters within this collective, which is what brought it to my attention in the first place. La and Zsa Zsa kindly support my non-participation of data-harvesting platforms by sending me Facebook screenshots and the like, keeping me in the loop, often punctuated with WOO!

With Zsa Zsa, it's usually to let me know when Meatraffle or Scud FM are playing, or to interrupt my day with some embryonic demo he's working on. It's not the listening that takes the time but delivering a considered, yet supportive response which he silently demands.

My final reason for this book's title, which I have to fess up is nothing more than gratuitous self-promotion, is because *if* this book makes it to print (and if you're reading this now, it has), every decent gig anyone attends anywhere ever, will be promoting it; for amongst all the applause and excitement, many a reveller will be shouting and screaming "WOO!"

***

"What's it about?" my bro asks.

"Well, er. . . everything, I guess?"

"Everything?"

"Okay, music mainly, but I'm keeping it open."

"What does that fucking mean?" laughs my bro?

"I don't wanna be fenced in by a subject."

"Okay, so you're writing a book called WOO! about music, but also about *everything*?"

"Okay, not everything. Anything."

"Anything?"

"Yep."

"What, anything that goes through your head?" he says, chuckling. "So, how on earth do you end a book about everything – I mean, *anything*?"

5TH JUNE 2020, KITCHEN TABLE, HOME

I could not answer that question then but since the end is nigh, I'll try and do so now, though I'm not going to insult your intelligence and give you some seismic revelation or cosmic twist, or anything remotely smart-arse, partly because I can't think of one, but also because it's just not that kind of book. It's about as honest an account I can give without lawsuits following (and even that's not guaranteed). They say, "Don't let the truth get in the way of a good story," so if you think this is all a load of old shite, well, that's because it's the truth.

I'm not special. We all have WOO! moments, I just wrote a few of mine down. It's a feeling we all know and much like an eighties Martini ad, it can happen anytime, anyplace, anywhere - and with anyone. For me the place was the Windmill and it was the Fat White Family who led me there.

I have no idea where all this will take me, but do any of us? The structure upon which we hang our lives, the plans we painstakingly make to give us direction, are nothing more than fictitious tramlines, a best guess, but no one has a fucking clue what lies ahead. Did anyone expect to be living like *this* a year ago?

Along the way, I lost my good friend Tigger. I cannot deny the pivotal role he played, not just the friendship, but also the loss of it, for it was this that ultimately led me to find my people, my tribe. I can see now he could never have been a part of this, we were too enclosed within our crazy, fun-seeking unit of two. We're estranged now, but it doesn't bother me. I have no animosity towards him, or Sadie, for that matter. In fact, when she recently stepped in front of my car, I instinctively went for the brake and not the accelerator, which surely must mean something? And just to underline the point, as if the universe were truly testing me, this happened, not once, but thrice.

When Tigger cut me loose it challenged me, to either crawl into a hole or push myself forward. I chose the latter and dis covered people with similar interests and political outlooks, but more than anything else, touched by just enough madness to be interesting without being total head-fucks. Like my good friends Dominick Hicks and Zsa Zsa. And of course, La, who happily occupies the Goldilocks zone of craziness, with whom one of the most powerful, multi-layered friendships has unexpectedly blossomed. It feels like we'll be friends for life, yet here I go again, battling against the prevailing winds of an unwritten future, as nothing in life can be taken for granted, most especially relationships.

I know the idea of social gatherings now feels like an alien concept, let alone large events, or piling into sweaty mosh pits. Being in close proximity to other fellow humans is going to be hard to reconcile for some considerable time, but things will change, humanity will move beyond this virus.

Of course, this will not be the end of it. There'll be other pandemics, but we could just as easily be hit by an asteroid, or the super volcano under Yellowstone Park might finally explode, black dust enveloping the entire planet, blocking out the sun and destroying all life.

There's myriad reasons why we could be wiped off the face of the earth, but we cannot go through life in fear of possibilities.

To look at it another way, humanity has unexpectedly found itself in a superposition, this virus exposing the structural weaknesses in this broken socioeconomic system, this globalised world with its consumption-based economy that's destroying the planet and forcing billions into poverty. Is it too optimistic to think this could be a pivotal moment in human history? That we might evolve as a species?

Maybe, during this lockdown hibernation we already have?

The constructs we live by and accept without interrogation are no longer reliable. We're all left questioning their worth.

All the shit we accumulate along the way is merely borrowed, yet it's easy to get lost in it all, to forget that in the final reckoning all that counts is our experience of living: our loves, our passions, our families, our friendships and the communities we build.

If this pandemic *has* changed us, if it *has* caused a shift in consciousness, a new way of thinking, then the idea of the world changing is now an inevitability. This is how it works.

I don't mean we should be sitting around in the lotus position, chanting, worthy as that may be. I just mean, when we do step out of our introspective isolation, we can look at the world afresh, be alive to what's around us, more available to experience, to those special, sometimes magical moments that cause every atom of our body, every synapse of our nervous system, every spark within our brain, every fibre of our being, to overwhelm our intellect, squeeze our lungs hard, force our mouths to open and yell "WOO!"

The End

Acknowledgments

What began as the germ of an idea during a drunken conversation turned into a psychological voyage, intensified further by the mind-bending impact of this pandemic. It has not just been the writing of it that has consumed me, but all the fiddly bits and legal requirements publishing requires, complicated further by my wish to head each chapter up with a song lyric, something I was constantly warned against due to the additional copyright protection lyrics enjoy and the fact that many are subject to publishing deals. So, instead of going through any formal channels, whenever possible, I approached the band/lyricist directly. The positive responses and messages of support I received just blew me away. I also discovered the only way to elicit a response from Jason Williamson, was to call him a cunt.

There are many, many people I need to thank for the part they played in this book's creation and I have a nagging fear I will miss people out, but here goes:

Stuart, not only my bro, but one of my dearest friends with whom I've enjoyed countless escapades, some of which made it through to this book. He was one of a tiny handful of people with whom I initially discussed the idea with, since he too had become smitten by the Windmill's inexplicable energy. He simply said, "Well someone's got to, it may as well be you." Thanks bro, for all your encouragement. May we have many voyages to come and may them all be unpredictably strange.

My other bro Jason: who has lived on the other side of the pond this past 25 years and as life goes on, I tend to see less and less. Yet, despite the distance, we are still steadfastly close. It was he I began writing with oh so many years ago, initially as pen pals exchanging surreal updates on our lives and eventually a screenplay; a metaphysical drama which was sadly cut short by real-life drama. Still, without

Jason turning me on to what can be achieved by arranging words in a particular order, I would never have discovered the therapeutic joy of writing. So, he's the one to blame for *all* of this.

Sean De Sparengo: my very good friend who ceaselessly pushed me to write more, bemoaning my lack of output, so genuinely thrilled when I sent him early drafts of various segments. Sean's belief in my abilities has always far outweighed my own, so his importance in coaxing this book into being cannot be overstated. He helped with typos, structure, layout, design work and was one of the first to read a full draft. His eventual response turned me into a blubbering mess, but in a good way. Thank you, Sean, for everything.

La Staunton: who, when shown some chapters early on pretty much insisted I continue. I'm not sure she felt quite the same way as the years progressed, for I could talk of nothing else, a man possessed, frothing at the mouth like a rabid dog. Nevertheless, she managed me well and our friendship not only survived this, but grew stronger. Throughout the writing, La has provided inciteful feedback, hands on help, even designing the front cover, adapting a photo provided by Lou Smith. Most of all, I would like to thank her for our friendship, which in many ways energised the writing of this book. Thank you La, as mates go, you're the gift that keeps on giving.

Anna Yorke: a professional copy editor by day, introduced by our mutual friend Dominic Hicks. She kindly offered to help and has been utterly stoic in her support ever since, tirelessly wading through various drafts, continually finding typos my brain refused to see. She is also a talented gig photographer possessing an uncanny ability to harness the intensity of a performance within a single frame and she has very kindly contributed some of her work to this book. Thank you, Anna, for your practical help, your saint-like patience and your friendship.

Beth Soan: a friendship born out of tragedy and for which I raise a glass to our departed comrade Jack Medley. Beth happens to be a massive bookworm with a BA in English and after reading a draft last year, she offered her help to get it print ready. A punctuation genius, Beth quickly assumed the role of English teacher, enlightening me to all the strange rules surrounding dialogue (she even used a red pen!)

and just before this global pandemic kicked off, she and La spent five intense days with me on a line by line edit. I am incredibly grateful for all their loving help and support and Beth, I'm so very happy we became mates!

Lou Smith: who apart from being the Windmill's chief videographer and T-shirt producer, is also in possession of an ever-growing and already stupendous collection of photographs of all that is happening here, documenting many bands from their infancy, most especially Fat White Family, Warmduscher and Meatraffle. Lou has very kindly allowed me to reproduce some of his photographs within this book and did a very fine proofreading job of the very latest draft. Cheers Lou, for your friendship and for visually recording this important piece of musical history.

Finn Whitehead: not just for his feedback and ongoing encouragement, but for reluctantly allowing me to use the photograph of him with the royal couple. I did, however, promise to inform you readers that Finn is not a royalist, he was merely commenting on his experience of Harry and Meghan as people. So Finn, thanks for all your support and friendship.

Tim Perry: to whom I dispatched a draft of the book, unaware he is a published author in his own right. A couple of weeks later he got in touch and spent several hours offering corrections and very useful feedback. And once, perhaps by accident, an actual compliment slipped out his mouth, a moment I will forever cherish. So, thank you Tim, for your help during lockdown, your input was invaluable.

Cat Yong: who quite apart from playing base in MeU, is a professional copy editor by day and despite her insanely busy life she found time to help out. Cat possesses in-depth knowledge of politics, current affairs and obscure garage bands, so I ran a few pieces by her and in return she provided some particularly useful feedback. Thanks a million Cat.

Warren Mansfield (Zsa Zsa Sapien): not just for his continual support, but for being the madcap inspirational genius that he is. Thanks bruv, for your crispy fishfingers, your vocal support, your have-a-go attitude to life and for so badly pretending you'd actually read the book, (though, I do know he got as far as Chapter eight, as he forwarded me some appropriate introductory lyrics).

Dan Carey: not just for volunteering to be a test reader, but for giving me a much needed shot in the arm with his enthusiastic reaction. Please note, despite his enjoyment of the book, Dan would like to dissociate himself from any commentary concerning Alex Turner and Steve Lamacq.

Patrick Lyons: for his fascinating anecdotes, his unswerving support, his hyperactive energy and his unique spirit. Thank you Patrick for always making the impossible feel within reach, you're an inspiration to us all.

Chris OC for his help with Chapter 24 and for allowing me to retell a very personal account of his father's struggles after Pinochet's military coup in Chile.

Jamie Taylor for his help with Phobophobes backstory and the devastating impact caused by the tragic early death of their bandmate and friend; George Bedford Russel (RIP).

Clams Baker: for his positive support throughout and for very kindly allowing me to use his Peasant Vitality website (https://peasantvitality.com) to help distribute this limited run of hardbacks.

Rosalina Mansfield (Madame HiFi): for her friendship, support and lovely feedback after reading the copy Warren was supposed to read. He says he is waiting for the audio version.

Dominic Hicks: for his friendship, his steadfast support and his anarchic worldview. He has also offered his directorial help for a book launch and I might just take him up on it.

Simon Rumley: not just for his feedback, advice and encouragement, but for introducing me to some truly great bands along the way.

Alex Sebley: for the initial chat that gave birth to the idea and for his ongoing enthusiasm for the project.

Seamus and Kathleen, the most welcoming hosts of this most wonderful venue.

Toby, Piotr and Nasos for being such good natured all-round good eggs.

Alex Matthews, who can be found at bookeditingservices.co.uk for her superbly detailed work in helping polish the final draft in preparation for publishing.

I also have to pay immense gratitude to all the many minds I tapped along the way in the name of research (though rarely in a formal capacity), including (and in no particular order): Jamie Taylor, Patrick Lyons, Clams Baker, Simon Adamczewski, La Staunton, Chris OC, Beth Soan, Tim Perry, Lou Smith, Finn Whitehead, Anna Yorke, Dominic Hicks, Ollie Cookson, Lincoln Barrett, Cat Yong, Lias Saoudi, Rosalina Mansfield, Ben Wallers, Adam Brennan, James Sutcliffe, Alex White and many more I have undoubtedly failed to mention, some I will no doubt recall immediately after publishing, so if this you, please accept my heartfelt apologies.

I would like to thank Lou Smith, Anna Yorke, La Staunton, Holly Whitaker, Beth Soan, Cat Yong, George Cannell, Adam Herndon and whoever took the uncredited pictures* for providing some truly iconic photography and for so beautifully capturing such wonderful memories. Poignant reminders of a world we took so much for granted. (*If this happen to be yours, please get in touch and all will be rectified in future editions)

Also, I cannot thank enough all of the songwriters detailed at the front of this book for allowing me to reprint samples of their lyrics.

Special thanks must, of course, go to Fat White Family, for all the reasons previously stated.

Finally, my wonderful family (whose names have been omitted to protect the innocent), I cannot thank you enough for putting up with me during periods when I was physically present, but mentally absent. All my children, for being part of my listening group, with (carefully) selected chapters, my eldest daughter for her help with some of the editing, my youngest son for his input with Chapter 38 and to my amazing wife, who very early on prompted me to consider a more emotional narrative, a decision which helped the book write itself. To all my family, I remain eternally grateful for your love, care, patience and encouragement.

And last, but by no means least, I would like to express my warmest love and deepest appreciation to my dear mother. She became my first test audience, whisking through the entire manuscript in a couple of days at our kitchen table. Of course, she's biased, but it was heartening to hear her gasping and chuckling and advising me that I'll probably need a lawyer.

So, I dedicate this book to my very lively and incredibly loveable family, to my brilliant friends and to the Windmill Brixton and all who sail in her.

All UK proceeds of this book go to the Windmill Brixton

In memory of Jack Medley

Roofdog Ben
Adam Herndon

About the Author

Dave Thomson has a grade 3 Certificate of Secondary Education in English and lots of records.